Creating
Cultural Monsters

Serial Murder in America

Creating Cultural Monsters

Serial Murder in America

Julie B. Wiest

CRC Press
Taylor & Francis Group
Boca Raton London New York

CRC Press is an imprint of the
Taylor & Francis Group, an **informa** business

CRC Press
Taylor & Francis Group
6000 Broken Sound Parkway NW, Suite 300
Boca Raton, FL 33487-2742

© 2011 by Taylor and Francis Group, LLC
CRC Press is an imprint of Taylor & Francis Group, an Informa business

No claim to original U.S. Government works

Printed in the United States of America on acid-free paper
10 9 8 7 6 5 4 3 2 1

International Standard Book Number: 978-1-4398-5154-8 (Hardback)

This book contains information obtained from authentic and highly regarded sources. Reasonable efforts have been made to publish reliable data and information, but the author and publisher cannot assume responsibility for the validity of all materials or the consequences of their use. The authors and publishers have attempted to trace the copyright holders of all material reproduced in this publication and apologize to copyright holders if permission to publish in this form has not been obtained. If any copyright material has not been acknowledged please write and let us know so we may rectify in any future reprint.

Except as permitted under U.S. Copyright Law, no part of this book may be reprinted, reproduced, transmitted, or utilized in any form by any electronic, mechanical, or other means, now known or hereafter invented, including photocopying, microfilming, and recording, or in any information storage or retrieval system, without written permission from the publishers.

For permission to photocopy or use material electronically from this work, please access www.copyright.com (http://www.copyright.com/) or contact the Copyright Clearance Center, Inc. (CCC), 222 Rosewood Drive, Danvers, MA 01923, 978-750-8400. CCC is a not-for-profit organization that provides licenses and registration for a variety of users. For organizations that have been granted a photocopy license by the CCC, a separate system of payment has been arranged.

Trademark Notice: Product or corporate names may be trademarks or registered trademarks, and are used only for identification and explanation without intent to infringe.

Library of Congress Cataloging-in-Publication Data

Wiest, Julie B.
   Creating cultural monsters : serial murder in America / Julie B. Wiest.
      p. cm.
   Includes bibliographical references and index.
   ISBN 978-1-4398-5154-8
   1. Serial murders--United States. 2. Serial murders in mass media--United States. 3. Serial murderers--United States. 4. Violence in popular culture--United States. I. Title.

HV6529.W54 2011
364.152'320973--dc22
                                          2010051893

Visit the Taylor & Francis Web site at
http://www.taylorandfrancis.com

and the CRC Press Web site at
http://www.crcpress.com

To my family—your love and support make all the difference.

Contents

PREFACE		xi
ACKNOWLEDGMENTS		xiii
CHAPTER 1	INTRODUCTION	1
	Important Implications	2
	Major Contributions	2
	Book Organization	5

PART I WHAT WE (THINK WE) KNOW ABOUT SERIAL MURDER

CHAPTER 2	FUNDAMENTALS OF SERIAL MURDER	9
	Introduction	9
	Who Studies Serial Murder?	9
	Law Enforcement Personnel	9
	Academic Researchers	25
	Journalists and True Crime Writers	27
	Prevalence of Serial Murder	28
	Definitions of Serial Murder	29
	Distinguishing Serial Murder from Other Types of Murder	30
	Defining Serial Murder	32
	A Working Definition of Serial Murder	34
	Notes	34
CHAPTER 3	THE "TYPICAL" SERIAL MURDERER	37
	Introduction	37

VII

		Popular Portrayals in American Media	37
		Common Characteristics Identified by the FBI and Academic Researchers	45
		Race	63
		Gender	69
		Sexuality	72
		Nationality	73
		Similarities with Other Types of Offenses	77
		Other Serial Crimes	77
		School Shootings	78
		White Supremacy	79
		Notes	79
CHAPTER 4		EXISTING EXPLANATIONS FOR SERIAL MURDER	81
		Introduction	81
		Psychological Explanations	82
		Social Psychological Explanations	84
		Sociological Explanations	85
		A New Direction	86
		Notes	87

PART II A SOCIOCULTURAL APPROACH TO UNDERSTANDING SERIAL MURDER

CHAPTER 5	CULTURAL CONTEXT OF SERIAL MURDER	91
	Introduction	91
	Serial Murder in American Popular Culture	91
	Serial Murderers as Monsters and Celebrities	92
	Marketing Murderabilia	95
	Cultural Context of Human Behavior: How Culture "Works"	100
	Broadcasting Culture	101
	"Tuning In" and Cultural Competencies	101
	Building Lines of Action	104
	Note	106
CHAPTER 6	APPLYING THE MODEL OF AMERICAN CULTURE	107
	Introduction	107
	American Cultural Values: Contextual Features Suitable for Serial Murder	107
	Regard for Violence	108
	Individual Accomplishment and Competition	109
	Masculinities and Privilege	111
	The Criminal Experience	117
	Risk Taking and Thrill Seeking	118
	Power and Control	120

	Broadcasting Cultural Values: The Role of the American Mass Media	121
	Representations of Crime	121
	Model of Media Coverage	123
	Narrative Structure	126
	Initial Reports	128
	Notoriety and Record Setting	130
	Need to Know Why	131
	Anniversary Stories	134
	Missing Victims	134
	Social Typing	136
	Tuning In: Accepting the Messages	139
	Regard for Violence	140
	Individual Accomplishment and Competition	141
	Masculinities and Privilege	143
	The Criminal Experience	146
	Risk Taking and Thrill Seeking	146
	Power and Control	147
	Culturally Familiar Imagery	149
	Building Lines of Action: Using Cultural Values	150
	Notes	151
Chapter 7	**Implications**	153
	Introduction	153
	Toward a Deeper Understanding	153
	Investigative Considerations	158
	Decreasing the Incidence of Serial Murder	158
	Message Consistency	159
	Protections for All	160
	Note	161
Appendix: Methodology		163
References		187
Index		201
Author		223

Preface

Jeffrey Dahmer, John Wayne Gacy, Ted Bundy, "BTK," the "Night Stalker," and the "Green River Killer": The names are familiar, the men infamous. They have appeared on television, in newspapers and magazines. Their faces are displayed on merchandise like T-shirts, trading cards, comic books, calendars, and action figures. Web sites and fan clubs are devoted to them. Serial murderers have become perverse icons in the United States, cultural monsters as mythic as Frankenstein, the bogeyman, and Freddy Krueger—and American culture is substantially responsible.

A unique and comprehensive explanation of serial murder, *Creating Cultural Monsters: Serial Murder in America* draws on the years of dedicated research of Dr. Julie B. Wiest. This book examines connections between American culture and the incidence of serial murder and draws clear and well-supported conclusions. Wiest presents empirically supported arguments that have the potential to revolutionize how serial murder is understood, studied, and investigated, including a sociocultural explanation for the overrepresentation of white men as serial murderers. This text is suitable as a reference as well as a textbook for courses exploring serial murder, extreme violence, and criminal profiling.

Acknowledgments

I was extraordinarily fortunate to receive assistance from many people throughout the process of writing this text. First, I am inexpressibly grateful to Dr. Suzanne Kurth, who supported me throughout my doctoral program, was instrumental in the development and completion of my dissertation, and graciously agreed to read and critique drafts of this text. Her guidance greatly contributed to the development of the arguments herein. I am sincerely grateful to Dr. Jerry Morrow, my longtime mentor, who helped me take some of my first steps in academia and continues to walk beside me as I embark on new journeys. Thanks also to Drs. Hoan Bui, Tom Hood, and Cheryl Travis, who shared their valuable time and knowledge as members of my dissertation committee. Finally, I offer thanks to my kind High Point University colleagues, whose interest in the project was encouraging as its completion neared, as well as reviewers of the proposal and drafts for their thoughtful criticism and insights.

Thank you to graphic artist Rey Pineda for creating the series of figures that illustrate my model of American culture in Chapter 5 and Jim Goodman for conceiving the cover image.

1
Introduction

Jeffrey Dahmer, John Wayne Gacy, Ted Bundy, "BTK," the "Night Stalker," and the "Green River Killer." The names are familiar, the men infamous. Serial murderers have become perverse icons in the United States. Their activities, minds, and backgrounds have been extensively studied by law enforcement personnel, mental health experts, academic researchers, and the general public. Americans devour media accounts, true crime books, and television specials featuring numerous cases of serial murder to gain insight into the characteristics and behaviors of murderers. Many eagerly await the next episodes of *Dexter*, *Law and Order: Special Victims Unit*, and *CSI: Crime Scene Investigation* to indulge in a fascination with these killers, test amateur profiling skills, and—it is hoped—learn ways to reduce chances of victimization. Yet, after decades of studies, serial murder researchers have been unable to answer every American's most important question: Why?

This text presents a new approach to the study of U.S. serial murder by examining connections between American culture and the incidence of serial murder and drawing clear and well-supported conclusions. It represents the culmination of years of research into serial murder and is based on original research conducted for my doctoral dissertation, completed in 2009. Findings from that study provide evidentiary support for the arguments presented here and thus are referenced throughout. Although the framework explained here is specific to the American cultural context, findings have important implications for similar cultures. In addition, the approach could be adapted to explore the incidence and representations of serial murder in other cultures.

Important Implications

This book offers implications for law enforcement and mass media, as well as future research on serial murder, murder, and violence in general. Sociology and criminology generally have neglected the phenomenon of serial murder, with psychology responsible for most of the current knowledge and perspectives. Criminologists spend much time investigating variations in patterns of minor offending, perhaps finding studies of frequently occurring minor offending to be more useful because of the generalizability of their findings. Although serial murder is a rare phenomenon within a rare type of offending (homicide), it warrants study because it is among the most serious types of offending—in terms of harm caused and public fear aroused—with a limited understanding of its roots. Despite its rarity, serial murder has an enormous negative impact on society. It affects not only the actual victims but also their families, friends, the community, and sometimes the entire country. In addition, significant financial resources are dedicated to the investigation, apprehension, and legal proceedings of serial murderers. King County, Washington, officials interviewed for a *Seattle Times* article about the Green River Killer case compared the cost of the investigation and subsequent prosecution and defense of then-suspect Gary Ridgway to the cost of recovering from a natural disaster, estimating the case cost at $8 million to $12 million (Fryer and Ostrom 2001).

In addition, studying an extreme version of any phenomenon is useful in understanding more commonly occurring varieties. Studying serial murder not only serves to further our understanding of an atypical but serious type of murder but also can contribute to better understanding of ordinary murder and other types of violent behavior. Studying serial murder also may lead to a better understanding of cultural messages in the United States, how they are transmitted to the public through the mass media, how they influence violent behavior, and their possible consequences.

Major Contributions

Research on serial murder is full of inconsistency and discrepancy. Despite abundant public interest, media coverage, and law enforcement attention, there is limited knowledge and little agreement. No single definition of serial murder exists, which complicates efforts to determine its incidence. Profiles of serial murderers developed by social scientists differ from versions perpetuated in the media, in which many of the killers receive celebrity status. Explanations of serial murder range from biological to sociological, with much of the research from a psychological tradition and the cultural context generally neglected. But, to understand distinctive behavioral patterns, it is necessary to consider the influence of culture to identify those components that affect thoughts, attitudes, and behaviors.

The unique and comprehensive explanation of serial murder offered here draws clear connections to American culture; explains the reasons behind the higher incidence of serial murder in the United States when compared to other nations, as well as its omnipresence in American media; and investigates what it would take to decrease its occurrence. Six original contributions are emphasized here because of their potential to transform how serial murder in the United States is understood and studied.

1. **Serial murder is primarily a cultural phenomenon, not the result of individual deficiencies.** Much of the current research on serial murder hails from a psychological tradition and is individual centered. However, placing the phenomenon in a cultural context provides not only qualitative understanding but also the potential for reducing its frequency. Examining an individual's motivations or brain waves tells us little about the next individual, but understanding and exploring the cultural context help us develop explanations for patterned behaviors with the potential to intervene. Serial murder is a deviant means to gain culturally valued feelings of power, control, dominance, success, satisfaction, and pleasure through individualism, competition, and risk taking, especially for those with limited resources and legitimate power. It also offers a means to attain other cultural values—success and fame—that most forms of offending do not. Because masculine ideals mesh neatly with many American cultural values, adherence to those values also is a means for proving masculinity. American culture is full of inconsistent messages

and values that may be utilized in a number of legitimate and illegitimate ways. This contributes to the establishment of a cultural environment full of inconsistent messages, adjustable boundaries, and contradictions—an ideal environment for serial murder.

2. **An illustrated model is offered to explain how culture "works."** The model explains how people utilize cultural values to construct lines of action according to their cultural competencies. It is then used to help explain the ways in which the American cultural milieu fosters serial murder and the creation of white, male serial murderers. American cultural values—especially as they emphasize competition and individual achievement; white, male privilege; and hegemonic masculinity—along with the emotional appeal of crime commission appear to contribute to the development of serial murderers by making serial murder an available and desirable line of action for some men.

3. **A formula is suggested for predicting a serial murderer's potential notoriety.** The formula includes three components: the social status of the killer, the social status of the victims, and the shock factor of the murders. Those components, as well as their relationship, are explained and operationalized.

4. **Popular definitions of serial murder are critically analyzed and considered part of the problem.** Definitions of serial murder vary widely, with much of the discrepancy related to number of victims, distinctiveness of motivational factors, and the specificity of the time span involved. The framework on which the majority of definitions are based characterizes a serial murderer as a person who has killed three or more people previously unknown to him or her over a period of weeks, months, or years. Many definitions also require evidence of sadism and sexual overtones. Yet, the definitions appear to describe characteristics most associated with white, male serial murderers in the United States and exclude characteristics that may be associated with other groups and people acting with different motivations. Slight reformulations of these narrow definitions would fundamentally change the characterization of the "typical" serial murderer. I urge a

reexamination of the construction and representation of serial murderers in American culture and suggest consequences of a continued cultural blindness to multiple murderers who are not white men.

5. **Discrepancies between popular profiles and characteristics reported by social scientists are identified, and the use of criminal profiling is critiqued.** I explore the ways in which meanings are constructed about serial murder and serial murderers and how and why exaggerated and apparently inaccurate representations have gained acceptance. The (mis)representation of serial murderers is self-serving for those who create and perpetuate the profiles—the Federal Bureau of Investigation (FBI) and the media—and possibly counterproductive in solving serial murder cases.

6. **The requisites for decreasing the incidence of serial murder are discussed.** The glorification of serial murderers in omnipresent media representations, the exalted image of the FBI and its profilers, and U.S. economic and social structures are discussed as major contributors to the incidence of serial murder. Short- and long-term suggestions are offered to move toward decreasing its occurrence.

Book Organization

This book is divided into two parts. The first outlines established information about serial murder and its sources, especially focusing on definitions, common characteristics of serial murderers, and existing explanations for serial murder. The second part presents an original framework for exploring the sociocultural context of serial murder, including an examination of serial murder in popular culture; the presentation of a model for how culture "works" to influence thoughts and behaviors; the application of that model to serial murder cases; and a consideration of the implications of these arguments, how they may be used to decrease the incidence of serial murder in the United States, and recommendations for future research. Finally, the Appendix details the methodology employed in the 2009 study, including an explanation of the qualitative content analysis method, the employed sample, data collection sources, and the analytical procedure.

PART I
What We (Think We) Know about Serial Murder

2
FUNDAMENTALS OF SERIAL MURDER

Introduction

Before we begin to explore characteristics of serial murderers and explanations for serial murder, we must identify the sources of our knowledge and make clear our definitions. These are no easy tasks. Available information encompasses multiple disciplines and perspectives, and there are nearly as many definitions of serial murder as there are researchers. Acknowledging these varied perspectives and identifying definitional discrepancies will better equip us to sort through and evaluate the frameworks presented.

Who Studies Serial Murder?

Besides the large number of true crime fans and amateur profilers out there, most research into serial murder is conducted by three groups: law enforcement personnel, academic researchers, and journalists or true crime writers. Each group examines cases of serial murder with a distinct purpose and focus, and each contributes to our understanding of the phenomenon.

Law Enforcement Personnel

Law enforcement personnel can be divided into local officials and those in the Federal Bureau of Investigation (FBI; Figure 2.1), each serving a separate purpose. Local police officers and sheriff's deputies primarily are concerned with collecting information about crime scenes and victims—via crime scene investigation, witness statements, and forensic analysis—and then analyzing this information to determine a possible motive or uncover other clues about

Figure 2.1 **(See color insert.)** The FBI headquarters in Washington, D.C., is pictured at night (date unknown).

the perpetrator that may aid in solving the case. Throughout the course of their investigation, they may uncover behavioral patterns or forensic links that lead to an investigation of serial murder. Cases of serial murder, however, may present unique investigative challenges, particularly when the murders are committed across multiple law enforcement jurisdictions. Different law enforcement agencies have varying abilities and resources to process crime scenes and may or may not communicate with one another, issues that could complicate their ability to link murders in serial cases and ultimately apprehend an offender. State and national resources that aid in linking cases[1] are not consistently utilized, perhaps because of a lack of awareness or training.

The FBI aids serial murder investigations and contributes to knowledge of the phenomenon in two important ways: criminal profiling and disseminating knowledge. Since the term *serial killer* was coined by Special Agent Robert K. Ressler in the 1970s, the FBI has claimed to be the foremost authority on serial murder. The development and recognition of criminal profiling, a procedure that uses crime scene and victim analysis to create a sketch of the probable personality and behavioral characteristics of serial offenders, cemented that authority.

Although FBI agents claim ownership of the set of necessary skills needed to profile serial crimes (Morton and Hilts 2008) and are perhaps the most widely recognized group of profilers, they are not the only group, or even the most successful. Professors Ronald M. Holmes and Stephen T. Holmes, for example, have developed more than 600 profiles for police departments around the world and have had an impressive degree of success.

The profiling technique is rooted in nineteenth-century fiction (e.g., in Sir Arthur Conan Doyle's Sherlock Holmes stories), but its first known use in the United States was by psychiatrist James A. Brussel in the 1957 "Mad Bomber" case in New York. Brussel helped the police narrow their search for the suspect, and he later aided Behavioral Science Unit instructor Special Agent Howard Teton and Special Agent Patrick Mullaney in developing the technique for the FBI. Other prominent special agents and researchers who helped shape the technique over the years include Special Agent Richard Ault, who, with Special Agent Robert K. Ressler, applied the practice to better aid law enforcement agencies worldwide; Special Agent John Douglas, who with Ressler interviewed known serial murderers to create a database that further developed profiling techniques; and Behavioral Science Unit instructor Roy Hazelwood and Ann Burgess, of the University of Pennsylvania School of Nursing and associate director of nursing research for the Boston Department of Health and Hospitals, who further refined the procedures.

The National Center for the Analysis of Violent Crime (NCAVC) was established in 1984 at the FBI National Academy in Quantico, Virginia, as the major resource center aiding law enforcement agencies with unusual, high-risk, and serial crimes. It arose in the 1970s and 1980s from the Behavioral Science Unit, which in 1996 was known as the Investigative Support Unit. In the mid-1980s, the unit divided into the Behavioral Science Instruction, Behavioral Science Research, and Behavioral Science Investigative Support Units, all of which are now incorporated in the NCAVC. The center currently is organized into three components: the Behavioral Analysis Unit—East/West Regions, Child Abduction Serial Murder Investigative Resources Center, and Violent Criminal Apprehension Program. Using advanced behavioral science techniques and a sophisticated computer model, the components of the center work together to advise law enforcement

PROMINENT FBI CONTRIBUTORS TO SERIAL MURDER RESEARCH

- **During his 48-year tenure (1924–1972) as director of the FBI, J. Edgar Hoover helped establish**—and fiercely protected—the image of the FBI agent as an all-American hero. Under his leadership, the prestige of the bureau grew along with its responsibilities, quickly becoming a central component of the U.S. government and an icon in American popular culture and setting the stage for the modern image of the heroic, relentless FBI profiler made famous in American popular media.
- **Robert K. Ressler**, former program manager of the Violent Criminal Apprehension Program of the FBI, served in the FBI for 20 years (1970–1990) and is credited with coining the term *serial killer* in the 1970s. Along with agent John Douglas, he developed the database that led to the development of profiling techniques. He also coauthored two books in criminology—*Crime Classification Manual*, with Ann W. Burgess, Allen G. Burgess, and Douglas; and *Sexual Homicide: Patterns and Motives*, with Ann Burgess and Douglas, both published in 1992—and, with Thomas Schachtman, coauthored two books about profiling techniques and cases in which they were used, *Whoever Fights Monsters* (1992) and *I Have Lived in the Monster* (1997).
- **John E. Douglas** served in the FBI for 25 years (1970–1995); the last 5 years were spent leading the Investigative Support Unit, the branch of the FBI primarily responsible for criminal profiling. Although he did not develop criminal profiling, he is closely associated with it, reportedly serving as the model for character Jack Crawford, FBI agent in charge of the Behavioral Science Unit in *The Silence of the Lambs*, the Academy Award–winning film based on the novel by Thomas Harris. Along with agent Robert Ressler, he developed the database that led to

> the development of profiling techniques. He also coauthored two books in criminology—*Crime Classification Manual*, with Ann W. Burgess, Allen G. Burgess, and Ressler; and *Sexual Homicide: Patterns and Motives*, with Ann Burgess and Ressler, both published in 1992—and, with Mark Olshaker, he wrote several more books about profiling techniques and cases in which they were used, including *Mindhunter* (1995), *Journey into Darkness* (1997), and *Obsession* (1998).
>
> - **Patrick J. Mullaney**, who served in the FBI for 20 years (1966–1986), and **Howard Teton**, who served for 24 years (1962–1986), are recognized as the creators of the criminal profiling techniques used by the FBI. Teton is credited with developing the technique of using crime scene evidence to aid in the identification of an offender's behavior patterns and motivation.

agencies in focusing their investigations, suggest strategies for offender identification and apprehension, and develop strategies to be used in legal proceedings. Although the public and often the requesting law enforcement agency place a great deal of weight on criminal profiles in serial murder investigations, they should be viewed as one investigative tool among many. No profile has, or will, ever by itself solve a criminal case. (The methods and merits of psychological profiling are discussed further in this chapter.)

Profilers' specialized training in criminal investigative analysis—the process of reviewing crimes from both behavioral and investigative perspectives—has aided serial murder investigations in the United States and abroad. When the FBI is called to aid in cases of serial murder, agents employ behavioral, forensic, and investigative perspectives to develop an educated guess of the most probable perpetrator. They generally follow a series of steps (Woodworth and Porter 1999), including (1) collecting data from as many sources as possible, including police and medical examiner reports, crime scene photographs, and victim and witness statements; (2) identifying crime characteristics, including the apparent offending sequence, methods of crime commission (i.e., modus operandi), and victim behaviors and characteristics; and (3) considering background and physical characteristics of the offender, as well as habits and personality dynamics. The resulting profile may offer descriptions of the offender's physical characteristics, vehicle information, home location, employment type, relationship status, speech patterns, or other details—sometimes with surprising accuracy. In the 1980s, FBI profilers famously aided in the apprehension and conviction of Wayne Williams as the "Atlanta Child Killer," David Carpenter as the "Trailside Killer of San Francisco," and Alaskan serial murderer Robert Hansen.

David Carpenter

David Carpenter, the Trailside Killer, murdered at least five people (four women and one man), mostly by shooting, on hiking trails near San Francisco, California, from 1979 to 1980. He raped some of the victims and stole their money. He was suspected in 10 deaths, but prosecutors determined that there was enough evidence to try him for only half of those. Carpenter was convicted in two separate trials, in 1984 and 1988, and sentenced to death; he is still on death row at San Quentin State Prison in California.

Carpenter was raised by strict, sometimes neglectful, and abusive parents, an upbringing that some researchers cite as the cause of his severe stutter. After serving 1 year in prison for child molestation as a teenager, he worked mostly odd jobs, including a ship's purser, a salesman, and a printer. He married in 1955, but his wife divorced him in 1960 following the birth of their third child, after he was convicted of attacking a woman and received a 14-year sentence. He served 9 years of that sentence but was arrested shortly after his release for attacking another woman in 1970. He served another 9 years for kidnapping, robbery, and parole violations. In between his stints in prison, he remarried, but that marriage also failed. After prison, he received a degree from a trade school, worked as a typesetter instructor, and took up hiking as a hobby, which he found provided opportunities for attacking women without being seen.

Robert Christian Hansen

Robert Christian Hansen murdered at least 15 women (mostly prostitutes and topless dancers) by shooting and stabbing in Alaska from 1980 to 1983. He usually would pick up the women for sex and overpower them during the act. He then would force his victims into his plane and fly them to his remote cabin, where he would rape and torture them before stripping them, letting them loose in the wilderness, and finally hunting them down with a high-powered rifle or hunting knife. On June 13, 1983, one of his victims escaped, and her report led police to Hansen's door. He denied her accusations, however, and offered an alibi that police confirmed. He was finally arrested in October 1983, after investigators reexamined his alibi and found it was false; search warrants of Hansen's house and plane uncovered the rifle used in most of the murders and personal items he took from many of the victims. In February 1984, he confessed to 15 murders but was convicted of just 4 as part of a plea deal. He was sentenced to 461 years plus life in prison, with no chance for parole, and sent to Lewisburg Federal Penitentiary in Pennsylvania, where he remains today.

By all accounts, Hansen had a difficult childhood; his parents were strict and domineering, and he endured frequent teasing because of severe acne and a stutter. After graduating from high school, he enlisted in the Army Reserves and married at age 21. The marriage ended after less than a year, when Hansen was imprisoned for arson. After his release, he remarried, bounced from job to job, and was arrested several more times for thefts. In 1967, he moved to Alaska. He quickly earned a reputation as a great outdoorsman and hunter; opened a successful bakery; had two children with his second wife; and mostly managed to stay out of trouble, except for a 1-year imprisonment for stealing a chain saw, until his arrest for the murders.

Criminal profiling also led to the development of classification systems, or typologies, of serial murderers that generally classify differences in motivation and expected gains. The most common typology is the "organized/disorganized" categories developed by the FBI to classify homicides and provide clues about offenders. The FBI also developed classifications for sexual homicide (the category in which the FBI until recently placed serial murder) as organized, disorganized, or mixed.[2] Academic researchers also have developed typologies of murderers in general (e.g., Wille 1975; Lee 1988) and of serial murderers specifically (e.g., Holmes and De Burger 1988). Holmes and De Burger's (1988) categorization of serial murder into four major types—visionary, mission oriented, hedonistic, and power/control oriented—is frequently cited by serial murder researchers.[3] The utility of these typologies, however, is unclear, and even the FBI questioned their helpfulness in serial murder investigations, calling most typologies "too cumbersome" (Morton and Hilts 2008).

The successes of criminal profiling during the 1980s and the widespread attention generated by portrayals of the NCAVC and criminal profiling techniques in the 1991 film *The Silence of the Lambs* (and numerous films and television programs since) contributed to the creation of a glorified image for criminal profilers, who generally receive a large amount of public support for their work. The special agents who work as profilers are portrayed in American media as *superagents*—elite members of law enforcement and the "secret weapons" in serial murder investigations. Profilers rarely are blamed publicly when their profiles are less than helpful, which, by some accounts, occurs frequently. Two serial murder cases in which criminal profiles led the investigation astray and perhaps cost lives were those of the the "Baton Rouge Serial Killer" and the Green River Killer cases.

Derrick Todd Lee, the Baton Rouge Serial Killer, was convicted of killing two women in two trials in 2004 but is linked to the deaths of 7 to 10 women in the Baton Rouge and Lafayette areas of Louisiana from 1992 to 2003. Although the criminal profile provided during the investigation predicted an unskilled, white, male killer with poor relationships, Lee is black and personable, was employed, and lived with his wife and two children. The profile did get some points right, such as his age, gender, tight financial situation, physical strength, and controlling behavior. The accuracy of other profile points is unknown, but the discrepancies are significant.[4]

Gary Leon Ridgway, the Green River Killer, was convicted in 2003 of murdering 48 women in Washington, mostly from 1982 to

1984 but also in 1990 and 1998. He became a suspect in the murders in 1983 and provided DNA samples to police in 1987, but he was not captured until November 2001. Why did so much time elapse before he was apprehended? This was perhaps because he did not fit the criminal profile developed by the FBI during the investigation. Based on that profile, police were looking for a man incapable of holding a job or maintaining relationships with others and who was an avid outdoorsman, impulsive, drawn to the investigations, and hateful of women, especially prostitutes. The profile was accurate about the killer's gender and its last three predictions, but Ridgway was not an outdoorsman, held the same job for 32 years, and was happily married at the time of his arrest. In addition, profiler John Douglas asserted that a letter sent in 1984 to the *Seattle Post-Intelligencer* discussing the murders and purportedly from the killer was phony; Ridgway's later confessions revealed its authenticity and dealt another blow to the utility of profiling in this case. Again, while accuracies of the profile should be acknowledged, the discrepancies are noteworthy and, in this case, likely contributed to a years-long delay in Ridgway's apprehension.[5] Despite some problems with criminal profiling, the techniques have aided a number of investigations and should not be discounted. What is needed is more cooperation between FBI profilers, who contribute experience and expertise in crime scene analysis, and academic researchers, who contribute expertise in psychological or behavioral analysis.

Gary Leon Ridgway

Gary Leon Ridgway murdered 48 women (usually prostitutes and teenage runaways) by strangulation, mostly from 1982 to 1984 and also in 1990 and 1998 in Washington. He killed his victims in his home or outdoors and dumped all of the bodies outdoors, many in or near the Green River. He was a suspect in the murders since 1983 but was not captured until November 2001 after DNA analysis of hair and saliva samples he provided to police in 1987 matched DNA found in semen left on several victims. He accepted a plea deal, pled guilty on November 5, 2003 (Figures 2.2–2.7), and received 48 life sentences. He is serving his sentences in Washington.

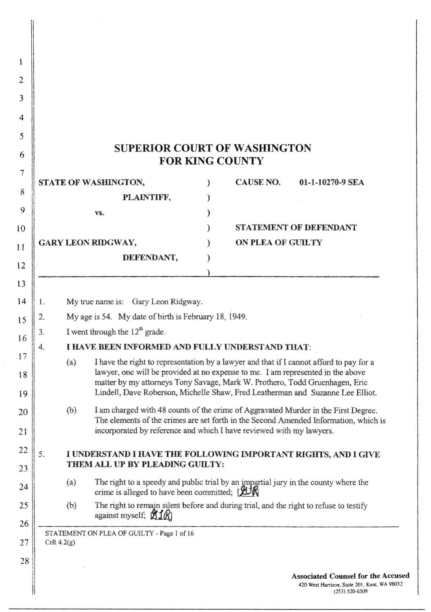

Figure 2.2 The first page of Gary Ridgway's ("Green River Killer") statement on plea of guilty, accepted by Judge Richard Jones on November 5, 2003, in King County Superior Court, Washington, in *The State of Washington v. Gary Leon Ridgway*.

(c) The right at trial to hear and question the witnesses who testify against me; [GJR]
(d) The right at trial to testify and to have witnesses testify for me. These witnesses can be made to appear at no expense to me; [GJR]
(e) I am presumed innocent unless the charge is proven beyond a reasonable doubt or I enter a plea of guilty; [GJR]
(f) The right to appeal a finding of guilt after a trial; [GJR]
(g) I have entered into a Plea Agreement with the King County Prosecuting Attorney, which is attached to this document. Under sections 11, 12 and 13 of that Agreement I have waived any rights to appeal directly or indirectly or through collateral attack, any aspect of my pleas of guilty, and any aspect of the sentence resulting from any of them. I hereby reaffirm that provision and waive these rights. [GJR]

6. **IN CONSIDERING THE CONSEQUENCES OF MY GUILTY PLEA, I UNDERSTAND THAT:**

(a) The crimes with which I am charged carries a maximum sentence and fine of:

COUNT NO.	OFFENDER SCORE	STANDARD RANGE ACTUAL CONFINEMENT (not including enhancements)	PLUS Enhancem*	TOTAL ACTUAL CONFINEMENT (standard range including enhancements)	COMMUNITY CUSTODY RANGE (Only applicable for crimes committed on or after July 1, 2000. For crimes committed prior to July 1, 2000, see paragraph 6(f))	MAXIMUM TERM AND FINE
1-47	N/A	N/A	N/A	Life Imprisonment without the possibility of early release or parole	N/A	Life Imprisonment w/o the possibility of early release or parole and/or a $50,000 fine
48	N/A	N/A	N/A	Life Imprisonment	N/A	Life Imprisonment

*(F) Firearm, (D) other deadly weapon, (V) VUCSA in protected zone, (VH) Veh. Hom, See RCW 46.61.520, (JP) Juvenile present

(b) The standard sentence range is based on the crime charged and my criminal history. Criminal history includes prior convictions and juvenile adjudications or convictions, whether in this state, in federal court, or elsewhere.

The crimes to which I am pleading guilty do not carry a Standard Range sentence. I understand that the only penalty which the Court may impose for counts 1 through 47 to which I am pleading guilty is life imprisonment without the possibility of early release or parole. Count 48 carries a minimum sentence of Life Imprisonment.

(c) The Prosecuting Attorney's statement of my criminal history is attached to this agreement. Unless I have attached a different statement, I agree that the Prosecuting Attorney's statement is correct and complete. If I have attached my own statement, I assert that it is correct and complete. If I am convicted of any additional crimes between now and the time I am sentenced, I am obligated to tell the sentencing Judge about those convictions.

(d) I understand that I may not seek to withdraw the pleas of guilty that I am entering,

STATEMENT ON PLEA OF GUILTY - Page 2 of 16
CrR 4.2(g)

Associated Counsel for the Accused
420 West Harrison, Suite 201, Kent, WA 98032
(253) 520-6509

Figure 2.3 Page 2 of Gary Ridgway's statement on plea of guilty.

Defendant and the Judge [initials] ___].

[bb] ~~I understand that if I am pleading guilty to the crime of unlawful practices in obtaining assistance as defined in RCW 74.08.331, no assistance payment shall be made for at least 6 months if this is my first conviction and for at least 12 months if this is my second or subsequent conviction. This suspension of benefits will apply even if I am not incarcerated. RCW 74.08.290.~~ [If not applicable, this paragraph should be stricken by the Defendant and the Judge [initials], ___].

7. I plead guilty to counts 1 through 48 in the Second Amended Information. I have received a copy of that Information and carefully reviewed it with my lawyers. [initials]

8. I make this plea freely and voluntarily. [initials]

9. No one has threatened harm of any kind to me or to any other person to cause me to make this plea. [initials]

10. No person has made promises of any kind to cause me to enter this plea except as set forth in this statement. [initials]

11. The Judge has asked me to state what I did in my own words that makes me guilty of these crimes. This is my statement:

I killed the forty-eight (48) women listed in the State's second amended information.

In most cases, when I murdered these women, I did not know their names. Most of the time, I killed them the first time I met them and I do not have a good memory for their faces. I killed so many women I have a hard time keeping them straight.

I have reviewed information and discovery about each of the murders with my attorneys, and I am positive that I killed each one of the women charged in the Second Amended Information. I killed them all in King County. I killed most of them in my house near Military Road, and I killed a lot of them in my truck, not far from where I picked them up. I killed some of them outside. I remember leaving each woman's body in the place where she was found.

I have discussed with my attorneys the "common scheme or plan" aggravating circumstance charged in all these murders. I agree that each of the murders I committed was part of a "common scheme or plan." The plan was: I wanted to kill as many women I thought were prostitutes as I possibly could.

I picked prostitutes as my victims because I hate most prostitutes and I did not want to pay them for sex. I also picked prostitutes as victims because they were easy to pick up without being noticed. I knew they would not be reported missing right away, and might never be reported missing. I picked prostitutes because I thought I could kill as many of them as I wanted without getting caught.

Another part of my plan was where I put the bodies of these women. Most of the time I took the women's jewelry and their clothes to get rid of any evidence and make them harder to identify. I placed most of the bodies in groups which I call "clusters." I did this because I wanted to keep track of all the women I killed. I liked to drive by the "clusters" around the county and think about the

STATEMENT ON PLEA OF GUILTY - Page 7 of 16
CrR 4.2(g)

Associated Counsel for the Accused
420 West Harrison, Suite 201, Kent, WA 98032
(253) 520-6509

Figure 2.4 Page 7 of Gary Ridgway's statement on plea of guilty.

women I placed there. I usually used a landmark to remember a "cluster" and the women I placed there. Sometimes I killed and dumped a woman, intending to start a new "cluster," and never returned because I thought I might get caught putting more women there.

My statements as to each count are as follows:

Count I (1):

In King County, Washington, sometime between July 8, 1982 through July 15, 1982, with premeditated intent to cause her death, I strangled Wendy Lee Coffield to death. I picked her up, planning to kill her. After killing her, I placed her body in the Green River.

Count II (2):

In King County, Washington, sometime between July 25, 1982 through August 12, 1982, with premeditated intent to cause her death, I strangled Debra Bonner to death. I picked her up, planning to kill her. After killing her, I placed her body in the Green River.

Count III (3):

In King County, Washington, sometime between August 1, 1982 through August 15, 1982, with premeditated intent to cause her death, I strangled Marcia Chapman to death. I picked her up, planning to kill her. After killing her, I placed her body in the Green River.

Count IV (4):

In King County, Washington, sometime between August 11, 1982 through August 15, 1982, with premeditated intent to cause her death, I strangled Cynthia Hinds to death. I picked her up, planning to kill her. After killing her, I placed her body in the Green River.

Count V (5):

In King County, Washington, sometime between August 12, 1982 through August 15, 1982, with premeditated intent to cause her death, I strangled Opal Mills to death. I picked her up, planning to kill her. After killing her, I placed her body next to the Green River.

Count VI (6):

In King County, Washington, sometime between September 20, 1982 through May 30, 1988, with premeditated intent to cause her death, I strangled Debra Estes to death. I picked her up, planning to kill her. After killing her, I buried her body near the Fox Run Apartments in Federal Way.

Count VII (7):

In King County, Washington, sometime between May 2, 1983 through May 8, 1983, with premeditated intent to cause her death, I strangled Carol Christensen to death. I picked her up, planning to kill her. After killing her, I placed her body in a wooded area in Maple Valley.

STATEMENT ON PLEA OF GUILTY - Page 8 of 16
CrR 4.2(g)

Associated Counsel for the Accused
420 West Harrison, Suite 201, Kent, WA 98032
(253) 520-6509

Figure 2.5 Page 8 of Gary Ridgway's statement on plea of guilty.

premeditated intent to cause her death, I strangled April D. Buttram to death. I picked her up, planning to kill her. After killing her, I left her body just off Highway 18 near I-90.

Count XXXIX (39):

In King County, Washington, on or about September 28, 1983, with premeditated intent to cause her death, I strangled Maureen Feeney to death. I picked her up, planning to kill her. After killing her, I left her body just off Highway 18 near I-90.

Count XL (40):

In King County, Washington, on or about September 12, 1983 through September 15, 1983, with premeditated intent to cause her death, I strangled Tracy A. Winston to death. I picked her up, planning to kill her. After killing her, I left her body in Cottonwood Park near the Green River.

Count XLI (41):

In King County, Washington, on or about October 30, 1983, with premeditated intent to cause her death, I strangled Delise L. Plager to death. I picked her up, planning to kill her. After killing her, I left her body at Exit 38, just off I-90.

Count XLII (42):

In King County, Washington, on or about November 1, 1983, with premeditated intent to cause her death, I strangled Kim L. Nelson to death. I picked her up, planning to kill her. After killing her, I left her body at Exit 38, just off I-90.

Count XLIII (43):

In King County, Washington, sometime in December of 1983, with premeditated intent to cause her death, I strangled Lisa L. Yates to death. I picked her up, planning to kill her. After killing her, I left her body at Exit 38, just off I-90.

Count XLIV (44):

In King County, Washington, on or about February 6, 1984, with premeditated intent to cause her death, I strangled Mary E. West to death. I picked her up, planning to kill her. After killing her, I left her body at Seward Park.

Count XLV (45):

In King County, Washington, on or about March 13, 1984, with premeditated intent to cause her death, I strangled Cindy A. Smith to death. I picked her up, planning to kill her. After killing her, I left her body near Green River Community College just off Highway 18.

Count XLVI (46):

In King County, Washington, on or about October 17, 1986, with premeditated intent to cause her

STATEMENT ON PLEA OF GUILTY - Page 13 of 16
CrR 4.2(g)

Associated Counsel for the Accused
420 West Harrison, Suite 201, Kent, WA 98032
(253) 520-6509

Figure 2.6 Page 13 of Gary Ridgway's statement on plea of guilty.

death, I strangled Patricia M. Barczak to death. I picked her up, planning to kill her. After killing her, I left her body near Seattle International Raceway, just off Highway 18.

Count XLVII (47):

In King County, Washington, sometime between August 4, 1998, through August 6, 1998 with premeditated intent to cause her death, I strangled Patricia Yellowrobe to death. After killing her, I left her body just off Des Moines Way South in South Park.

Count XLVIII (48):

In King County, Washington, sometime between July 23, 1971 through August 31, 1993, with premeditated intent to cause her death, I strangled an unidentified woman referred to as Jane Doe "B20," to death. I picked her up, planning to kill her. After killing her, I left her body just off Kent-Des Moines Road.

☒ In addition to this statement, I agree the Court can also consider the Prosecutor's Summary of the Evidence to determine the factual basis of my plea and at my sentencing.

12. My lawyer has explained to me, and we have fully discussed, all of the above paragraphs. I understand them all. I have been given a copy of this "Statement of Defendant on Plea of Guilty." I have no further questions to ask the Judge.

Defendant

Gary Leon Ridgway
Print Name

I have read and discussed this statement with the Defendant and believe that the Defendant is competent and fully understands the statement.

_____
Senior Deputy Prosecuting Attorney Bar #   Defendant's Lawyer   Bar # 12400

_____
Print Name   *Mark W. Prothero*
                                                                Print Name

_____
Senior Deputy Prosecuting Attorney Bar #   Defendant's Lawyer   Bar # 12340

_____
Print Name   *Todd M. Gruenhagen*
                                                                Print Name

_____
Senior Deputy Prosecuting Attorney Bar #   Defendant's Lawyer   Bar #

STATEMENT ON PLEA OF GUILTY - Page 14 of 16
CrR 4.2(g)

Associated Counsel for the Accused
420 West Harrison, Suite 201, Kent, WA 98032
(253) 520-6509

Figure 2.7 Page 14 of Gary Ridgway's statement on plea of guilty.

Ridgway was described as having low intelligence with poor school performance. He worked as a truck painter for Kenworth Truck Company for 32 years, acquiring that job after his release from the U.S. Navy and keeping it until his apprehension. He was heterosexual and married with one child at the time of his apprehension. He started killing women at age 33. He had no known history of abuse and had previous convictions for patronizing prostitutes. He showed no interest in law enforcement work.

As a child, Ridgway was described as a loner and outcast who had difficulty relating to his peers and did not participate in school or community activities. He was held back two grades in high school, embarrassing him and making him feel like a failure. In explaining his murders, Ridgway claimed to be cleaning up society by ridding it of prostitutes, whom he saw as trash. He took photographs and personal items from his victims but did not keep them long.

Academic serial murder researchers frequently argue that neither the foundations for the techniques of the FBI (Canter 2000; Torres, Boccaccini, and Miller 2006; Woodworth and Porter 1999), with profilers frequently relying on intuition or speculation, nor claims about the success of FBI profilers (Woodworth and Porter 1999) are well supported empirically. In a test of the assertion of the FBI that investigative experience is necessary for effective profiling, Kocsis, Hayes, and Irwin (2002) found evidence to the contrary. The researchers (two Australian and one American) tested the profiling abilities of four groups of Australian law enforcement personnel—homicide detectives, senior police detectives, trainee detectives, and police recruits—compared to a group of Australian undergraduate chemistry students. Their findings were surprising: The chemistry students consistently outperformed all law enforcement groups in profiling offenders of closed homicide cases; on a number of scales, the second-highest-performing group (after the chemistry students) was the recruits, and in many cases, the homicide detectives performed significantly worse than the chemistry students. Our knowledge about the utility of criminal profiling in America would be advanced by the performance of a similar study in the United States.

Finally, some research suggests that the use of algorithms or simple scientific procedures in investigations of serial offenses can be as effective as human knowledge and experience. Software packages known as geographic profiling systems (e.g., Dragnet) have been found effective in predicting the home location of serial offenders (Canter et al. 2000). Snook, Canter, and Bennell (2002) concluded that what we know about offender spatial behaviors can be summarized as simple heuristics that people with no special law enforcement training, no knowledge of geographic profiling or criminal behavior, and no investigative experience can quickly understand and utilize to make predictions as accurately as geographic profiling systems.

Regardless of the utility or futility of criminal profiling techniques, the FBI plays an instrumental role in building and sharing knowledge about serial murder and serial murderers. Members of NCAVC, a branch of the agency's Critical Incident Response Group (CIRG), periodically conduct training programs and seminars[6] to exchange knowledge about serial murder with other experts (i.e., law enforcement personnel, academics, mental health specialists, and members of the media) in a cooperative effort to establish more consensus on the subject and best practices that will lead to more effective working relationships. In addition, FBI publications that describe findings from interviews with identified serial murderers and case analysis have helped establish the basis for much of what we know about serial murder and serial murderers.

Academic Researchers

Published academic research into serial murder is sparse but began to appear in the mid-1980s. These studies have been overwhelmingly theoretical because quantitative data on serial murder are nearly impossible to collect. Serial murder is lumped into the broad category of homicide in official crime statistics; thus, no data specific to serial murder are readily available, although researchers have struggled to extrapolate these cases using a variety of sources. The focus and scope of academic research on serial murder depends on the discipline from which the researcher hails, although psychology has long been the dominant perspective and the individual the paramount focus.

> ## PROMINENT SERIAL MURDER RESEARCHERS IN ACADEMIA
>
> - Sociologist Dr. James De Burger
> - Dr. Steven A. Egger, associate professor of criminology at the University of Houston at Clear Lake in Texas
> - Dr. James Alan Fox, Lipman Family Professor of Criminology, Law, and Public Policy at Northeastern University
> - Dr. Eric W. Hickey, director of the Center for Forensic Studies at Alliant International University and professor of criminal psychology at California State University, Fresno
> - Dr. Ronald M. Holmes, emeritus professor in the Department of Justice Administration at the University of Louisville
> - Dr. Stephen T. Holmes, assistant professor of criminal justice at the University of Central Florida
> - Dr. Philip Jenkins, Edwin Erle Sparks Professor of History and Religious Studies at Pennsylvania State University
> - Dr. Jack Levin, Brudnick Professor of Sociology and Criminology at Northeastern University and codirector of the Center on Violence and Conflict at the university
> - Dr. Elliott Leyton, professor emeritus in the Department of Anthropology at Memorial University
> - Dr. Harold Schechter, professor of American Literature and Culture at Queens College, the City University of New York
> - Dr. Mark Seltzer, the Evan Frankel Professor of Literature at the University of California, Los Angeles

Journalists and True Crime Writers

Finally, media reports are the most accessible source of information on serial murder (in terms of availability and ease of comprehension) and thus are popular with the general public. They are also frequently utilized by academic researchers and law enforcement; even the FBI collects data about serial murder cases from media reports (Egger 1998). Media reports include news stories about new and existing cases; in-depth or investigative reporting about the murders, perpetrators, victims, and the communities in which the murders took place; and commentary (generally in the form of editorials, letters to the editor, or guest columns) on social issues surrounding the cases or criticism of police performance. Crime reporters covering sensational serial murder cases and freelance journalists frequently author books narrating the cases and offering analysis. Some find such success in this genre that they become full-time true crime writers.

> **WELL-KNOWN TRUE CRIME AUTHORS**
>
> - Journalist **Philip Carlo** is best known for his true crime books about mafia activities, such as *Ice Man: Confessions of a Mafia Contract Killer* (2006), but he also is known for his book *Night Stalker: The Life and Crimes of Richard Ramirez* (1996), for which he spent 200 hours with the serial murderer on San Quentin's death row.
> - One of the best-known true crime writers in the United States, **Ann Rule**, a former police officer and caseworker, has published more than 30 books in the genre, including *Green River Running Red* (2004), about the Green River Killer in Washington, and *The Stranger Beside Me* (1980), about serial murderer Ted Bundy, whom Rule knew personally.
> - **Carlton Smith**, a former journalist, has published nearly 20 books in the genre, including *The BTK Murders* (2006) and, with Tomas Guillen, *The Search for the Green River Killer* (1991).

Prevalence of Serial Murder

What we now call serial murder has occurred throughout the history of the United States and presumably the world, but law enforcement officials and social scientists suggest that there appears to have been a surge in serial murders in the United States within the past 30 to 50 years (Holmes and De Burger 1988; Lane 1997; Vronsky 2004). This interestingly fits within the time frame in which the phenomenon was labeled "serial murder" and began receiving increasing recognition through media coverage. The perceived surge in serial murder could be explained by an increased awareness of the phenomenon, better record keeping and crime scene analysis, increased media attention, or an increase in the number of serial murderers. Some serial murder researchers (e.g., Vronsky 2004) suggest that any rise in the number of serial murderers (or victims, for that matter) could be explained by a proportionate rise in the general population: More people means more serial murderers and more victims.

It is impossible to know whether there has been a surge in serial murder, most simply because we have no data to compare—we do not know how many serial murderers are active now or how many were active at any other previous point in time. Serial murderers are not counted in official crime statistics, and many likely are never identified, either because they manage to avoid capture or because their murders are never linked. If the killer does not display an obvious pattern or if the killer crosses law enforcement jurisdictions, the murders likely will be treated as separate cases. Cases of serial murder also are difficult to solve because there frequently is no apparent link between the killer and victim, complicating law enforcement personnel's search for a motive and the perpetrator.

Likewise, victims of serial murder are unlikely to be identified as such unless they were killed in a relatively small geographic region, within one law enforcement jurisdiction, in a similar manner as one or more other murders, and within a relatively short time span of other similar murders—or if the killer confesses and is believed. Some victims may never be found or identified. Frequent victims of serial murderers, including prostitutes, runaways, and homosexuals, may lead secretive lives, with pseudonyms, temporary dwellings, and few close friends, making identification more difficult. For those with transient lifestyles, it could be days, weeks, or even months before anyone knows they are missing. In addition, anyone with information in these communities may be reluctant to come forward with what they know out of fear for their own safety or because of a distrust of the police or legal system.

Law enforcement officials have ventured estimates of the number of active serial murderers in the United States and the average number of yearly victims, but these estimates vary greatly, ranging from the low 30s to 100 or more (Holmes and De Burger 1988; Caputi 1989). The U.S. Department of Justice approximates the number of active serial murderers at 35 and the number of annual victims at 540 (Schmid 2005). In the 1980s and 1990s, highly publicized estimates were much greater, chiefly because of an erroneous statement made at a 1983 news conference by then-director of the Behavioral Science Unit (now the Behavioral Analysis Units) of the FBI, Roger Depue, that serial murderers claim 4,000 victims each year (Schmid 2005). Since then, the estimated number of yearly victims has still frequently been reported as between 3,500 and 5,000, and the estimate of 4,000 is commonly cited in media reports. The FBI no longer provides official estimates, declaring only that serial murder is rare, comprising less than 1 percent of all murders in a year (Morton and Hilts 2008).

Divergent definitions of serial murder also complicate efforts to create a list of known serial murderers. Without a single definition of serial murder that is generally agreed on by researchers, there are no real criteria for identifying which killers should be classified as serial murderers and thus no agreement on numbers. Definitional considerations are more thoroughly discussed in the following section, but suffice it to say that definitions that are more limited identify fewer serial murderers and broader definitions identify more.

Definitions of Serial Murder

What constitutes murder and distinguishes it from natural death and other forms of violent deaths due to accidents or suicides are widely agreed on, albeit less distinct in practice. Definitions of serial murder vary, however, with much of the discrepancy related to number of victims and distinctiveness of motivational factors. Less ambiguous is how serial murder differs from single murder and other types of multiple murder.

Distinguishing Serial Murder from Other Types of Murder

Serial murder is distinguished from single murder in several ways in addition to number of victims. Single murders are more likely than serial murders to be committed by intimates or acquaintances and to be motivated by hatred, anger, revenge, or rage. Most serial murder researchers concur that serial murderers almost exclusively kill strangers (Holmes and De Burger 1988; Holmes and Holmes 2002; Morton and Hilts 2008), and serial murder victims often are members of vulnerable populations, such as children, elderly, prostitutes, runaways, and homosexuals (Fox, Levin, and Quinet 2005; Hickey 2006; Holmes and De Burger 1988; Vronsky 2007). In contrast to patterns in single murder, in which men represent the largest percentage of victims, the most frequent victims of serial murder are women (Hickey 2006; Kraemer, Lord, and Heilbrun 2004; Schechter and Everitt 1997).

Serial murder also is distinguished from other types of multiple murder—mass murder and spree murder—by the time frame in which the murders are committed. *Mass murder* is the killing of at

---

EXAMPLES OF INDIVIDUAL MASS MURDERERS

- **Richard Speck** killed eight student nurses in their Chicago townhouse on July 14, 1966.
- **James Huberty** killed 22 people inside a San Diego McDonald's restaurant on July 18, 1984.
- **Richard Farley** killed seven people at his former workplace, Electromagnetic Systems Labs, in Sunnyvale, California, on February 16, 1988.
- **Timothy McVeigh** killed 168 people in the Oklahoma City bombings on April 19, 1995.
- **Eric Harris** and **Dylan Klebold** killed 13 people at Columbine High School in Columbine, Colorado, on April 20, 1999. Harris was believed to be the mastermind of the massacre (Cullen 2009).

least several people in one place at the same time (Holmes and De Burger 1988). Mass murder frequently is committed—or at least masterminded—by one person, but genocide and acts of terrorism, including the September 11, 2001, terrorist attacks on the United States, also would fall under this category.

Spree murder, on the other hand, is the killing of at least several people within a short time frame (during a period of hours or weeks)

EXAMPLES OF SPREE MURDERERS

- **Charles Whitman** killed his mother and wife in their homes approximately 12 hours before fatally shooting 14 people from a tower on the University of Texas at Austin campus on August 1, 1966 (Figure 2.8).
- **John Allen Muhammad** and **Lee Boyd Malvo** killed 10 people in various locations throughout the Washington, D.C., metropolitan area and along Interstate 95 in Virginia over a period of 3 weeks in October 2002.
- **Seung-Hui Cho** killed 32 people in two separate attacks (about 2 hours apart) on the campus of Virginia Polytechnic Institute and State University in Blacksburg, Virginia, on April 16, 2007.

Figure 2.8 Charles Whitman, a spree murderer.

in multiple locations, usually by one impulsive killer (Holmes and De Burger 1988).

Defining Serial Murder

Although not intended to be a general definition of serial murder, a definition does appear in a federal law passed by the U.S. Congress in 1998, called the Protection of Children from Sexual Predator Act of 1998 (Protection of Children from Sexual Predator Act of 1998, 15). The law includes new language regarding investigative authority in serial murder cases, establishes a resource center to provide support for serial murder investigations, and offers the following working definition: "The term 'serial killings' means a series of three or more killings, not less than one of which was committed within the United States, having common characteristics such as to suggest the reasonable possibility that the crimes were committed by the same actor or actors" (14).

Most serial murder researchers employ a definition of serial murder developed by the FBI (although no longer used by the agency) or some close variation. The FBI has long defined a serial murderer as a person who killed three or more people over a period of weeks, months, or years with an emotional cooling-off period between murders (Branttey and Kosky 2005). The time element not only distinguishes serial murder from other forms of multiple murder but also addresses differences between serial murderers and other murderers. The National Institute of Justice and others include in the definition evidence of "sadistic, sexual overtones" in the commission of the murders (Schechter and Everitt 1997). Consonant with this qualification, serial murder is most often classified as "sexual homicide," with varying degrees of organization, by law enforcement agencies, including until recently the FBI.

The FBI updated its definition of serial murder in a document published in 2008 on its Web site and now defines serial murder as follows: "The unlawful killing of two or more victims by the same offender(s), in separate events" (Morton and Hilts 2008, 9). This definition is substantially more expansive than the previous FBI definition in a number of ways: It reduces the requisite number of victims from three to two, eliminates the "cooling-off period" requirement, removes any motivational condition, and allows for the possibility of multiple killers in a single serial murder case. However, a significant restriction on this definition appears later in the same document: "For the most part, the serial murder involves strangers with no visible relationship between the offender and the victim" (Morton and Hilts 2008, 17). The new FBI definition, then, is more limited than it at first appears and would more accurately read: The unlawful killing of two or more victims by the same offender(s), in separate events, with no visible relationship between the offender and the victim.

Criminal profiler Brent Turvey (1999) requires only "two or more related cases involving homicide behavior" (287).[7] Social scientists frequently incorporate a number of motivational, behavioral, and psychological qualifiers. Academic researchers Holmes and De Burger (1988) define a serial murderer as a solo killer whose attacks are unprovoked and target those with whom he has little-to-no relationship, and they exclude murders committed for passion, profit, or other personal gain. Academic researcher Hickey's (2006) definition requires three or more victims killed "over time" and a pattern connecting the murders, but he includes murders for financial or personal gain and allows relationships between killers and victims. Academic researcher Egger's (1998) definition is particularly exclusive:

> A serial murder occurs when (1) one or more individuals (in many cases, males) commit(s) a second murder and/or subsequent murder; (2) there is generally no prior relationship between victim and attacker (if there is a relationship, such a relationship will place the victim in a subjugated role to the killer); (3) subsequent murders are at different times and have no apparent connection to the initial murder; and (4) are usually committed in a different geographical location. Further, (5) the motive is not for material gain and is for the murderer's desire to have power or dominance over his victims. (6) Victims may have symbolic value for the murderer and/or are perceived to be prestigeless and in most instances are unable to defend themselves or alert others to their plight, or are perceived as powerless given their situation in time, place, or status within their immediate surroundings, examples being (7) vagrants, the homeless, prostitutes, migrant workers, homosexuals, missing children, single women (out by themselves), elderly women, college students, and hospital patients. (5–6)

Most definitions of serial murder exclude murders committed by a person serving as an agent of someone or something else, such as killings during military service, political terrorism, murder for hire, and organized crime (Heide and Keeney 1994; Ferguson et al. 2003; Walsh 2005). However, the new broad definition of the FBI of serial murder could be interpreted to include a majority of these cases.

A Working Definition of Serial Murder

The definition of serial murder employed in my previous analysis (Wiest 2009) was based on the original FBI definition, as well as common characteristics established in the literature (discussed in the next chapter): *Serial murder is defined as three or more homicides that were intentionally and willingly committed by a single offender acting alone for personal gratification over a period of weeks, months, or years.* The motivational qualifier helps distinguish serial murder from homicides motivated by material or financial gain, sympathy, revenge, passion, or temporary rage, which can be demonstrated to be qualitatively different types of homicide.

A *serial murderer*, then, would be defined as a person who has been convicted of serial murder as defined in the preceding paragraph. Among types of killers that may be considered serial murderers elsewhere but are not included in this definition are those who have been suspected but not convicted of at least three murders; those who murdered family members or other intimates; those who killed as part of a partnership; and health care or child care workers who killed in those settings or while on duty. These offenders appear to differ in killing methods, targeted victims, and apparent motivation from the "typical" serial murderer (further explained in the next chapter) and generally are treated as atypical in popular portrayals.

Notes

1. National-level resources include the National Center for the Analysis of Violent Crime of the FBI (including its Behavioral Analysis Units and Violent Criminal Apprehension Program); the Law Enforcement Online Web site; and forensic databases like the Combined DNA Index System (CODIS), various Automated Fingerprint Identification Systems (AFIS),

and the National Integrated Ballistics Identification Network (NIBIN). CODIS, a national database designed to link DNA evidence in criminal cases, is divided into three levels—the National DNA Index System, the State SNA Index System, and the Local DNA Index System—that should all be considered in serial murder cases that may cross multiple jurisdictions.
2. For a detailed explanation of typologies developed by the FBI, see Douglas et al. (1997) and Vronsky (2004).
3. For a detailed explanation of this categorization, see Holmes and De Burger (1988) and Holmes and Holmes (2002).
4. For more information about the Baton Rouge Serial Killer case and an evaluation of the criminal profile of the FBI, see Ramsland ("Criminal Profiling") and Ramsland ("The Profile Evaluated").
5. For more information about the Green River Killer case and an evaluation of the criminal profile of the FBI, see Levi-Minzi and Shields (2007).
6. A symposium, "Serial Murder: Multi-Disciplinary Perspectives for Investigators," was held August 29 to September 2, 2005, in San Antonio, Texas. Its primary goal was to identify commonalities of knowledge on an array of topics related to serial murder among recognized experts in various fields (i.e., law enforcement, medical, legal, academic, and media) and specialties.
7. Related cases are those in which substantial similarities in modus operandi or crime scene characteristics are found such that the cases are considered by law enforcement officials as likely committed by the same perpetrator or perpetrators.

3

THE "TYPICAL" SERIAL MURDERER

Introduction

Definitions of serial murder were developed after a great deal of analysis of known cases, with a particular focus on identifying common characteristics of known serial murderers. There is a great difference, however, between popular media portrayals of the "typical" American serial murderer and common characteristics of American serial murderers identified by the Federal Bureau of Investigation (FBI) and academic researchers. Both representations are explored here.

Popular Portrayals in American Media

Popular portrayals of serial murderers found in American media are generally of two types: the hideous, monstrous loner and the intelligent, handsome, charming guy next door. Egger (1998) offers a clear description of the first type:

> The serial killer is a sex-starved man-beast who is driven to kill because of a horrible childhood and the way society has treated him. He has had an unusual relationship with his mother. He travels alone across large geographic areas of the country and has an in-depth knowledge of police criminal investigative procedures, which allows him to elude the local, state, and federal law enforcement. He is an insane and cowardly maniac who preys on the weak and helpless. (14)

Vronsky (2004, 2007) argues that after Jack the Ripper's murders in 1888 in London (Figures 3.1–3.2), serial murderers were portrayed as "depraved monsters—freaks of nature—outcasts and drifters whose demented criminal features should have given them away" (2004, 6). This is the type portrayed most often when the serial murderers play supporting roles to the "star" detectives or other officials in movies such as *Copycat* (1995), *Red Dragon* (2002), and *Untraceable*

38   CREATING CULTURAL MONSTERS

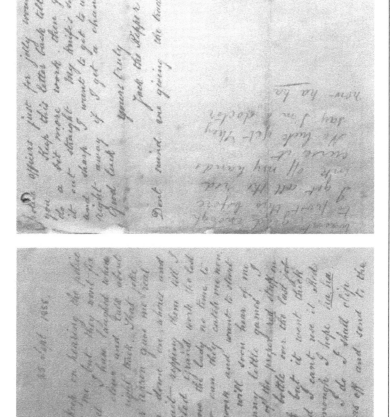

Figure 3.1 (See color insert.) Jack the Ripper letter dated September 25, 1888.

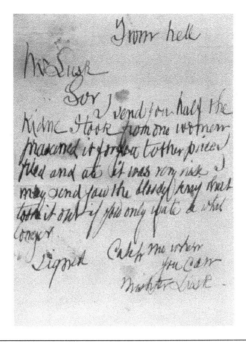

Figure 3.2 **(See color insert.)** Jack the Ripper "From hell" letter postmarked October 15, 1888.

(2008); television shows such as *Law & Order: Special Victims Unit* (1999–2010) and *CSI: Crime Scene Investigation* (2000–2010); and books such as the *In Death* novels by J. D. Robb (1995–2010), the Kay Scarpetta novels by Patricia Cornwell (1990–2010), and the Temperance Brennan novels by Kathy Reichs (1997–2010). Although this image is still common, a shift appears to have occurred, with the second type—the intelligent, handsome, charming guy next door—increasingly represented in American media.

Vronsky (2004, 2007) identifies this shift as beginning with representations of serial murderer Ted Bundy in the 1970s, who was depicted as handsome, intelligent, charming, and sociable. Vronsky (2004, 6) sees Bundy as the killer who defined the "new postmodern serial killer role model," which he argues is no longer a hideous, depraved monster but more representative of an ordinary person, if not better than an ordinary person. Fox et al. (2005) agree, calling the "human monster" image of serial murderers a "Hollywood stereotype" and claiming that a "more modern image describes these killers as unusually handsome and charming" (107), an image that does not appear to be any more accurate. This type is best depicted by the fictional Hannibal Lecter, the psychiatrist and cannibalistic serial murderer in the films *The Silence of the Lambs* (1991), *Red Dragon* (2002), and *Hannibal Rising* (2007); the Earl Brooks character, a successful business owner, family man, and serial murderer, in the film *Mr. Brooks* (2007); and the Dexter Morgan character, a Miami police department blood-spatter expert and vigilante serial murderer in the *Dexter* book series by Jeff Lindsay (2004–2010) and subsequent Showtime television series *Dexter* (2006–2010).

Theodore Robert Bundy

Theodore Robert (Ted) Bundy murdered at least 3 women (but is believed to have killed approximately 35) by strangulation and bludgeoning from 1974 to 1978 in Washington, Utah, Colorado, and Florida (Figures 3.3–3.5). He killed some of his victims in their homes, leaving the bodies there, and others outside, in his vehicle, or in some unknown location, dumping the bodies in remote outdoor areas. He was arrested in Utah in August 1975 for failing to stop for a police officer and for possession of burglary tools. He was convicted of kidnapping, sentenced to 15 years in prison, and then extradited to Colorado to face a murder charge. He escaped custody in Colorado in June 1977, was captured 6 days

Figure 3.3 Ted Bundy's FBI photo when he was placed on the Ten Most Wanted Fugitives list in 1978.

THE "TYPICAL" SERIAL MURDERER

Figure 3.4 **(See color insert.)** Serial murderer Ted Bundy escaped from the Pitkin County Courthouse in Aspen, Colorado, by jumping from the second window from left, second story, on June 7, 1977. Bundy murdered at least three women (the actual number of victims is believed to be closer to 35) by strangulation and bludgeoning from 1974 to 1978 in Washington, Utah, Colorado, and Florida. He was executed on January 24, 1989, in Florida.

Figure 3.5 Ted Bundy's Florida Department of Corrections mug shot on February 13, 1980.

later, and escaped again in December 1977, this time making it to Florida. He killed two women and one girl and severely wounded three other women before being captured for good after a traffic stop. He was convicted of two murders in Florida on July 23, 1979, and sentenced to death twice. He was then convicted of one murder in Florida in February 1980 and sentenced to death. He was executed on January 24, 1989.

Bundy was described as highly intelligent and performed well in school. He earned a college degree in psychology and attended law school for a while. He had worked on local political campaigns, for a crisis hotline, and for a while as a campus security guard, but he had a fairly inconsistent employment history. He was heterosexual, never married, and had no children. He started killing women at age 28. He had no history of abuse, although he discovered while in his 20s that who he thought was his sister was really his mother and that who he thought were his parents were really his grandparents. He was arrested on suspicion of burglary during his killing spree but otherwise had no prior history of arrests. He did not serve in the military and showed no interest in law enforcement work, except to occasionally pose as a police officer to lure victims.

Bundy was described as a loner and socially awkward, with difficulty relating to his peers. He was a good athlete and joined the football team at school, but he quit after a short time because of a lack of interest. As an adult, he was a Republican campaign worker and crisis counselor and was generally described as well adjusted. No explanation was offered for his murders, and he did not keep trophies.

Vronsky (2007, 138) also suggests a shift in the portrayal of female multiple murderers, from one of "respectable and sometimes attractive women who harbored homicidal intentions behind a façade of feminine mystique" to one of an unattractive, hardened woman who is comfortable on the streets and promiscuous, based on representations of Aileen Wuornos, a prostitute who murdered at least six men from 1989 to 1990 in Florida. He argues that this supposed shift "might be signaling the shape of things to come" (Vronsky 2007, 138), suggesting that representations of female multiple murderers may become more similar to the male model.

Aileen Carol Wuornos

Aileen Carol Wuornos murdered at least six men by shooting from 1989 to 1990 in Florida (Figure 3.6). Working as a prostitute, she was picked up by her victims and driven to remote locations, where she killed them in their vehicles or outdoors and left their bodies. She was identified after crashing and abandoning a car belonging to one of her victims. Witnesses provided descriptions of Wuornos and a female companion, others who had seen the pair driving the car provided their names, police found Wuornos's palm print on the car, and her fingerprints were found on pawned items belonging to her victims. She was convicted of one murder on January 27, 1992, and received a death sentence. On March 31, 1992, she pled guilty to three murders and received three death sentences. Then, in June 1992 and February 1993, she pled guilty to two more murders and received two more death sentences. She was executed on October 9, 2002.

Wuornos was described as of low intelligence with poor school performance (she dropped out of high school). She began working as a prostitute as a young teenager and continued prostitution

Figure 3.6 **(See color insert.)** Mug shot of multiple murderer Aileen Wuornos from the Florida Department of Corrections (date unknown). Wuornos murdered at least six men from 1989 to 1990 in Florida. She was executed on October 9, 2002.

until her apprehension. She was a lesbian, divorced from a man and involved with a woman when she was apprehended, and had one child as a young teenager whom she immediately gave up for adoption. She started killing men at age 33. She was sexually and physically abused by her grandfather, whom she thought was her father (she, like Bundy, had been told that her mother was her sister and her grandparents her parents). She had prior convictions for disorderly conduct, driving under the influence (DUI), and weapons offenses. She reportedly tried to join the military and become a corrections officer.

Wuornos was described as a loner and social outcast as a child who had difficulty relating to her peers and would often act out to gain their attention. She also appeared to have difficulty building and maintaining close relationships as an adult. She explained her murders in terms of her prior victimization but also argued that they were all committed in self-defense. She stole items of value from her victims, such as cars, jewelry, and money, but did not keep trophies.

For both types, fictional representations and purported biographical accounts of actual killers frequently portray the investigation like a game of cat and mouse, with the killers repeatedly contacting police before their apprehension. The representations also depict substantial contact with the media and exaggerate the killers' abilities and intelligence. Although some serial murderers do contact police and media and express feelings of enjoyment from doing so, social scientists have found these activities more the exception than the rule. Serial murderers Ted Bundy and Gary Ridgway were portrayed as engaged in a cat-and-mouse game with police—Bundy because of his multiple escapes from jail, frequent changes in appearance, and high mobility and Ridgway because he rotated among several locations to dispose of bodies. These behaviors do not necessarily indicate enjoyment of the chase; they can be explained by efforts to avoid (or end) capture.

The version of the typical serial murderer suggested by FBI and academic studies is categorically different from popular media portrayals. Both versions begin with the murderer as white, male, and American, but there is much discrepancy in the portrayals of other personal and background characteristics, as well as motivations and activities. The following section presents information about the characteristics of identified serial murderers reported by social scientists and law enforcement officials.

Common Characteristics Identified by the FBI and Academic Researchers

Identified serial murderers are overwhelmingly white men, typically between the ages of 25 and 35, although the age ranges of their victims vary widely (Douglas and Olshaker 1997; Fox et al. 2005; Holmes 1985; Holmes and De Burger 1988; Holmes and Holmes 2002; Vronsky 2004). Yet, serial murderers who begin killing after age 35 exist. Albert Fish, a pedophile and cannibal, murdered at least three children in New York in the 1920s; he was 54 years old when he started killing.

Hamilton Howard Fish

Hamilton Howard (Albert) Fish murdered at least three children by strangulation and torture in New York between 1924 and 1928 (Figure 3.7). He also was a child molester and cannibal and a suspect in two other murders. He worked as a house painter for a while, married four times (although the first marriage was

Figure 3.7 Mug shot of serial murderer Albert Fish from a 1903 arrest for grand larceny in New York. Fish, a pedophile and cannibal, murdered at least three children in New York in the 1920s. He was executed on January 16, 1936.

never legally dissolved), and had six children with his first wife. Fish enjoyed sending obscene letters to women he found in classified advertisements and self-injury—at the time of his arrest, an X-ray revealed at least 29 needles that had been inserted and lodged in his pelvic region. He was imprisoned for grand larceny, sending obscene letters, and petty thefts, and he spent time in psychiatric facilities more than once. In 1928, he kidnapped, killed, and cannibalized a 10-year-old girl, his last known victim. Six years later, he sent a letter to her mother describing the crime in detail. A small emblem on the envelope in which the letter was sent led police to Fish, who admitted to the murder. He was convicted of that murder in March 1935 and sentenced to death. He was executed by electric chair on January 16, 1936, at Sing Sing Correctional Facility in New York.

Ed Gein, known as the "Plainfield Ghoul" and credited as the source for several fictional serial murderers, including Norman Bates from *Psycho* (1960), Leatherface from *The Texas Chainsaw Massacre* (1974), and Buffalo Bill from *The Silence of the Lambs* (1991), murdered two women[1] in Plainfield, Wisconsin, in the 1950s; he was approximately 48 years old when he started killing. In addition, Bob Berdella, who murdered six men from 1980 to 1984 in Kansas City, Missouri, began killing at age 41; and Joel Rifkin, who murdered nine women from 1989 to 1993 in New York City, began killing at age 40.

Robert Berdella

Robert (Bob) Berdella murdered six men by torture, suffocation, and drug injections from 1980 to 1984 in Kansas City, Missouri. He killed his victims in his home after extensive torture, then dismembered the bodies and put the body pieces out with the trash. He was caught after one of his victims escaped and notified police. In a plea bargain, he confessed to the murders on December 19, 1988, and received a life sentence. He died of a heart attack in prison on October 8, 1992.

In biographical narratives, Berdella was described as highly intelligent, performing well in school. He attended art school after high school but dropped out. He worked as a cook before opening a curio shop, selling mostly rare artifacts, replica skulls, lava lamps, incense, and the like. The business was only moderately successful, and he periodically worked a second job as a cook. He was homosexual, never married, and had no children. He started killing men at age 41. He had no known history of abuse. Prior convictions were for drug offenses. He never served in the military or showed interest in law enforcement work. Berdella took photographs of his victims throughout the torture he inflicted and after their deaths; kept journals and audiocassette tapes documenting the torture and deaths; and saved two heads as souvenirs, or trophies. He blamed the movie *The Collector* (based on the book of the same name) for influencing his desires to kill.

Berdella was described by family members, neighbors, and former classmates as a loner and outcast as a child; he had difficulty relating to his peers and did not participate in school or community activities. As an adult, however, he was described as a community leader who was instrumental in revitalizing his neighborhood and forming a crime watch group, although he had few friends.

Joel David Rifkin

Joel David Rifkin murdered nine women (mostly drug addicts and prostitutes) by strangulation from 1989 to 1993 in New York City. He killed his victims either in the home he shared with his mother and sister or in his vehicle, dismembered the bodies, and scattered the body parts throughout the city. He was caught in June 1993 when he fled in his pickup truck from a police officer attempting to pull him over for missing license plates and crashed into a utility pole, at which time the officer discovered the body of his last victim in the bed of the truck. After several trials, he was convicted in 1994 and sentenced to 203 years to life in prison. In 2000, he was transferred from Attica State Prison to Clinton Correctional Facility at Dannemora.

Rifkin, adopted as an infant, was described as highly intelligent with poor school performance. He attended college but dropped out. He owned an unprofitable landscaping business. He was heterosexual, was never married, and had no children. He started killing women at age 40 and had a prior conviction for patronizing a prostitute. He had no known history of abuse and never served in the military or showed any interest in law enforcement work.

Rifkin was described as socially awkward as a child, with difficulty relating to his peers. He found some acceptance after joining the track team in school but did not stay a member long. He said he began patronizing prostitutes after high school as a way to gain sexual experience without being rejected by women he knew. He said he killed as a form of revenge against his biological mother, whom he believed to be a prostitute, and said the movie *Frenzy* further influenced his desire to kill. He saved personal items from his victims, such as driver's licenses or other identification cards, credit cards, clothing, and jewelry.

Adolescent serial murderers are rare, just as single murderers younger than 18 are relatively rare. Myers (2004) studied cases of serial murderers who were younger than 18 during the entire series of their crimes, identifying only six in the past 150 years. At least two serial murderers began killing as teenagers, with the majority of their crimes occurring later. Edmund Kemper, known as the "Coed Killer," murdered six female hitchhikers in the Santa Cruz, California, area in the early 1970s; before that series, he killed his paternal grandparents at age 15. Jeffery Dahmer, who murdered 17 men and boys from 1978 to 1991 in Milwaukee, Wisconsin, killed his first victim at age 18.

Jeffrey Lionel Dahmer

Jeffrey Lionel Dahmer (known as the "Milwaukee Monster") murdered 17 men and boys by strangulation from 1978 to 1991 in Milwaukee, Wisconsin. He killed his victims in his parents' home, his grandmother's home, or his apartment, depending on where he was living at the time of each murder, and dismembered the bodies, which he then either saved or disposed of by burying under his parents' or grandmother's house (when he lived there), putting the body pieces out with the garbage, or storing the body pieces in a vat of acid. He was caught after one of his victims escaped and notified police. He pled guilty, although claimed insanity, to 15 murders on July 13, 1992, and received 15 consecutive life sentences. He was beaten to death in prison on November 28, 1994.

Dahmer was described as average in intelligence with poor school performance. He briefly attended college, dropping out after failing his first quarter. He was employed inconsistently but just prior to his apprehension worked at a chocolate factory. He was homosexual, never married, and had no children. He started killing men and boys at age 18. He had no known history of abuse. Prior convictions included sexual offenses (indecent exposure and sexual assault). He served in the Army but was honorably discharged because of alcoholism. He showed no interest in law enforcement work.

Dahmer was described as a loner and outcast as a child; he had difficulty relating to his peers, would often act out to gain their attention, and appeared indifferent toward school and community activities. He also appeared to have difficulty building and maintaining close relationships as an adult. His murders were explained at trial as due to a fear of abandonment and insanity. He saved photographs and body parts as trophies.

Identified serial murderers are of average intelligence (Fox and Levin 2005; Fox et al. 2005; Morton and Hilts 2008; Ressler et al. 1992; Wiest 2009), contrary to the notion frequently included in popular profiles of serial murderers that they are extraordinarily intelligent.[2] Regardless of intelligence, they tend to have performed poorly in school (Schechter and Everitt 1997; Wiest 2009). Some researchers contend that most serial murderers work as unskilled laborers (Schechter and Everitt 1997). Of the 15 serial murderers analyzed in my study (Wiest 2009), most held working-class occupations (e.g., factory worker, warehouse worker, auto mechanic, delivery driver, construction worker, and painter) and had difficulty maintaining a steady work history.

Past research has found that serial murderers frequently have difficulty maintaining relationships with others (e.g., Douglas et al. 1997; Vronsky 2004), and this was supported in my analysis. Fourteen of the 15 serial murderers included in the study were described by family members, neighbors, and former classmates as loners or outcasts as children. Most were described as socially awkward, with difficulty relating to their peers, a lack of ability for participating in socially valued activities (e.g., athletics or clubs), or indifference toward such activities. Several did participate in socially valued activities as children or teenagers, but they still often reported feeling ostracized by their peers—although this feeling is not uncommon among teenagers. A couple of those in the study participated in socially valued activities as adults. John Gacy, who murdered 33 boys and young men in the 1970s in Chicago, was a Boy Scout, an active member of the Jaycees, and later a Democratic precinct captain.

John Wayne Gacy

John Wayne Gacy (known as the "Killer Clown") murdered 33 boys and young men by strangulation from 1972 to 1978 in Chicago, Illinois (Figure 3.8). He killed all of his victims in his home and buried most of the bodies in the crawl space under his home or elsewhere on his property; several were placed in nearby rivers. He was caught when police searched his house after his last victim went missing; the police discovered items they considered suspicious and a foul odor emanating from the crawl space. He pled not guilty by reason of insanity but was convicted on March 13, 1980, and sentenced to death. He was executed on May 10, 1994.

Gacy was described as average in intelligence with poor school performance, although he did attend business school after high school. He had a fairly consistent work record and at the time of his arrest owned a profitable construction business. He was often described as homosexual, although he said on several occasions that he was bisexual. He was divorced at the time of his apprehension and had children who lived with their mother. He started killing young men at age 30; had no known history of abuse; and had various prior arrests and convictions for sodomy (an arrest

Figure 3.8 **(See color insert.)** An active member of the Democratic Party, serial murderer John Gacy was photographed with then-First Lady Rosalynn Carter on May 6, 1978. Gacy murdered 33 boys and young men by strangulation from 1972 to 1978 in Chicago, Illinois. He was executed on May 10, 1994.

that he indicated deeply embarrassed him), breaking and entering, conspiracy, assault, disorderly conduct, battery and aggravated battery, and reckless conduct. He did not serve in the military and showed no interest in law enforcement except to occasionally pose as a police officer (he drove a late-model black Oldsmobile, equipped with a red light and police radio scanner, and often carried handcuffs and a phony police badge) to lure victims.

As a child, Gacy was described as well behaved with good relationships with his teachers and other children. He was a Boy Scout, an active member of the Jaycees, and later a Democratic precinct captain. He claimed mental illness and explained the murders as ridding society of its "bad element." He kept small personal items from his victims, such as wallets and clothing.

Dennis Rader, who murdered 10 men, women, and children from 1974 to 1986 in Wichita, Kansas, earned a criminal justice degree from Wichita State University and was active and well known in his community, a Boy Scout leader, and congregation president at his church. Most of the serial murderers in my study appeared to have difficulty building and maintaining close relationships as adults, although marriage was common.[3] A few remained loners into adulthood, and none had more than a couple of close friends at one time.

Dennis Lynn Rader

Dennis Lynn Rader (known as the "BTK Killer") murdered 10 men, women, and children by strangulation and stabbing from 1974 to 1986 in Wichita, Kansas (Figures 3.9–3.14). He killed the victims in their homes, gaining access by breaking in while they were not home and waiting; pretending to be a police officer or phone company worker; slipping in through an unlocked door; or in one case, throwing a concrete block through a plate glass window. Police traced a computer disk he sent to a local television station to a church where he was congregation council president, then made a familial match of his daughter's DNA obtained from a subpoena of medical records with the DNA in semen found at one of the murder scenes. He was captured in February 2005; pled guilty on June 27, 2005; and received 10 consecutive life sentences. He is serving his sentences in Kansas.

Rader was described as of average intelligence with average school performance, and he eventually earned a criminal justice degree from Wichita State University. He had previously worked for a home security company but was employed as a community compliance officer at the time of his apprehension. He was heterosexual and married with grown children at the time of his apprehension. He started killing mostly women at age 29. He had no known history of abuse and no prior convictions. He served in the U.S. Air Force and showed an interest in law enforcement work, evidenced by his college major and employment.

Rader was described as socially awkward as a child, with difficulty relating to his peers. As an adult, he became active and well known in his community. He was a Boy Scout leader and congregation president at his church. He kept a diary of his murders and collected newspaper clippings about his and other serial murder cases; he also took photographs of his victims and kept small items like driver's licenses. He blamed a "demon" or "dark side" inside of him for the murders.

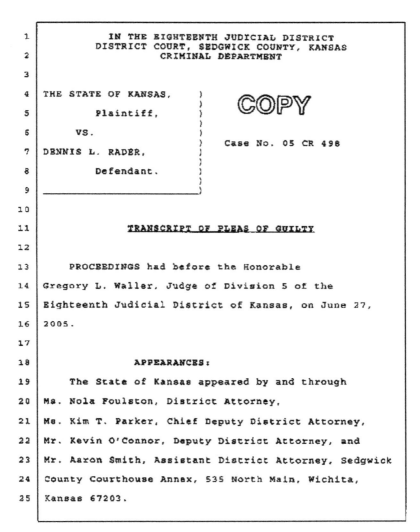

Figure 3.9 The first page of the transcript from Dennis Rader's ("BTK Killer") pleas of guilty, delivered before Judge Greg Waller on June 27, 2005, in the Eighteenth Judicial District Court, Sedgwick County, Kansas, in *The State of Kansas v. Dennis L. Rader*.

```
STATE V. DENNIS L. RADER   05 CR 498   GUILTY PLEAS   6/27/2005
 1    you did on that day?
 2              THE DEFENDANT: As before, Vian was a --
 3    Actually on that one she was completely random.
 4    There was actually someone that across from Dillons
 5    was potential target. It was called Project Green,
 6    I think. I had project numbers assigned to it. And
 7    that particular day I drove to Dillons, parked in
 8    the parking lot, watched this particular residence,
 9    and then got out of the car and walked over to it.
10    It's probably in the police report, the address. I
11    don't remember the address now. Knocked. Nobody --
12    Nobody answered it. So I was all keyed up, so I
13    just started going through the neighborhood. I had
14    been through the neighborhood before. I kind of
15    knew a little -- little of the layout of the
16    neighborhood. I'd been through the back alleys,
17    knew where some -- certain people lived. While I
18    was walking down Hydraulic I met a -- a young boy
19    and asked him if he would ID some pictures, kind of
20    as a russ (sic), I guess, or ruse as you call it,
21    and kind of feel it out, and saw where he went, and
22    I went to another address, knocked on the door.
23    Nobody opened the door, so I just noticed where he
24    went and went to that house, and we went from there.
25              THE COURT: Now, you -- you call these
                    DAVID G. HOLT, CSR, RMR, CRR
                    OFFICIAL COURT REPORTER
```

Figure 3.10   Page 46 of the transcript from Dennis Rader's pleas of guilty.

```
STATE V. DENNIS L. RADER  05 CR 498  GUILTY PLEAS  6/27/2005
 1              THE DEFENDANT:  And I watched -- I
 2   watched where he went.
 3              THE COURT:  What happened then?
 4              THE DEFENDANT:  After I tried this once,
 5   the residence, nobody came to the door.  I went to
 6   this house where he went in, knocked on the door and
 7   told 'em I was a private detective, showed 'em a
 8   picture that I had just showed the boy and asked 'em
 9   if they could ID the picture; and that time I -- I
10   had the gun here and I just kind of forced myself
11   in.  I just, you know, walked in -- just opened the
12   door and walked in and then pulled a pistol.
13              THE COURT:  What gun?  What pistol?
14              THE DEFENDANT:  The .357 magnum.
15              THE COURT:  All right.  So you only had
16   one gun with you this time?
17              THE DEFENDANT:  Yes, sir, uh-huh.
18              THE COURT:  What happened then?
19              THE DEFENDANT:  I told Mrs. -- Miss Vian
20   that I had a problem with sexual fantasies, that I
21   was going to tie her up, and that -- and I might
22   have to tie the kids up, and that she would
23   cooperate with this -- cooperate with me at that
24   time.  We went back.  She was extremely nervous.  I
25   think she even smoked a cigarette.  And we went back

                DAVID G. HOLT, CSR, RMR, CRR
                   OFFICIAL COURT REPORTER
```

Figure 3.11 Page 48 of the transcript from Dennis Rader's pleas of guilty.

```
STATE V. DENNIS L. RADER   05 CR 498   GUILTY PLEAS   6/27/2005
 1    to the -- one of the back -- back areas of the
 2    porch, explained to her that I had done this before,
 3    and, you know, I think she -- at that point in time
 4    I think she was sick 'cause she had a night robe on,
 5    and I think, if I remember right, she was -- she had
 6    been sick.  I think -- I think she came out of the
 7    bedroom when I went in the house.  So anyway, we
 8    went back to the -- her bedroom, and I proceeded to
 9    tie the kids up, and they started crying and got
10    real upset.  So I said oh, this is not gonna work,
11    so we moved 'em to the bathroom.  She helped me.
12         And then I tied the door shut.  We put some toys
13    and blankets and odds and ends in there for the
14    kids, make them as comfortable as we could.  Tied
15    the -- We tied one of the bathroom doors shut so
16    they couldn't open it, and we shoved -- she went
17    back and helped me shove the bed up against the
18    other bathroom door, and then I proceeded to tie her
19    up.  She got sick, threw up.  Got her a glass of
20    water, comforted her a little bit, and then went
21    ahead and tied her up and then put a blag (sic) -- a
22    bag over her head and strangled her.
23              THE COURT:  All right.  Was this a
24    plastic bag also?
25              THE DEFENDANT:  Yes, sir.  I think it

              DAVID G. HOLT, CSR, RMR, CRR
                 OFFICIAL COURT REPORTER
```

Figure 3.12 Page 49 of the transcript from Dennis Rader's pleas of guilty.

THE "TYPICAL" SERIAL MURDERER

```
STATE V. DENNIS L. RADER    05 CR 498    GUILTY PLEAS    6/27/2005
 1              THE COURT:  So you were not working in
 2    any form or fashion.  You were just --
 3              THE DEFENDANT:  Well, I don't know, if --
 4    you know, if you read much about serial killers,
 5    they go through what they call the different
 6    phases.  That's one of the phases they go through is
 7    a -- as a trolling stage.  You're lay -- Basically
 8    you're looking for a victim at that time, and that
 9    can either be trolling for months or years.  But
10    once you lock in on a certain person then you become
11    stalking, and that might be several of them, but you
12    really home in on that person.  They -- They
13    basically come the -- That's -- That's the victim,
14    or at least that's what you want 'em to be.
15              MS. FOULSTON:  Excuse me, Your Honor.  I
16    think he said "trolling," with a T, not
17    "patrolling."
18              THE COURT:  He did say "trolling" with a
19    T.  I thought he said "patrolling."
20              THE DEFENDANT:  Oh, okay.
21              THE COURT:  All right, sir.
22              THE DEFENDANT:  No, no.  I wasn't
23    working, sir.
24              THE COURT:  All right.
25              THE DEFENDANT:  No, this was -- No, this

                    DAVID G. HOLT, CSR, RMR, CRR
                         OFFICIAL COURT REPORTER
```

Figure 3.13 Page 53 of the transcript from Dennis Rader's pleas of guilty.

> STATE V. DENNIS L. RADER   05 CR 498   GUILTY PLEAS   6/27/2005
>
> 1 bed when you turned on the lights in the bathroom?
> 2   THE DEFENDANT: Yeah, the bathroom, yeah,
> 3 just to -- so I could get some light in there.
> 4   THE COURT: All right. What did you do
> 5 then?
> 6   THE DEFENDANT: Oh, I manually strangled
> 7 her when she started to scream.
> 8   THE COURT: So you used your hands?
> 9   THE DEFENDANT: Yes, sir.
> 10   THE COURT: And you strangled her? Did
> 11 she die?
> 12   THE DEFENDANT: Yes.
> 13   THE COURT: All right. What did you do
> 14 then?
> 15   THE DEFENDANT: After that, since I was
> 16 in the sexual fantasy, I went ahead and stripped her
> 17 and probably went ahead and -- I'm not for sure if I
> 18 tied her up at that point in time, but anyway, she
> 19 was nude, and I put her on a blanket, went through
> 20 her purse, some personal items in the house, figured
> 21 out how I was gonna get her out of there.
> 22 Eventually moved her to the trunk of the car. Took
> 23 the car over to Christ Lutheran Church -- This is
> 24 with the older church -- and took some pictures of
> 25 her.
>
>   DAVID G. HOLT, CSR, RMR, CRR
>   OFFICIAL COURT REPORTER

Figure 3.14 Page 61 of the transcript from Dennis Rader's pleas of guilty.

Serial murderers and their victims come from all social classes, although some researchers suggest that they are mostly in the lower-to-middle strata (e.g., Holmes and De Burger 1988). Some researchers claim that serial murderers frequently show an interest in police work and security-type jobs (Holmes and De Burger 1988; Holmes and Holmes 2002), but this claim was not support by my study, in which just 3 (Keith Jesperson, Rader, and Wuornos) of the 15 serial murderers analyzed showed such interest. Two others—Bundy and Gacy—posed as police officers to lure their victims, but this does not necessarily indicate an interest in police work; instead, it suggests a cultural awareness of obedience to authority. Researchers have suggested that many serial murderers have military experience (Castle and Hensley 2002; Ressler et al. 1992), and according to the FBI, most receive other-than-honorable discharges (Ressler et al. 1992). This also was unsupported in my study: While 5 of the 15 serial murderers served in the military, just 1—Eddie Cole—was dishonorably discharged. Cole, who murdered 13 women from 1971 to 1980 in Texas, California, and Nevada, was discharged from the U.S. Navy after being arrested on suspicion of burglary and auto theft.

Carroll Edward Cole

Carroll Edward (Eddie) Cole confessed to murdering 13 women by strangulation from 1971 to 1980 in Dallas, Texas; San Diego, California; and Las Vegas, Nevada. He killed each victim either in her home, leaving the body there, or outside, finding a disposal site a short distance from the murder. He was tried for five murders total, three in Dallas and two in Las Vegas. He pled not guilty to the Dallas murders but was found guilty on April 9, 1981, and sentenced to life in prison. He pled guilty to the Las Vegas murders on August 16, 1984, and received another life sentence and a death sentence. He was executed on December 6, 1985.

Cole was described as highly intelligent but with poor school performance (he dropped out of high school). He was employed inconsistently but at the time of his apprehension worked in a Toys "R" Us warehouse. He was heterosexual and divorced at the time of his apprehension, with no children. He started killing women at age 33. He had various prior convictions, mostly for property and conduct offenses. He was dishonorably discharged from the U.S. Navy and showed no interest in law enforcement work.

Cole was described as a loner and outcast as a child; he had difficulty relating to his peers and did not participate in school or community activities. He was abused by his mother as a child and was not enrolled in school until he was 7 years old, putting him a year behind his peers. He said he killed as a form of revenge against his abusive and adulterous mother. He did not keep trophies from his murders.

Serial murder researchers often depict these murderers as commonly from unstable or physically, psychologically, and mentally abusive families with histories of alcohol, drug, criminal, and psychiatric problems; as having high rates of psychiatric problems; and as frequently showing an early interest in voyeurism, fetishism, and sadomasochistic pornography (Fox et al. 2005; Schechter and Everitt 1997).[4] Inconsistent with findings of other studies, abuse was not a characteristic shared by the majority of serial murderers in my study: Just five claimed to have been victims of abuse as children; one had a strained relationship with his mother, and two had arduous relationships with their fathers, but this does not seem unusual when compared to the general population. Dayton Rogers, who murdered at least seven women in the 1980s in Oregon, suggested that his strict religious upbringing might have been influential in his development into a serial murderer.

Dayton Leroy Rogers

Dayton Leroy Rogers (known as the "Molalla Forest Killer") murdered seven (possibly eight) women by stabbing in the 1980s in Oregon. He killed all but one of his victims in his vehicle or outdoors and dumped the bodies in the Molalla Forest. He was captured when witnesses saw him attack his last victim while parked in a parking lot and provided his license plate number to police. He pled self-defense but was convicted of one murder in 1988 and sentenced to life in prison. He then was convicted of six murders on June 7, 1989, and sentenced to death. The death sentence was overturned in 2000, but he again was sentenced to death in 2006.

Rogers was described as highly intelligent with poor school performance (he dropped out of high school). He owned an engine repair business, but despite the profitability of his company, he was deeply in debt. He was heterosexual and married at the time of his apprehension with one child. He started killing women at approximately age 27 (the date of his first murder is unknown). He was physically abused by his father as a child and had been accused of rape and violent assaults as a young adult. He did not serve in the military and showed no interest in law enforcement work.

Rogers was described as a loner and outcast as a child; he had difficulty relating to his peers and did not participate in school or community activities. Little explanation was offered for his murders, but he claimed self-defense at trial for one of them and suggested that his strict religious upbringing may have been influential. He kept victims' clothing and jewelry as trophies.

Some serial murderers were raised by adoptive parents (Fox et al. 2005), but no connection has been established. Rifkin, who was adopted as an infant, said he killed as a form of revenge against his biological mother, whom he believed to be a prostitute. Three childhood "symptoms" allegedly appear in the backgrounds of many serial murderers: enuresis (bed-wetting), fire starting, and sadistic activity (often in the form of animal torture) (Schechter and Everitt 1997). Some psychological studies have sought to identify a link between serial murderers and this triad of childhood activities (e.g., Singer and Hensley 2004). These activities appeared in the backgrounds of several of the serial murderers in my study, although no conclusions were drawn because of the difficulty of finding information for every serial murderer.

To be a serial murderer, an offender by definition must avoid apprehension for a period of time, and researchers try to identify conditions contributing to serial murderers' ability to avoid detection. Serial murderers usually "maintain a low profile ... and do not come across as 'crazies'" (Holmes and De Burger 1988, 20).

Some serial murderers hold jobs, attend church services, and generally blend in as "normal" members of their communities. Others are highly mobile, and their crimes may be spread over years across several law enforcement jurisdictions, complicating detection. As an example, Keith Jesperson, who murdered at least four women in the 1990s in Oregon, Wyoming, Washington, and possibly Florida and California, was a long-haul truck driver, killing most of his victims inside his truck before dumping the bodies and driving miles away. Bundy, also highly mobile, killed victims in Washington, Utah, Colorado, and Florida.

Keith Hunter Jesperson

Keith Hunter Jesperson (known as the "Happy Face Killer"), a long-haul truck driver, murdered at least 4 women (he confessed to 160) by strangulation from 1990 to 1995 in Oregon, Wyoming, Washington, and possibly Florida and California. He killed one victim in his home and the rest in his truck, then dumped the bodies outdoors. He was caught when he called police from a truck stop to turn himself in for one of the murders. He pled guilty to one murder in Washington in October 1995 and received a life sentence; pled no contest to two murders in Oregon in November 1995 and received a life sentence; and accepted a plea deal and pled guilty to one murder in Wyoming in June 1998 and received another life term. He is serving his sentences in the Oregon State Penitentiary.

Jesperson was described as of average intelligence with poor school performance. He said that he wanted to go to college after high school but that his father refused to pay for it. He was heterosexual, divorced at the time of his apprehension, and had children who lived with their mother. He started killing women at age 35. He has no known history of abuse and no prior convictions. He never served in the military, but as a boy dreamed of joining the Royal Canadian Mounted Police.

Jesperson was described as a loner and outcast as a child; he was socially awkward and had difficulty relating to his peers. He joined the football team at school but quit after a short time, complaining of cruelty from the coaches and other players. He said he killed as a form of revenge against his former wife. He did not keep trophies from his murders.

Because motives are often used to solve murder cases, an apparent lack of traditional motive may impede identification (Holmes and De Burger 1988). Serial murderers are often characterized as highly organized and careful, rather than impulsive. It should be considered, however, that only those killers with these characteristics reach the status of serial murderers because other, less-skillful or less-organized killers may be captured before killing enough people to qualify.

Analysts often link the commission of serial murder to an exertion of power over the victim, ritualized performance, dehumanization of the victim, and sexually sadistic fantasy (Claus and Lidberg 1999; Warren, Hazelwood, and Dietz 1996), all of which were supported in my analysis. Serial murderers usually do not appear to kill for financial or material gain, although taking small personal items from victims as "trophies" is common (Hickey 2006; Wiest 2009). Holmes and De Burger (1988, 50) claim the gain for most serial murderers is psychological and that accompanying homicidal fantasies serve to "reward, reinforce, and restimulate" the killer to continue killing. In my study, there was evidence of a desire for power in most of the serial murderers included, some claiming that they killed as a form of revenge against a powerful female figure in their lives (e.g., mother or former lover), others claiming self-defense or reclaiming power after prior victimization, and still others claiming that they were "cleaning up" society by killing undesirable people.

Race

Identified American serial murderers—and their victims—are overwhelming white (Holmes and De Burger 1988; Holmes and Holmes 2002; Vronsky 2004). The fact that most victims and perpetrators of serial murder are white corresponds to the long-documented trend of intraracial homicide (Garfinkel 1949) and social segregation in the United States, but explanations for white men's apparent overrepresentation as serial murderers have not been offered.

Fox et al. (2005), Kraemer et al. (2004), and Seltzer (1995) claim that the disproportionate percentage of white to African American serial murderers is consistent with the racial composition of the United States. According to the 2000 census, however, African Americans made up 12.1 percent of the U.S. population, while non-Hispanic whites made up 69.1 percent. White men constituted almost 37 percent of the American population, yet represented a much higher proportion of serial murderers, estimated as high as 95 percent (Warren et al. 1996). The proportion of white, male serial murderers also is higher than the typical racial and gendered patterns found in murder rates and other types of violence, in which men and African Americans are overrepresented (U.S. Department of Justice 2006). With homicide in general, men are overrepresented as victims compared to women (U.S. Department of Justice 2006), but the opposite is the case for serial murder victims.

Several social scientists argue, however, that African Americans constitute a larger percentage of serial murderers than most previous studies suggest. Walsh (2005) asserts that African Americans are overrepresented as serial murderers "at a rate approximately twice one would expect based on the average percentage of African Americans in the population" (281). Hickey (2006, 141) claims that there have been 200 African American serial murderers in the United States since the mid-1800s, and Vronsky (2004) argues that the number of African American serial murderers is increasing rapidly, from 10 percent of the total number of serial murderers before 1975 to 21 percent now.

The divergence in the number of African American serial murderers reported may be explained by the employed definition of serial murder. The studies that find a higher incidence of African American serial murderers seem to employ a definition that is on the inclusive end of the serial murder definitional spectrum. Conversely, the studies that find a lower incidence seem to employ a more exclusive definition.[5] Wayne Williams, an African American man, was convicted in 1982 of murdering 2 men in Atlanta, although he is widely believed to be the man responsible for at least 22 of the 29 deaths of African American children, known as the "Atlanta child murders," from 1979 to 1981 (Figure 3.15). Because he was convicted of just two murders, Williams's status as a serial murderer is not widely accepted. Paul

THE "TYPICAL" SERIAL MURDERER

Figure 3.15 (**See color insert.**) Mug shot of multiple murderer Wayne Williams from Fulton County Police, Atlanta, Georgia, on June 21, 1981. Williams was convicted in 1982 of murdering two men in Atlanta, although he is believed to be the man responsible for at least 22 of the 29 deaths of African American children, known as the "Atlanta child murders," from 1979 to 1981. He is currently serving two life sentences.

Durousseau, an African American man, murdered at least five women from 1997 to 2003 in Florida and Georgia (Figure 3.16). Henry Wallace, an African American man, murdered at least nine young African American women from 1992 to 1994 in North Carolina. Because their victims were acquaintances, Durousseau and Wallace would not fit many definitions of a serial murderer.

Figure 3.16 Mug shot of serial murderer Paul Durousseau from the Florida Department of Corrections (date unknown). Durousseau murdered at least five women from 1997 to 2003 in Florida and Georgia. He was given a death sentence on December 13, 2007, and resides on Florida State Prison's death row.

Henry Louis Wallace

Henry Louis Wallace, an African American man, murdered at least 9 young African American women (but admitted to 10, including 1 prostitute) mostly by strangulation but also by stabbing from 1992 to 1994 in Charlotte, North Carolina. He killed his victims, all of whom were acquaintances (either co-workers or friends or family of people he knew well), in their homes and either left the bodies there or dumped them outdoors. He also raped and robbed most of his victims. He was captured after police found his fingerprints on a car stolen from one of the dead women and discovered that Wallace knew most of the victims. He promptly confessed to the murders after his capture in March 1994, but at trial, his attorneys argued that he suffered from mental illness. He was convicted of nine counts of first-degree murder, as well as additional charges, including rape, and sentenced to death in January 1997. He awaits execution at Central Prison in Raleigh, North Carolina.

Wallace was described as of average intelligence with poor school performance. He attended college for a while but failed out twice. He worked at various fast-food restaurants. He was heterosexual, was never married, and had no children. He started killing women at age 27. He had no history of abuse and showed no interest in law enforcement work. He had a prior arrest for rape and served in the U.S. Navy.

Wallace was described as a loner and social outcast as a child and appeared to have difficulty building and maintaining close relationships as an adult. Insanity was alleged as an explanation for his murders. He did not keep trophies.

African American serial murderers have not received as much media attention as white serial murderers, which Hickey (2006) suggests is because black-on-black crime "doesn't sell papers." It is possible that in the past these murders more often were given scant attention by law enforcement and media, particularly if the African American murderers murdered other African Americans, but whether that has occurred or to what extent is unknown. There were plenty of reasons to publicize the crimes of Coral Watts—an African American man who murdered at least 14 white women from 1974 to 1982 in Houston, Texas, and Michigan and who in 2004 nearly became the first serial murderer released from prison—but his crimes and near release received little media attention nonetheless.

Coral Eugene Watts

Coral Eugene Watts (known as the "Sunday Morning Slasher"), an African American man, murdered at least 14 (but admitted to more than 80) white women by drowning, stabbing, hanging, or strangulation from 1974 to 1982 in Houston, Texas, and Michigan. He killed his victims in their homes or outdoors and left the bodies where they were killed. He was caught when neighbors called police while he attempted to kill two women after breaking into their apartment. In 1982, he received an unusual plea deal in Texas in which he confessed to 12 murders in exchange for immunity, pled guilty to "burglary with intent to commit murder," and received 60 years in prison. As he was on the verge of being released in 2004 because of an appellate court ruling and mandatory release laws, Michigan charged him with first-degree murder, and he was found guilty on November 18, 2004, and sentenced to a life term. On July 27, 2007, he was found guilty of a second Michigan murder and received another life term. He died September 21, 2007, of prostate cancer.

Watts was described as of average intelligence with poor school performance. He started college but dropped out 3 months into his first semester. He worked as an automobile mechanic. He was heterosexual, was divorced at the time of his apprehension, and had one child whom he had abandoned. He started killing at age 21. He claimed to have been abused by his stepfather as a child and had prior convictions for harassment, theft, and assault. He did not serve in the military and showed no interest in law enforcement work.

As a child, Watts was described as a loner and socially awkward. He was a good athlete but had difficulty relating to his peers. He appeared to have difficulty building and maintaining close relationships as an adult. He said that he killed his victims because they had "evil eyes," and he took small personal items, which he disposed of within days of the murders.

Serial murderers of other races or ethnicities are even less recognized, but there are several identified cases in the United States. Richard Ramirez, born in El Paso, Texas, to Mexican immigrants, murdered at least 13 women and men in the 1980s in Southern California. Mexican-born Juan Corona murdered 25 men in 1971 in California. Rory Conde, a native Colombian, murdered 6 prostitutes in the 1990s in Miami. Chinese American Charles Ng, along with Leonard Lake, murdered 11 people (6 men, 3 women, and 2 male babies) in the 1980s in California.

Richard Munoz Ramirez

Richard Munoz Ramirez, born in El Paso, Texas, to Mexican immigrants, murdered at least 13 women and men by shooting or stabbing from 1984 to 1985 in Southern California. He killed all his victims in their homes after breaking in at night. Several of his victims did not die and were able to give descriptions of their attacker. Those descriptions were used, along with fingerprints lifted from a stolen car and distinct shoe prints found at several of the murder scenes, to identify Ramirez as the suspect. His photograph was printed and broadcast through mass media, and citizens recognized him in the street, captured him, and waited for police to arrive. He was convicted on September 20, 1989, and received 19 death sentences. He awaits execution at San Quentin State Prison.

Ramirez was described as of average intelligence with poor school performance (he dropped out of high school) and no legitimate employment history. He was heterosexual, never married, and had no children. He began killing mostly women at age 24. He had no history of abuse and had prior convictions for theft and auto theft. He did not serve in the military and showed no interest in law enforcement work.

Ramirez was described as a loner and social outcast as a child and did not participate in school or community activities. No explanation was offered for his murders. He stole items of value from his victims, such as jewelry and money, but he did not keep trophies.

Gender

Estimates of the number of female serial murderers also vary because of definitional discrepancies. Women identified as serial or multiple murderers generally fit into one of three categories: those who kill family members, those who kill on the job (health care workers who kill patients or child care workers who kill children), or those who kill with a male partner (often a husband or lover) (Davis 2001; Fox and Levin 2005; Hickey 2006; Schechter and Everitt 1997; Vronsky 2004, 2007). When women are involved in partner serial killings, the man is almost always depicted as the "mastermind," while the woman is an accomplice or follower (Hickey 2006, 194–195).[6] Carol Bundy murdered at least two women in Los Angeles in 1980 with her lover David Clark. Clark, who started killing prostitutes and runaways first and later brought Bundy in as an accomplice, was widely portrayed as the dominant partner in their murderous relationship.

Carol M. Bundy

Carol M. Bundy, with David Clark (known as the "Sunset Strip Killers"), murdered at least two women by shooting in Los Angeles in 1980, although they each murdered additional victims separately. Several of their victims also were beheaded, and Bundy admitted using at least one victim's head during sexual activity with Clark. The pair met in December 1979 at a bar, which Bundy frequented to watch her landlord and love interest, Jack Murray. Clark had grown up in a privileged home and was well educated, but he lacked motivation and worked sporadically as a mechanic. Bundy was divorced from an abusive husband (her third marriage), had two children, was overweight, wore thick glasses, and desperately sought male affection. Clark was intuitive about Bundy's feelings and saw her as a meal ticket; the pair soon became lovers and moved in together.

Clark started killing prostitutes and runaways first and later brought Bundy in as an accomplice. Clark reportedly was the dominant partner in their murderous relationship, and Bundy submitted to his wishes out of a desire to please him. After two bodies were found in June 1980, Bundy called the police to report her lover. It was assumed to be a crank call, although the caller knew many details of the crimes not released to the media, but the switchboard cut her off, and Bundy did not call back. In August 1980, Bundy and Murray were friendly, and Bundy began dropping hints to him about the murders. According to Bundy, Murray suggested turning Clark in to the police, so Bundy killed Murray in his van. Police eventually found the decomposing body in the van, and witness statements led them to Bundy, who blamed the crime on Clark. Clark also turned on Bundy, calling her crazy.

On May 31, 1983, Bundy accepted a plea deal; she received two consecutive prison terms of 27 years to life for a murder she participated in with Clark and for Murray's murder. She was sent to the California Institute for Women at Frontera and died of heart failure on December 9, 2003. On January 28, 1988, Clark was convicted of six murders and one attempted murder and in March was given six death sentences. He is currently on death row in San Quentin State Prison in California.

Female multiple murderers kill family members more often than male multiple murderers (Hickey 2006; Vronsky 2007). Marie Noe killed eight of her 10 children in Philadelphia, Pennsylvania, between 1949 and 1968; Nannie Doss was convicted of killing her fifth husband in 1955 in Oklahoma after confessing to the murders of seven other family members (three other husbands, her mother, her sister, her nephew, and her mother-in-law) by poisoning or smothering over a decade in several states; and Tillie Klimek killed four husbands by poisoning in Chicago from 1919 to 1921. Female multiple murderers acting alone are most often found in hospitals or other health care or child care settings (Hickey 2006; Vronsky 2004). For example,

Kristen Gilbert, a nurse, murdered four patients by injecting them with epinephrine in the 1990s in Massachusetts.

Marie Noe

Marie Noe killed 8 of her 10 children (1 was stillborn and 1 died at the hospital shortly after birth) in Philadelphia, Pennsylvania, between 1949 and 1968. She killed most of them within months of their birth, and none made it to his or her second birthday. After each death, an investigation showed the same cause: sudden infant death syndrome (SIDS). Her husband was not home at the time of any of the children's deaths, and insurance policies had been taken out on six of the children. Noe was charged with eight counts of second-degree murder in 1998—30 years after the last death—and in 1999, she confessed to smothering them. She pleaded guilty and was sentenced to 20 years of probation.

The reasons these women kill appear to be different from those of the prototypical male serial murderer. "These often fall into the category of either 'mercy homicide,' in which the killer believes he or she is relieving great suffering, or the 'hero homicide,' in which the death is the unintentional result of causing the victim distress so he (or she) can be revived by the offender, who is then declared a hero" (Douglas and Olshaker 1997, 27). Financial gain is another common reason for murder among female multiple murderers. Doss and Klimek purchased life insurance policies on their husbands before murdering them; Noe had insurance policies on six of the eight children she killed; and Dana Sue Gray, a former nurse who strangled three women (ages 57–87) in the 1990s in California, went on shopping sprees with her victims' credit cards.

Women's methods of committing suicide and killing tend to be different from males, and this is also true for multiple murder. "A woman is unlikely to kill repeatedly with a gun or knife. It does happen with something 'clean' like drugs" (Douglas and Olshaker 1997, 27). Vronsky (2007, 43) claims that female multiple murderers "overwhelmingly" choose poison as their killing method, just as Doss and

Klimek did. Women's use of drugs and poison may imply that the act of killing itself is not the focus, but instead it is a means toward some ultimate goal, such as financial gain or others' recognition or sympathy (Douglas and Olshaker 1997; Vronsky 2007). Vronsky (2007, 33) suggests that the female multiple murderer is "all business," meaning she does not often participate in behaviors unnecessary to the killing itself, like kidnapping, confinement, rape, mutilation, cannibalism, sexual gratification, or necrophilia, which are more common with male offenders.

Social scientists who employ a more exclusive definition of serial murder assert that there are no known female serial murderers (e.g., Silvio, McCloskey, and Ramos-Grenier 2006), and others with more inclusive definitions claim that women account for 10 to 15 percent of known U.S. serial murderers (e.g., Seltzer 1995). Hickey (2006), who allows in his definition murders for financial or personal gain and relationships between killers and victims, identified 64 female serial murderers. Still others identify solo killer Aileen Wuornos as the only known female serial murderer (Shipley and Arrigo 2004; Arrigo and Griffin 2004), but her serial murderer designation is disputed (Myers, Gooch, and Meloy 2005; Schechter and Everitt 1997; Silvio et al. 2006).

The existence of female serial murderers depends on the employed definition of serial murder. The broad definition of the FBI would include a number of women. If the additional component of the National Institute of Justice of "sadistic, sexual overtones" is incorporated, then there are many fewer. If women who kill family members, women who kill for financial gain, women in the health care or child care settings, and women who kill as part of a male-female team are excluded, the number drops even further. No known female serial murderers match the popular portrayal of the typical serial murderer—"the lone psychopathic lust murderer, coolly stalking and snaring his victims, then butchering and mutilating them in a sex-crazed frenzy" (Schechter and Everitt 1997, 311)—or most definitions of serial murder.

Sexuality

Defining serial murder in terms of sexual motive establishes a link between the killer's sexuality and the sex of the victims. The majority of identified serial murderers—about 86 percent—are heterosexual men and kill women (Schechter and Everitt 1997). Likewise, homosexual male serial murderers often kill males, typically other homosexuals (Schechter and Everitt 1997). Jeffery Dahmer and John Gacy were both homosexual men (Gacy may have been bisexual) who murdered boys and young men, as were Randy Kraft, who murdered at least 16 boys and men in the 1970s and 1980s in California, and Ronald Dominique, who murdered at least 8 men (he confessed to 23 victims) from 1997 to 2006 in Louisiana. When a heterosexual male serial murderer kills men, the male victims usually do not appear to be the killer's intended targets (i.e., their murder is a "necessity" to carry out the murder of the intended female target). Each male victim of Richard Ramirez and David Carpenter was killed while in the company of his wife or fiancée; when Ramirez encountered a couple, he generally killed the man first and then raped and killed the woman.

Both male and female children also are victims of serial murderers (Fox and Levin 1998; Hickey 2006). Albert Fish molested and killed male and female children, although he had an apparent preference for boys, and Mack Ray Edwards, who murdered at least three children in the 1950s and 1960s in California, also killed children of both sexes. Children may be sexual objects for some adults (Finkelhor and Araji 1986; Freund and Watson 1990), and medical studies have shown that pedophiles are less likely than other types of sex offenders to have a strong gender preference in victims (e.g., Freund et al. 1991). These patterns were consistent with findings in my study.

Nationality

The United States appears to have many more serial murderers than any other industrialized county (Egger 1998; Newton 1991). The serial murderer with the highest number of victims, however, was Russian: Andrei Chikatilo murdered at least 53 children (boys and girls) and young women from 1978 to 1990 in the Soviet Union. Newton (1991) contends that 74 percent of all serial murderers in the twentieth century came from the United States. Vronsky (2007) sets that number at 76 percent, with 21 percent of serial murders occurring in Europe, where England claimed the majority of those with 28 percent, followed by Germany with 27 percent and France with 13 percent. Jenkins (1994,

41) qualifies that perhaps the rate of serial murder in the United States is merely a product of greater awareness of the offense, differences in the legal systems, or differences in media coverage. It is also important to point out that most definitions of serial murder would exclude more commonly occurring cases of multiple killings in other countries (e.g., the legally sanctioned killing of homosexuals in Iran), which raises the question of whether there are more serial murderers in other countries than have been identified. If the rate of serial murder is higher in the United States than in any other industrial nation, as it seems, no explanation has been formulated.

Andrei Chikatilo

Andrei Chikatilo murdered at least 53 children (boys and girls) and young women by strangulation and stabbing from 1978 to 1990 mostly in the Russian port city of Rostov, but some victims were killed in other regions in Russia and in the Ukraine and Uzbek republics of the Soviet Union. He usually would lure his victims away from bus stops with a ruse—often a promise of a ride or candy for children or a promise of alcohol or money for women (many of whom were homeless, prostitutes, or both). He would then take them into a secluded wooded area and savagely murder them, frequently committing acts of torture, mutilation, and cannibalism.

Chikatilo was married with two children. He was college educated and worked as a teacher for 10 years until he was fired because of several complaints of child molestation. He later worked as a supply clerk, although he was fired from one such job and spent a short time in prison for theft. Despite having been questioned about the murders in 1984 and identified as a suspect in 1987, Chikatilo was not captured until November 20, 1990, after nearly a week under surveillance. During his trial, Chikatilo was kept in a locked steel cage to protect him from the furious family members of his victims, and he frequently interrupted the proceedings by exposing himself, shouting, singing, and refusing to answer questions. Despite questions of his sanity, Chikatilo was convicted on October 14, 1992, of 52 of the 53 murder charges, as well as five charges of molestation, and sentenced to death. On February 15, 1994, he was executed. It was discovered later that another man, Alexsandr Kravchenko, had been tried, convicted, and executed for the first murder committed by Chikatilo.

Several social scientists have compared characteristics and the incidence of U.S. serial murder to those of other countries, often basing their studies on theories and perspectives developed in the United States, with mixed results. Capp (1996) studied serial murderers in seventeenth-century England, and Grover and Soothill (1999) studied serial murder in Britain from 1960 to the 1990s. In the latter study, Grover and Soothill applied the theoretical arguments of Elliott Leyton, a Canadian anthropologist recognized for his studies of American serial murder, and they concluded that his structural arguments and focus on socioeconomic factors could not explain British serial murder. They did find similarities in American and British serial murder, including characteristics of offenders (overwhelmingly white, male, and of lower-to-middle social class) and type of victims (those in vulnerable groups, including prostitutes, children, young adults, gay men, and the elderly). In my study, there were many similar characteristics between typical American serial murderers and Robert Black, a Scottish white man who murdered at least three girls from 1982 to 1990 in Scotland and England.

Robert Black

Robert Black murdered at least three girls (and is suspected of more) by strangulation from 1982 to 1990 in Scotland and England. He abducted his victims from public areas, killed them in his van, and dumped the bodies outdoors. He was captured during a failed abduction attempt. He was convicted of three murders on May 19, 1994, and received a life sentence with the possibility of parole.

Black was described as of average intelligence with average school performance. He was adopted as an infant after being abandoned by his biological mother. When his adoptive parents died, he was sent to a children's home. He was expelled for unclear reasons and then sent to a home for male juvenile offenders. The school helped him get a welding apprenticeship, which he lost before even starting, and he had an inconsistent employment history until becoming a delivery driver for Poster Dispatch and Storage. He was heterosexual, never married, and had no children. He began killing female children at age 35. He claimed to have been sexually abused by a male staff member at the boys' home, and he had prior convictions for pedophilia, theft, auto theft, and assault. He did not serve in the military and showed no interest in law enforcement work.

As a child, Black was described as a loner and socially awkward. He was a good athlete but had difficulty relating to his peers. In explaining why he killed the children, he said he wanted to molest them without "hurting" them. He did not keep trophies from the murders.

Grover and Soothill (1999, 13) suggest a cultural difference between the United States and Britain, placing emphasis on Britain's supposedly harsher "engine of patriarchal capitalism." They argue that British men who cannot compete in the economic system are "cast out" and subsequently provided "minimal social and economic protection" by the state "because it is thought such provision will merely exacerbate their 'idleness.'" "At this juncture, the inability of individuals to compete on the terms of patriarchal capitalism and a lack of social provision" contributes to "'creating' serial killers who simply but grotesquely exploit many of the cultural meanings of a society." They also suggest that pervasive homophobia and a "more exaggerated form" of oppression of homosexuals in Britain may explain instances of heterosexual serial murderers victimizing gay men in Britain.

Harbort and Mokros (2001) suggest similarities between characteristics of U.S. and German serial murderers, although there are far fewer of the latter, even relative to population size. Hodgskiss (2004, 90) compared the characteristics of South African serial murderers with those of serial murderers in other nations, concluding that killers in South Africa are most similar to those in Europe, with both distinguished from North American serial murderers because of a "seeming lack of sexually violent conscious fantasy."[7] Although Hodgskiss suggests that the presence of a sexual component is characteristic of serial murder in the United States, not all researchers of American serial murderers include a sexual qualifier.

Finally, Hickey (2006) reviews cases of serial murder in 22 countries besides the United States (including Canada, Germany, Britain, France, Hungary, Australia, South Africa, Russia, and Iran). He identifies differences in the ways serial murder is defined and viewed and argues that "cultural differences influence the methods and motives" (Hickey 2006, 291) of serial murderers. Most notably, he found many similarities among industrialized nations and more discrepancy when comparing industrialized and developing nations. Albeit with limited empirical support, there appear to be differences in cases of serial murder in the United States as compared to other countries, even those with similar economic and political ideologies.

Similarities with Other Types of Offenses

It appears that particular deviant activities are chosen by fairly homogeneous groups. Serial murder is one such activity, which the literature indicates most frequently is chosen by white, working-class men. Many of the typical offenders in other deviant activities have similar characteristics and exhibit similar behaviors. Other scholars have discussed similarities between serial murderers and other types of offenders (e.g., Levin 2008). This section briefly illustrates the fact that serial murder is not unique in its offender profile.

Other Serial Crimes

Characteristics of serial burglars vary; the most frequently reported motivation is for material gain, but sexually motivated burglaries have been found in a small number of cases (Schlesinger 2000). Schlesinger and Revitch (1999) identified 14 sexual murderers, including several serial murderers, who had a history of burglaries, including Richard Ramirez and Ted Bundy.

Lloyd-Goldstein (2000) argues that serial stalkers display similar behaviors to those associated with serial murderers, although the apparent motivations of serial stalkers appear more varied. Most serial stalkers are unmarried men in their mid-30s with a higher-than-average education, unstable work history, and a poor ability to form and maintain relationships (Lloyd-Goldstein 2000), much like serial murderers. In addition, serial stalkers and serial murderers target similar victims; the most frequent victims of each are women, although serial stalkers usually know their victims (Lloyd-Goldstein 2000), while serial murderers most often do not, and homosexual men are much more likely to be victims than heterosexual men (Lloyd-Goldstein 2000). Most serial stalkers are not violent, but when they do assault their victims, they are unlikely to use a weapon, and the assaults are rarely sexual in nature (Lloyd-Goldstein 2000).

Serial arsonists are predominantly white men (Lewis and Yarnell 1951) who, like serial murderers, display a need for ownership, power, and control (Brogan 2006; Lewis and Yarnell 1951). In their study of 1,145 cases of males older than 15 who engaged in what they called "pathological firestarting," Lewis and Yarnell (1951) identified several common characteristics of serial arsonists: Most were of below-average intelligence, between ages 16 and 28, and frequently diagnosed with psychopathology or psychosis, frequently had physical defects, used alcohol, and had difficulty maintaining relationships. Mavromatis (2000) compared serial arsonists with serial murderers, finding similar apparent motivations and that several serial murderers were arsonists prior to killing.

In serial rape, women are the most frequent victims, and men—although not necessarily white—are the most frequent offenders (Goldsworthy 2006; Palmer and Thornhill 2000). As in serial murder, serial rapists display a need for power and control, yet the average age of serial rapists is lower than that of serial murderers, and rage is more typical in serial rapists.

School Shootings

The "U.S. Secret Service Safe School Initiative Report" (National Institute of Justice 2002) reports that there is no typical school shooter, although boys and young men still appear to be the primary offenders. The report indicates variation in socioeconomic background, age, race and ethnicity, family situations, academic performance, history of drug and alcohol abuse, and mental health history. School shooters share with some serial murderers an apparent desire for fame or recognition, as well as a need for power and control, and have little or no history of violent offending. In addition, both types of offending evoke community shock and command media attention.

White Supremacy

White supremacy differs somewhat from serial murder in that it is group oriented, although there appears to be an increasing push for members to carry out acts of violence on their own or in small groups (Ferber 2004). Also, members frequently are of a lower socioeconomic status, with sympathizers in all socioeconomic levels (Daniels 1997; Ezekiel 1995). However, there are several similarities between the two types of offending. The white supremacist movement is almost entirely comprised of men (Ezekiel 1995), and it is based on a desire for power and control and provides a means for white men to "prove their masculinity" (Ferber 2004; Ferber and Kimmel 2004). Like serial murderers, white supremacists target members of vulnerable populations for violence, and they attempt to portray images of strength, bravery, and skill (Ezekiel 1995).

Notes

1. Gein's status as a serial murderer depends on the definition employed.
2. Vronsky (2004), an investigative journalist, and Holmes and Holmes (2002) are among few serial murder researchers who still include "above-average intelligence" in their profiles of typical serial murderers. Egger (1998), an academic researcher, as well as Morton and Hilts (2008), with the FBI, identify the supposed high level of intelligence and extraordinary ability of serial murderers to outsmart police and avoid capture as myths perpetuated in American popular culture.
3. Of the 15 serial murderers in the study, 3 were married at the time of their arrest, and 5 more had been married and divorced at least once. Five of those currently or previously married had children, 2 were divorced at the times of their arrests and did not have custody of their children, and 2 had children but never had contact with them.
4. These characteristics are not unique among offenders in general.
5. Further research is needed because definitions are not stated in all studies examined in this review.

6. Well-known male-female serial murderer teams in which the women were depicted as subservient include Paul Bernardo and Karla Homolka; Fred and Rosemary West; and Doug Clark and Carol Bundy.
7. Hodgskiss (2004, 82) recognizes, then quickly dismisses, the possibility that this finding could be explained by an unwillingness of the offenders to express their desires to the researchers, arguing that "it does not explain why South African offenders would be systematically reticent about their fantasies, while admitting to a range of offences and freely discussing some of the most private areas of their lives."

4
EXISTING EXPLANATIONS FOR SERIAL MURDER

Introduction

Explanations for serial murder have been offered throughout the past few decades, with little variation in perspective. Biological explanations of serial murder show up from time to time, but psychological explanations continue to dominate research on serial murder. In recent years, however, serial murder researchers have increasingly been examining the influence of social and cultural variables.

Arguments linking media consumption to aggression and violence are also suggested in some of the serial murder literature. Samenow (2004) and other psychologists argue that media do not *create* aggression or crime, and that if they did, everyone would be a criminal. People who are predisposed to and have at least nascent thoughts about committing a crime may gain ideas or confidence from media reports, but what is critical for the commission of a crime "is not what plays on the screen but what lies in the mind of the viewer. Television, movies, video games, magazines, or books will not turn a responsible person into a criminal" (Samenow 2004, 7). The same could be said for the often-cited "facilitators" (e.g., alcohol, drugs, and pornography) that may precede serial murder (Vronsky 2004), in that they are not *causes*.

Vronsky (2004, 286) and others claim that a person develops into a serial murderer through a combination of environmental factors, parental effects, and a biological and genetic predisposition that creates "a pattern of often violent fantasies and obsessive thoughts that the serial killer has difficulty separating from reality." Media exposure alone does not lead to particular forms of antisocial behavior.

Psychological Explanations

Psychological researchers propose various configurations of causes, such as combinations of social isolation, stress, sexual or physical abuse, parental absence in early life, neglect, personal failures, and rejection as precipitators or causes of serial murder (Claus and Lidberg 1999). Drawing on attachment theory, serial murder may be explained as a product of the killer's failure to form symbiotic attachment with his or her mother as an infant. This mother–child relationship is "crucial" for the infant's development of a "stable ego structure" and learning (Claus and Lidberg 1999, 430). "The serial murder(er) is therefore engaged in a delusive striving towards a pathological symbiotic unity with the victim" (Claus and Lidberg 1999, 430). Based on interviews with several serial murderers, Hickey (2006) in a similar vein concluded that serial murderers' predilection to kill grows out of an unstable, abusive, or otherwise dysfunctional childhood environment. Again drawing on attachment theory, Shipley and Arrigo (2004) argue that adolescent delinquency and adult criminality are related to childhood trauma and poor childhood attachments to parents.

The psychological explanations do not account for the overrepresentation of men as perpetrators in all violent crime, particularly serial murder, or why only a small proportion of people who experienced trauma, abuse, or neglect as children become criminal offenders. Most people who grow up with strict, domineering, or even abusive parents do not become criminals, just as most people who grow up with easygoing, indecisive, or absent parents do not. Criminals often do come from volatile, abusive, or neglectful circumstances, but there likely is more to their stories (Samenow 2004, 8–9).

Another frequent type of psychological explanation is that serial murderers are psychopathic, sociopathic, psychotic, or schizophrenic or have some other psychiatric disorder[1] that propels them to kill.[2] Most known serial murderers, however, are not classified as mentally ill, and even when they do show symptoms of mental illness, their disorders do not normally qualify them as insane (Fox et al. 2005; Holmes and De Burger 1988). Fox et al. (2005) suggest that the majority of serial murderers are sociopathic yet still may have a conscience and the capacity for remorse. By dehumanizing their victims (viewing them as less than human and therefore worthless and expendable), serial murderers may be able to lessen their feelings of guilt and may convince themselves that the killing actually is a good thing—or at least not that bad. Fox et al. (2005, 113) argue that compartmentalization allows the killers to divide the world into two groups of people: "those whom they care about and everyone else." This process is used to explain how many serial murderers may also be kind and loving husbands, fathers, sons, and community leaders.

Consonant with their psychological orientations, various serial murder researchers argue that the gain for a serial murderer in killing others is purely psychological. For example, Skrapec (2001, 49) contends that serial murderers kill "first and foremost for personal gratification." She urges the study of the individual, subjective experiences of these killers to understand the phenomenon and sees as less significant the "objective realties of his life or the evaluations we make of those objective realities" (Skrapec 2001, 51). Some researchers suggest the killers may experience sexual satisfaction through the commission of murder. Drawing on 12 case examples of serial murderers, Myers et al. (2006, 902) concluded that they "reveal the positive feelings of sexual pleasure, even exhilaration—rather than anger or other unpleasant states—are the driving psychological force in the crimes."

Based on interviews with 36 sexual murderers, most of whom were serial murderers, and other data, Burgess et al. (1986) developed a motivational model for sexually oriented and sadistic violence, with five components: ineffective social environment; formative events (including trauma, developmental failure, and interpersonal failure); patterned responses; action toward others; and feedback filter (system for justifying actions). This model neglects contributing social factors beyond ineffective child–parent bonds. In a follow-up report based on the same data, Ressler et al. (1992) consider the effects of social environment on the development of future serial murderers, although their arguments still ignore the cultural context.

Finally, criminal profiling represents a large segment of the psychological literature on serial murder. Various analytical methods are studied as possibly useful in identifying a killer's motivations and behavior patterns, including examining serial murderers' victims (Godwin 1998), as well as body disposal sites (Godwin 1998; Lundrigan and Canter 2001) and sites of initial killer–victim contact (Godwin 1998). Mott (1999) compares variables such as rate of killing, vulnerability, and body disposal in solved and unsolved cases of serial murder in an effort to develop investigative and preventive tools. Finally, researchers in the United Kingdom (Canter et al. 2000; Snook et al. 2002) have found support for the utility of a geographic profiling system called Dragnet in predicting the home location of serial offenders.

Social Psychological Explanations

A social psychological explanation of serial murder is offered in the fractured identity theory developed by Holmes, Tewksbury, and Holmes (1999). Drawing on the work of social psychologists Erving Goffman and Charles Horton Cooley, they argue that some social event or series of events may occur in adolescence that results in a fractured personality for the future serial murderer. This fracture does not affect the entire personality and may not be recognizable by others, and after a killing, the fracture may become temporarily dormant, which addresses why serial murderers generally appear "normal" in everyday life. The sequence of social events and the timing of the fracture are identified as affecting whether a person becomes a serial murderer or develops some other pathology.

Drawing on Goffman's work, Levin and Fox (2007) have described serial murderers as especially adept at impression management. One of the reasons serial murderers are able to avoid detection is because they "perform" ordinariness well. "They are seen as unusually capable of looking and acting beyond suspicion, of appearing to be more innocent than a truly innocent person, of being able to lure their victims with charm and cunning" (Levin and Fox 2007, 5). They also point out that their heightened self-awareness and proficiency in managing impressions is not fundamentally different from the persuasive and sometimes manipulative tactics employed by salespeople and "successful" people in other culturally legitimate occupations, such as financial investors and politicians.

Although few social psychologists study serial murder, their studies of other phenomena can provide insights. Utilizing findings from his famous 1971 Stanford prison experiment and examinations of cults and the Abu Ghraib prisoner abuses, Zimbardo (2007) argues that anyone is capable of committing atrocities within certain social settings. Ordinary, good people "can be seduced, recruited, initiated into behaving in evil ways under the sway of powerful systematic and situational forces" (Zimbardo 2007, 443). The social system can corrupt otherwise good people, rather than evil people corrupting the system. Zimbardo also argues that, in particular situations and times, anyone is capable of committing acts of heroism. Most people do not enter a situation with any special attributes of evil or goodness, but some can be transformed by the situation into evildoers or heroes.

Sociological Explanations

Psychologists tend to downplay the effects of socialization in individual development and behavior patterns. Citing "attempts to improve the environment" like social programs designed to provide criminals with education, job training, or counseling, Samenow (2004) argues that such programs do not aid in rehabilitation because they do not change criminals' personalities or ways of thinking. In this way, Samenow and other psychologists for the most part discount the role of socialization and culture in *shaping* the thoughts and behaviors of criminals. The argument that criminals grow up in all kinds of environments and that we therefore cannot pick out particular causal factors that determine criminality is shortsighted. Socialization is just one piece of the complex interrelationship of components that influence behavior, which also includes psychological and biological processes and mass media.

Some serial murder researchers (e.g., Douglas and Olshaker 1997; Grover and Soothill 1999; Holmes and De Burger 1988; Leyton 1986) urge the recognition of sociological variables in analyzing serial murder. Leyton (1986) proposed that serial murder may be socially constituted, or a consequence of the social structure, and that studying serial murder within a sociological framework is crucial for better understanding of the phenomenon. Grover and Soothill (1999) argue that biological and psychological explanations for crime may be useful but are usually presented without regard to the potential effects of social and cultural variables. The historical and cultural contexts of crime typically are ignored.

Environmental influences and patterns of early interaction in the family setting are important (Holmes and De Burger 1988), as "many more serial killers are *made* than *born*" (Douglas and Olshaker 1997,

20; italics in original). Athens (1992) and Rhodes (1999) situate violence as an outcome of social experiences, arguing that, given suitable circumstances, virtually anyone can develop the capacity for violence.

Also, serial murder may be framed as a consequence of a patriarchal culture. Caputi (1989, 1993) refers to serial murder as "sexually political murders" rooted in "a system of male supremacy." She sees America's fascination with serial murder, as evidenced by its vast presence in popular culture, as a way to "terrorize women and to empower and inspire men" (Caputi 1989, 445). Similar arguments have been used by others to explain rape and domestic violence (e.g., Sheffield 2004).

A New Direction

Despite the hard work of many researchers, there is still so much we do not know. In addition to the disputes over the definition and characteristics of serial murder and serial murderers, the explanations of the phenomenon are seriously lacking. Biological and psychological explanations do not account for historical or cultural differences in the incidence of serial murder or for the preponderance of white, heterosexual males as the murderers. While some social scientists and law enforcement officials encourage the examination of the role of social variables on the development of serial murderers, and findings from other studies implore an examination of the cultural context, no sociocultural model has been offered.

Taking a more reserved and inclusive stance on studying serial murder, recent published Federal Bureau of Investigation (FBI) reports suggest that all three components—biological, psychological, and social—contribute to the development of a serial murderer: "They have the appropriate biological predisposition, molded by their psychological makeup, which is present at a critical time in their social development" (Morton and Hilts 2008, 11). Although this confluence-of-components theory appears to be a solution to the inadequacies of each separate component, it brings us no closer to an explanation, and its breadth may actually push us further away. Indeed, the FBI urges further research to better understand the development of serial murderers (Morton and Hilts 2008).

We can no longer ignore the sociocultural context. We must examine cultural values transmitted through socialization to understand how American culture fosters the creation of serial murderers. In addition, an examination of the cultural context aids in an understanding of the creation of the image of the violent, white, male sexual predators depicted in the media, as well as the preoccupation of the public with them. The next part of this book examines the cultural context of serial murder in America and explains how a sociocultural approach can guide us toward greater understanding and possibilities for change.

Notes

1. Although sociopathy and psychopathy are grouped with antisocial personality disorder in the *Diagnostic and Statistical Manual of Mental Disorders* (American Psychiatric Association 2000), some psychologists argue that there are enough differences between the three disorders to maintain their separation (e.g., Skilling et al. 2002). Fox and Levin (2005) argue that it is unnecessary to make distinctions among the disorders when trying to understand serial murder because the characteristics prevalent in serial murderers are common to all three, although these authors frequently refer to sociopathy in their research.
2. See Fox et al. 2005; Hickey 2006; Ramsland 2006; and Vronsky 2004, 2007.

Figure 2.1 The FBI headquarters in Washington, D.C., is pictured at night (date unknown).

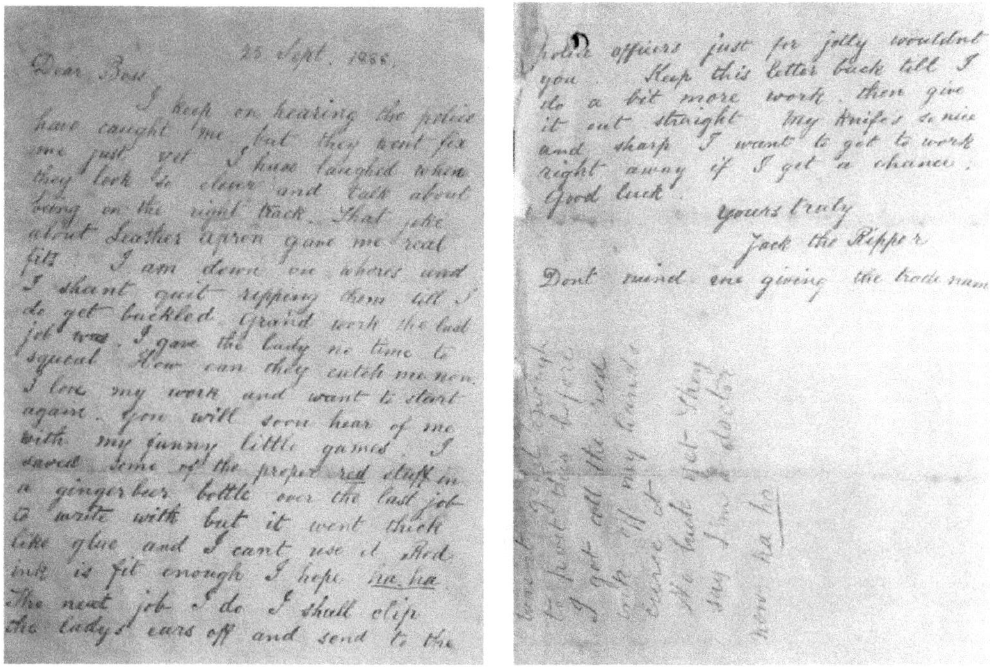

25 Sept. 1888.

Dear Boss,

I keep on hearing the police have caught me but they wont fix me just yet. I have laughed when they look so clever and talk about being on the right track. That joke about Leather Apron gave me real fits. I am down on whores and I shant quit ripping them till I do get buckled. Grand work the last job was. I gave the lady no time to squeal. How can they catch me now. I love my work and want to start again. You will soon hear of me with my funny little games. I saved some of the proper red stuff in a ginger beer bottle over the last job to write with but it went thick like glue and I cant use it. Red ink is fit enough I hope ha. ha. The next job I do I shall clip the ladys ears off and send to the police officers just for jolly wouldnt you. Keep this letter back till I do a bit more work, then give it out straight. My knife's so nice and sharp I want to get to work right away if I get a chance. Good luck.

Yours truly

Jack the Ripper

Dont mind me giving the trade name

wasnt good enough to post this before I got all the red ink off my hands curse it. No luck yet. They say I'm a doctor now. ha ha

Figure 3.1 Jack the Ripper letter dated September 25, 1888.

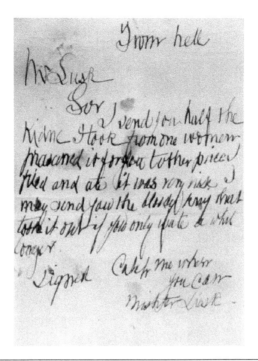

Figure 3.2 Jack the Ripper "From hell" letter postmarked October 15, 1888.

Figure 3.4 Serial murderer Ted Bundy escaped from the Pitkin County Courthouse in Aspen, Colorado, by jumping from the second window from left, second story, on June 7, 1977. Bundy murdered at least three women (the actual number of victims is believed to be closer to 35) by strangulation and bludgeoning from 1974 to 1978 in Washington, Utah, Colorado, and Florida. He was executed on January 24, 1989, in Florida.

Figure 3.6 Mug shot of multiple murderer Aileen Wuornos from the Florida Department of Corrections (date unknown). Wuornos murdered at least six men from 1989 to 1990 in Florida. She was executed on October 9, 2002.

Figure 3.8 An active member of the Democratic Party, serial murderer John Gacy was photographed with then-First Lady Rosalynn Carter on May 6, 1978. Gacy murdered 33 boys and young men by strangulation from 1972 to 1978 in Chicago, Illinois. He was executed on May 10, 1994.

Figure 3.15 Mug shot of multiple murderer Wayne Williams from Fulton County Police, Atlanta, Georgia, on June 21, 1981. Williams was convicted in 1982 of murdering two men in Atlanta, although he is believed to be the man responsible for at least 22 of the 29 deaths of African American children, known as the "Atlanta child murders," from 1979 to 1981. He is currently serving two life sentences.

Figure 5.1 The Serial Killer Museum is part of the Museo Criminale on Via Cavour in Florence, Italy.

Figure 5.2 A close-up of the sign for the Serial Killer Museum in Florence, Italy.

Figure 5.3 A close-up of the outside displays at the Serial Killer Museum in Florence, Italy.

PART II

A Sociocultural Approach to Understanding Serial Murder

5
Cultural Context of Serial Murder

Introduction

Serial murder is deeply embedded in American culture, and serial murderers have become perverse icons in the United States, as legendary as other monsters known throughout history in cultural myths. Public fascination with serial murder is evidenced by widespread media coverage of serial murder cases; the popularity of the true crime genre and serial murder storylines in mainstream media; the existence of Web sites and fan clubs devoted to serial murder as well as particular killers; sales of T-shirts, trading cards, comic books, calendars, and action figures; and the assortment of serial murder artifacts that are housed in museums or exchanged by collectors. This chapter establishes the cultural context of serial murder by examining the public fascination with the phenomenon, as well as representations of serial murder in American popular culture, and then explaining how culture "works" to influence thoughts and behaviors.

Serial Murder in American Popular Culture

As evidenced by reading weekly program summaries and movie and book reviews, serial murder storylines are a mainstay of contemporary fiction, film, television crime drama, and true crime narratives. Serial murder as a theme has even crept into so-called high culture. The musical *Sweeney Todd* (also produced as a ballet and film) features a murderous barber who is aided by a female baker who tricks the town into cannibalism to dispose of the bodies; and the opera *The Infernal Comedy*, which was released on DVD in 2010 but first debuted on stage in Santa Monica, California, in 2008 under a different title, tells a fictional tale about real-life Austrian serial murderer Jack Unterweger (performed by American actor John Malkovich).

Widespread media coverage and intensive public interest are familiar subjects in scholarly studies of serial murder (e.g., Grover and Soothill 1999; Schmid 2005), and several scholars have remarked on the contemporary ubiquitous presence of serial murder in American entertainment and popular culture (Beasley 2004; Caputi 1993; Eschholz and Bufkin 2001; Holmes et al. 1999; Jenkins 1994; Schmid 2005). Schmid (2005, 17) argues that the serial murderer fulfills a "double need" in society: "the need for representations of death, and a need for celebrities" and that the representation of serial murderers as celebrities may serve to ease our anxieties about death, as we are able to confront death by reading or hearing about it in a safe, controlled setting.

Serial Murderers as Monsters and Celebrities

Monstropedia, the Monstrous Encyclopedia, Web site (http://www.monstropedia.com) claims to be "the largest encyclopedia about monsters." Although its primary focus is on more traditional monster imagery (e.g., fairy creatures, beasts, paranormal entities, the undead, dinosaurs, and demons), it also maintains a category for "human monsters," which includes serial murderers and "homicidal maniacs" as subcategories (the difference between the two categories is not explicit), as well as several other subcategories for specific killers. Indeed, the most common word used in the news and popular media to describe a serial murderer is *monster*. Many serial murderers use that description for themselves. *Monster* has become a familiar label used to describe people who commit acts of depravity and cruelty that are difficult to understand. Because of culturally familiar myths and legends about monsters, the term conjures an image that is readily understood.

Monsters in various forms have held a place in every culture throughout history (Hickey 2006), from demons, ghouls, and evil spirits; to vampires, werewolves, witches, and zombies; to mythic creatures such as Big Foot, the Abominable Snowman, and the Loch Ness monster. Despite differences in form and period of popularity, the representations of various "cultural monsters" have remained relatively consistent, including elements of insanity or possession, depravity, and wickedness. These monsters frequently take human form but are depicted with animalistic characteristics—emotionally void, predatory, and savage. They live on through cultural stories and remind us that evil resides in our world. Here, we find the basis for representations of serial murderers, a type of modern cultural monster. Their association with traditional monster imagery is especially clear when considering the nicknames given to many serial murderers by the media, which frequently include the words "ripper," "stalker," "slasher," "butcher," "vampire," and even "monster."

As described in Chapter 3, popular portrayals of serial murderers in American culture have shifted away from the human monster image and toward a perverse celebrity image. Recent media portrayals of serial murderers tend to be attractive and appealing, and some serial murderers receive more national publicity than movie stars, musicians, and professional athletes. Perhaps fueled by this modern image for serial murderers, the public anxiously awaits every detail in these cases as if the killers were Lindsay Lohan or Brad Pitt. "Serial killer groupies" flock to courtrooms during serial murder trials and prison visitation rooms after convictions. Serial murderers in prison get a substantial amount of letters, visitors, and even marriage proposals (Levin 2008). They sit for numerous interviews with law enforcement personnel, psychiatrists, social scientists, journalists, authors, and television and movie producers, all eager to hang on their every word. Their photographs and words appear in publications and on merchandise distributed worldwide.

The serial murderers included in my study (Wiest 2009) appeared to recognize the media as an available outlet for fame, and some used the media to attain recognition and seek celebrity status. Keith Jesperson and Dennis Rader actively sought attention from the media by sending numerous letters to media outlets and, in Rader's case, threatening to kill more if he did not see news coverage of his killings. After his confession, Rader said: "I feel like a star right now" (Smith 2006, 305). Eddie Cole signed autographs for prison guards, and Ted Bundy discussed others' apparent fascination with him: "They all want to see Bundy. A lot of 'em do. 'Where's Bundy?' I'll hear. 'Let's go see Bundy.' They'll drift by. There've been a lot of 'em" (Michaud and Aynesworth 2000, 294). Even after his sentencing, Jesperson continued to contact the media, apparently attempting to keep his name in the news.

Although they did not actively seek coverage, Joel Rifkin, Bundy, and Richard Ramirez apparently enjoyed the attention they received from the media and the many women who sought them out after their arrests, and Coral Watts was delighted to have police investigators' attention. The learned enjoyment of celebrity status was observed in college athletes by Adler and Adler (1989) in their concept of the "glorified self," which is an identity that is formed through forced fame. They argue that it "arises when individuals become the focus of intense interpersonal and media attention, leading to their achieving celebrity" (Adler and Adler 1989, 299). Some of the serial murderers, like the athletes, did not seek fame but learned to play—and enjoy—the celebrity part.

Even after their convictions or deaths, serial murderers may live on in the press. Nearly 12 years after his death, Bundy was featured in an article in which he was called "one of the most notorious serial killers the world has known" (Powell 2000). In a brief story published 9 years after his death, Bundy was used as a measuring stick by which other killers would be compared: "A 69-year-old woman accused of killing eight of her infant children is a mass murderer just like Ted Bundy and should not be allowed back on the streets, prosecutors argued" ("Woman Described as Killer Like Bundy" 1998). Bundy's case apparently was the career highlight of the judge who presided over his trial, as evidenced by the first sentence of a story announcing the judge's death: "Judge Edward D. Cowart of Dade County Circuit Court, whose regretful post-sentencing remarks to serial slayer Theodore R. Bundy were widely noted, died of a heart attack at Coral Reef Hospital early today" ("Edward D. Cowart, 62, Judge in Florida Trial of Ted Bundy" 1987). Ramirez was similarly mentioned in a story announcing the death of the prosecutor in his trial: "Retired Los Angeles Deputy District Attorney Phil Halpin, the prosecutor in the murder trial of 'Night Stalker' Richard Ramirez and in the 'Onion Field' retrial, has died after a lengthy battle with cancer" ("Former Los Angeles Prosecutor Phil Halpin Dies at 65" 2003).

The celebrity status of some serial murderers is also acknowledged by courts in references to the killers in unrelated cases (including a range of case types, from insurance lawsuits to other serial murder cases) and in the ways in which the killers are described. In three separate court cases regarding Jeffrey Dahmer's case, he was described as "well known," "infamous," and "legendary in the annals of serial killers in America." The substantial publicity surrounding accused killers' actions was acknowledged in several court cases, particularly those in which a change of venue had been requested:

> This case had enormous pretrial publicity. The newspapers, magazines, TV and radio were filled with daily accounts of the recovery of bodies from Gacy's crawlspace and other places where he had put them. ... It would have been difficult to find any venue in which the facts of the case were not common knowledge, since the publicity was national. Two of the jurors mentioned on voir dire that they had read about the case in *Time* and *Newsweek*. (*United States of America, ex rel. John Gacy N-00921 v. George Welborn, Warden, Menard Correctional Center, and Roland W. Burris, Attorney General of the State of Illinois*)

The court described the news coverage of this case as "saturation, as much as they possibly can give," but noted that this was not the only case in Los Angeles that had received such extensive news coverage. (*The People v. Richard Ramirez*)

In other cases, the killer's widespread public recognition was apparent by the court's use of his nickname, as in the case of Ramirez: "The Superior Court of Los Angeles County, California, sentenced defendant to death for the so-called Night Stalker murders" (*The People v. Richard Ramirez*). In the more notorious cases, the nickname of the killer appears to become a cultural reference point on its own, as illustrated in a reference in a legal journal article comparing Dayton Rogers's murders to Gary Ridgway's: "Oregon seemed to have its own 'Green River killer,' dubbed by the press the 'Molalla Forest killer,' in its midst" (Long 2002).

Marketing Murderabilia

As with other celebrities, there is an abundance of memorabilia related to serial murder that is available to collect. *Murderabilia* refers to two types of merchandise: (1) commercially available products related to murder and violent crime, especially serial murder, including T-shirts, trading cards, magazines, comic books, calendars, and action figures; and (2) items produced by or formerly belonging to the offenders, including created artwork, writings, jewelry, and musical recordings; previously owned vehicles, clothing, and personal items; and intimate artifacts such as locks of hair, childhood photographs, and autographs.

Murderabilia items of the first type are widely available on the Internet and in novelty stores. One of the largest Web sites specializing in such sales (http://www.serialkillercalendar.com) offers a huge array of "macabre merchandise" featuring serial murderers and other killers, including T-shirts; calendars; DVD sets; three series of trading cards; wall posters; wall clocks; throw pillows; action figures; postcards; mugs and steins; wooden keepsake boxes; notebooks; artwork; tote and messenger bags; aprons featuring cannibal killers; eight issues of the *Serial Killer Magazine*; energy drinks; and recordings of news footage, interviews, and confessions. Similar Web sites offer additional clothing and household items, apparel for children and pets, skateboards, and even computer fonts resembling serial murderers' handwriting. One site, CafePress (http://www.cafepress.com) allows users to create their own items with images and words of their choosing, and this has produced T-shirts, stickers, magnets, buttons, travel cups, and mouse pads with creepy slogans and quoted words of serial murderers.

Murderabilia items of the second type are primarily purchased or sold by collectors via private sales, police auctions, and online auction sites. In May 2001, eBay banned the sale of this type of murderabilia, although many items of the first type remain available, and other online auction sites exist to handle the demand. Several serial murderers have used Web sites and accomplices to sell various items, including locks of hair, fingernail clippings, artwork, letters, and autobiographical accounts. John Gacy reportedly made $100,000 from sales of his paintings while he was awaiting execution (Ramsland and Pepper "Serial Killer Culture"), and his artwork is still in high demand. Actor Johnny Depp once owned a painting by Gacy, and Massachusetts musician Nikki Stone purchased a Gacy piece for $3,000 (Ramsland and Pepper "Serial Killer Culture"). Jonathan Davis, singer for the band Korn, is one of the most prominent and devoted collectors of murderabilia. Davis owns Ted Bundy's Volkswagen bug (the vehicle he used to pick up victims and transport bodies), Gacy's clown suit, and legal documents signed by various high-profile killers (Ramsland and Pepper "Serial Killer Culture").

Not all serial murderers are permitted to profit from their notoriety in this way. Since 1977, so-called Son of Sam laws[1] have been passed by 42 states; these laws forbid criminals from making money through the sale of expressive works about their crimes. Many of these statutes require that any profits made from such sales be designated for the victims or their families. These laws, however, have been challenged by First Amendment rights groups, and the Nevada Supreme Court in 2004 struck down that state's Son of Sam law after a legal challenge by a former prison inmate.

Some items of the second type of murderabilia become part of museum exhibits. The Museum of Death in Hollywood, California (http://http://www.museumofdeath.net), boasts on its Web site "the world's largest collection of serial murderer artwork," crime scene and morgue photographs, a body bag and coffin collection, replicas of execution devices, autopsy videos, and more. Plans for a museum devoted to American serial murderers in California, with Korn's Davis as a major supporter, have been on hold since 2004. Davis's public announcement of the museum in 2002 led to a lawsuit by former partner and murderabilia collector/dealer Arthur Rosenblatt, who apparently had a different understanding of their agreement (Ramsland "Serial Killer Art"). The only museum in the world devoted to serial murderers is located in Florence, Italy (Figures 5.1–5.3). Affiliated with the Museo Criminale on Via Cavour, the museum primarily features American killers and offers a self-guided audio tour (available in several languages), leading visitors through exhibits featuring infamous serial murderers, as well as a capital punishment artifact exhibit. The infamous serial murderer of Florence—the never-captured "Monster of Florence," who killed 16 people from 1968 to 1985 in the hills of Tuscany—is conspicuously absent from this museum, perhaps contributing to the perception of serial murder as primarily an American affliction. Finally, the Federal Bureau of Investigation (FBI) operates a serial murder museum of sorts as the Evil Minds Research Museum of the Behavioral Science Unit. The appointment-only display was founded in 2008 in the basement of the FBI Academy in Quantico, Virginia, and is dedicated to studying "serial killer and other offender artifacts for the purpose of developing a deeper understanding of offender motivation, personality, and intent in order to assist and enhance investigative strategies and techniques" (Vecchi 2009, 14).

Figure 5.1 **(See color insert.)** The Serial Killer Museum is part of the Museo Criminale on Via Cavour in Florence, Italy.

CULTURAL CONTEXT OF SERIAL MURDER 99

Figure 5.2 **(See color insert.)** A close-up of the sign for the Serial Killer Museum in Florence, Italy.

Figure 5.3 **(See color insert.)** A close-up of the outside displays at the Serial Killer Museum in Florence, Italy.

It is clear that serial murder has deep roots in American culture. We now explore how culture influences people's thoughts and behaviors. Understanding the *workings* of culture will provide a framework for identifying cultural elements that contribute to the development of serial murderers in the United States.

Cultural Context of Human Behavior: How Culture "Works"

Culture incorporates language, ideas, beliefs, values, traditions, and a range of other vehicles used to experience and express meaning. Denzin (1992, 22) argues that culture is "the taken-for-granted and problematic webs of significance and meaning that human beings produce and act on when they do things together" and that culture "is shaped by the larger meaning-making institutions of society-at-large." Culture and forms of social power are bound to one another, as culture is constantly shaped and perpetuated by powerful institutions and groups in society. As a consequence, culture helps reproduce the power of the dominant class by offering support for dominant ideas, beliefs, and values through their perpetuation in cultural messages.

Culture is meaningful in that it offers a means for people to perceive, think about, and make sense of the world around them. Hall (1997, 2) emphasizes meaning in the cultural "process," arguing, "To say that two people belong to the same culture is to say that they interpret the world in roughly the same ways and can express themselves, their thoughts and feelings about the world, in ways which will be understood by each other." In other words, the establishment of language, ideas, beliefs, values, traditions, and other vehicles of meaning create a framework for us to make sense of our world and provide a link to others so that we can share our experiences in ways that are understandable and continually perpetuate the dominant culture.

The influential power of culture lies in its ability to produce shared meanings about cultural objects that become institutionalized and deeply part of the ways in which we think about our world. Culture links people, events, experiences, and things to concepts people share about them through symbols (Hall 1997). Cultural messages contain "codes" that indicate meanings—linking the "thing" to its concept. The messages are "encoded" by the sender and then "decoded" by the receiver, producing meaning. Cultural values and meanings change over time, and inevitably so do symbols and codes. Hall (1997, 62) argues that what is important is that cultural concepts and classifications "enable us to *think* about things, whether they are there, present, or not" (italics in original). Culture enables us to understand our world and adapt to changes in it.

Broadcasting Culture

Cultural messages provide information about what we should value and the legitimate uses for those values. These messages are transmitted through a variety of social institutions, including the family, schools, the state, mass media, religious and community groups, and peer groups, but mass media have a distinctive ability to spread cultural messages rapidly to an enormous audience. The mass media constantly transmit cultural messages and, because of their substantial reach, constitute one of the central socializing agencies in the world. Mass media not only provide people with information about the world around them, but also, because of their ubiquity, influence how we think and behave. Cultural messages transmitted through mass media generally correspond with dominate cultural values and expectations, aiding in their acceptance and subsequent reinforcement. Thus, media messages are both *influenced by* culture and *influence* culture. To illustrate how culture "works," we can think of culture as a "broadcast" of values transmitted especially through mass media (see Figure 5.4).

"Tuning In" and Cultural Competencies

Despite their mass broadcast, values are not accepted by every member of the culture or employed in the same ways. We are aware of some objects more than others and more or less likely to use some over others depending on our cultural competencies and which objects are useful for our purposes at the time. Being "culturally competent" means having the ability to understand the ideas, beliefs, and values held by dominant groups in society and to incorporate them into daily life through culturally legitimate means. Variations in individual abilities, as well as access to power and other resources, help shape this capacity. In Figure 5.5, the thicknesses of the arrows represent the various

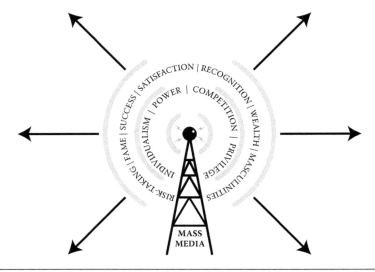

Figure 5.4 Model of American culture, phase 1. We can think of culture as a "broadcast" of values transmitted especially through mass media. Mass media not only provide people with information about the world around them, but also, because of their ubiquity, influence how we think and behave. Along with messages about cultural values, we receive information about legitimate uses for those values.

quantities of values that may be drawn on, while the gray circle depicts a cultural competency "filter" through which the selected values then pass. The filter represents an individual's capacity for understanding and using dominant cultural ideas, beliefs, and values, so it may vary considerably from individual to individual.

People make various choices about which and how many values to "tune in" from the cultural milieu. Schudson (1989, 160) explores the "conditions—both of the cultural object and its environment—that are likely to make the culture or cultural object work more or less." Specifically, he examines five dimensions of a cultural object that contribute to its strength or power: retrievability (the likelihood that the object will be drawn on by an audience in a variety of situations); rhetorical force (the indefinable quality of the object that produces intensity, grabs attention, and generates beliefs); resonance (its utility or relevance to the audience); institutional retention (the production of a set of concrete meanings people share about it); and resolution (its likelihood to influence action). The influence of culture varies with deviations in these dimensions—a cultural object may have a large impact on few people, a small impact on many people, a large impact on many people, or a small impact on few people (Schudson 1989).

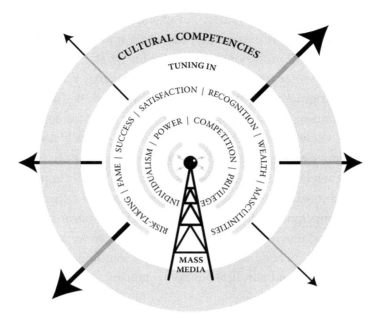

Figure 5.5 Model of American culture, phase 2. Cultural values are not accepted by every person, or employed in the same ways, depending on our cultural competencies and which objects are useful for our purposes at the time. The thicknesses of the arrows represent the various quantities of values that may be drawn on, while the gray circle depicts a cultural competency "filter" through which the selected values then pass. The filter represents an individual's capacity for understanding and using dominant cultural ideas, beliefs, and values, so it may vary considerably from individual to individual.

Lieberson (2000) offers the "cultural surface" as a way to understand a culture as a representation of the many processes that result in the formation of the various cultural elements (i.e., ideas, beliefs, and values) on which actors draw. Cultural elements come from different time periods for different reasons and have various shelf lives: some survive, some disappear, and others lay dormant for a time (Lieberson 2000). Because there is a variety of related and unrelated elements from which to choose on the cultural surface, individuals may utilize particular ones at particular times for particular reasons. Which cultural elements they choose to acknowledge or utilize is influenced by various external and internal factors.

Although individuals have options about which cultural values to select and utilize, these options are finite; individuals do not form their own values from infinite possibilities but must pick from available elements in their culture. Individuals do not all strive to reach the same goals, yet the goals they select are drawn from messages about dominant cultural values. For example, Americans may strive for wealth via various means (e.g., earning a master's degree in business, becoming a professional athlete or movie star, or winning the lottery), but we generally do not strive for poverty. Americans may strive for recognition via different means (e.g., working hard at school or work, running for political office, entering contests, appearing on reality TV shows, or breaking records), but we generally do not strive for anonymity or mediocrity. Similarly, there is a variety of possible paths to reach culturally valued goals—some culturally approved and some deviant—and our selection of a line of action depends on our cultural competencies. We cannot all be CEOs, astronauts, professional athletes, movie stars, or even "A" students, so we strive to find a path to wealth, success, satisfaction, recognition, fame, or power that works best for us and parallels our competencies.

Building Lines of Action

Although cultural messages impart what people *should* believe and think and how they *should* behave, people are differentially provided with the cultural competencies to build lines of action for reaching culturally valued goals. People generally strive toward culturally valued goals that they have the cultural means—opportunities and know-how—to attain. To construct a line of action, an actor must have an awareness of dominant culture values, a desire to achieve culturally valued goals, a sense that he or she can fairly accurately measure success or failure, and the ability to choose among alternative paths (Swidler 1998). Developing a line of action is not necessarily a smooth process. Indeed, a series of failures may precede a successful progression as the actor tries out a variety of available paths toward culturally valued goals before finding one that suits his or her cultural competencies. Because of differentiation in how people adapt to the dominant culture, various paths to social goods are possible. As cultural values pass through the cultural competency filter, their culturally legitimate uses may be distorted to build lines of action compatible with both the values and those competencies (see Figure 5.6).

CULTURAL CONTEXT OF SERIAL MURDER

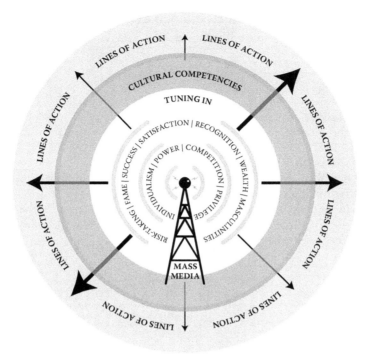

Figure 5.6 Model of American culture, phase 3. People are differentially provided with the cultural competencies to build lines of action for reaching culturally valued goals, so various paths to social goods are possible. As cultural values pass through the cultural competency filter, their culturally legitimate uses may be distorted to build lines of action compatible with both the values and those competencies.

Not only do cultural competencies vary, but also cultural messages may be inconsistent, helping to explain variations in ideas, beliefs, and values held by members of the same culture. To account for apparent contradictions in messages from various cultural values, we must recognize that not all cultural values are connected; some are, many are not, and some have only loose links. In addition, race, ethnicity, gender, and social class are important in studies of culture because they may affect how people receive, interpret, and respond to cultural messages. Because people form lines of action according to their cultural competencies, members of dominant and subordinate groups in society likely will respond to cultural messages differently.

In the following chapter, the model of American culture is applied specifically to the case of serial murder. Shown is how an understanding of the workings of culture—and particular contextual features of

American culture—leads to a better understanding of the creation of serial murderers in the United States.

Note

1. These laws were named for David Berkowitz, a serial murderer known as the "Son of Sam," who killed six people in New York between 1976 and 1977. After his conviction, Berkowitz was offered substantial sums of money for the rights to his story. When members of the New York Assembly discovered this, they passed a statute requiring that any profits made by an accused or convicted criminal from the sale of works related to his or her crimes must be placed into an escrow account for the victims. Perhaps ironically, Berkowitz was never subject to New York's Son of Sam law because it was not applied retroactively.

6
APPLYING THE MODEL OF AMERICAN CULTURE

Introduction

The model of American culture explained in Chapter 5 is applied here to demonstrate that deviant lines of action (e.g., serial murder) do not necessarily result from the employment of divergent values. Instead, legitimate *and* deviant lines of action are outcomes of a cultural process that includes variations in the selection of dominant cultural values for use; variations in competencies for using values in culturally legitimate ways; and variations in constructed lines of action according to those values and competencies. In this chapter, several cultural values are categorized as contextual features suitable for serial murder, all of which are related but influential in differing ways. Examining these features separately offers a deeper understanding of the cultural messages and influential elements of each, but combining them provides a powerful framework that can be used to understand how serial murderers are created in the United States. The role of the American mass media in broadcasting messages about cultural values is explored, and the ways in which serial murderers "tune in" the messages and subsequently build lines of action are examined with specific examples drawn from my study (Wiest 2009).

American Cultural Values: Contextual
Features Suitable for Serial Murder

Identifying the features of American society that make serial murder one path to social goods contributes to an understanding of American culture and how people construct lines of action according to their cultural competencies. Holmes and De Burger (1988, 44) argue that contextual features of American society "all too well serve the homicidal propensities of the serial killer." Features such as "redundant violence" and dehumanization, as represented in American popular culture; a cultural importance placed on individualism and competition; privilege associated with whiteness and maleness; an emphasis on thrill seeking; situational justifications and the normalization of violence; increased anonymity and depravity in urban life; and spatial mobility (Holmes and De Burger 1988; Jenkins 1994) are components of American culture and the nature of social life in American society that may increase the probability of serial murder (Holmes and De Burger 1988, 44) and Americans' fascination with it.

Regard for Violence

Violence has long been a form of entertainment in many cultures, from public executions, to images in television and movies, to lyrics in popular music, to norms in sports. While many acts of violence are generally condemned (e.g., violent acts perpetrated on innocent victims, domestic violence, and indiscriminate violence), social groups construct circumstances in which violence is considered legitimate (Cerulo 1998; Collins 2008). For instance, a degree of violence and deviant behavior is acceptable on Halloween (including vandalism, looting, and arson) and especially the night before, popularly known as Devil's Night. Violence is allowed in particular arenas, including wild parties and mosh pits at hard-rock concerts. And, deviant behavior is tolerated during mass celebrations, including Mardi Gras. Violence in sports is common. Some sports include elements of violence in the ways they are played, including contact sports like football, hockey, and rugby, and a degree of illegitimate violence also is pervasive in most sports, both by players (e.g., fouls, unnecessary roughness, and outright brawls) and by spectators (e.g., heckling, throwing objects, storming the field, or rioting in the streets) (Collins 2008).

Norms and boundaries associated with fighting in American culture distinguish fair fights from unfair fights (Collins 2008). Staged fights, whether planned schoolyard brawls or professional boxing matches, are often considered heroic for both the winner and the loser, and dueling historically was seen as a display of risk and manipulation of danger. Gunfighting replaced dueling as a fair fight between two skilled opponents, but gunfighting became more associated with unfair fighting as it was no longer an activity of the elite class, and often the fighting was not staged with implicit norms. Fights that are carried out because of a vendetta, those in which only one participant possesses a gun or other deadly weapon, and those that are numerically imbalanced are included in unfair fights and lack social support. Collins (2008) argues that vendetta fights engaged in by gangs are considered unfair and dishonorable by most people outside the gangs, but that vendetta fights engaged in by the Mafia are generally considered honorable or impressive, as they are related to careful, intelligent planning and a high degree of success, characteristics that are highly valued in American culture and associated with hegemonic masculinity.

Individual Accomplishment and Competition

Individualism, competition, and personal achievement are highly valued in American culture (Mount 1981; Reisman 1967; Williams 1962) and often are used as markers of a person's worth. Values such as cooperation, sympathy, and teamwork also are pervasive in American culture (Mount 1981) but generally are not seen as means for idealized success.

The ordinary American is celebrated in popular culture, as well as the exceptional—good or bad—individual (Rossides 2003). Familiar stories like those of the frontiersman, the outlaw, the rebellious loner, and the "self-made man" emphasize individualism as a path to success in the United States (Mount 1981). "Americans love to think of themselves as pioneers, men who have conquered a continent and sired on it a new society" (Cawelti 1984, 86). While many scholars point to the Western genre—with the long-celebrated American frontiersmen—as symbolizing American individualism, ruggedness, strength, and honor (e.g., Cawelti 1984; Collins 2008; Slotkin 1992), these values also are manifest in modern forms of entertainment, including crime dramas, sports, and video games.

Recognition and celebrity are emphasized in American culture, as indicated by the notion that everyone deserves "15 minutes of fame" at some point in their lives. It matters little whether the fame is earned for positive or negative reasons, as "we accord status and recognition for both fame and notoriety" (Adler and Adler 1989, 299). This is dramatically evident in the popularity of reality television programming, in which it is clear that being known for something—anything—is better than not being known. Every reality show has a villain, and even the worst singers on *American Idol* get recognition on prime-time television. Some of these reality programs have combined the values of recognition and competition, for example, like *The Amazing Race*, *America's Got Talent*, *America's Best Dance Crew*, and *America's Next Top Model*. Recognition of talents, hard work, and accomplishments, however, is most important to Americans, and others' deference or esteem may be thought of as an end in itself (Goode 1978).

The most celebrated in American culture are those perceived as fighting the "good" fight, and these stories are especially poignant when the actors apparently conquer incredible odds. Stories about people taking on nature, outer space and aliens, war, bullies, or the frontier—and winning—are ubiquitous in popular culture, which also romanticizes fantasies of being captain of the ship, a military hero, or an astronaut. Popular television shows like *Survivor*, *I Survived*, *Man vs. Wild*, and *Deadliest Catch* illustrate this well.

Individual accomplishment, whether it is through legitimate or illegitimate means, is well regarded in American culture. Entrepreneurs are praised for succeeding through hard work, perseverance, and having that extra something that boosted them above the competition. Others who achieve individualized success through deviant means may be admired if they or their offense are seen as somehow superior. Ted Kaczynski is known as much for his superior intellect as the destruction he caused as the Unabomber. Butch Cassidy and Bonnie and Clyde are legendary robbers, perceived as highly skilled and elusive. Charles Ponzi is perceived as a highly intelligent and skilled swindler, and Bernard Madoff, who pled guilty to perpetrating the largest Ponzi scheme in history, is regarded with awe because of the magnitude of his con and ability to avoid detection for nearly 20 years.

An emphasis on individual accomplishment also is evident in the ambivalence—and sometimes admiration—shown for a person who takes the law into his or her own hands by performing some justice-oriented deed through illegal means. Figures like Rambo and Robin Hood are exalted, despite their use of illegitimate means for good ends (Madsen 1998). Detectives, police officers, doctors, and lawyers in popular television shows and movies frequently are seen bending the rules to attain a desirable result.

Acknowledging an American aversion to authority and regard for frontiersmen and others who supposedly follow a "higher law," Graham (1970, 79) argues that "it is not difficult to fathom why America—despite official rhetoric to the contrary—has never been a very law-abiding society." The American cultural emphasis on achievement not only promotes productivity, efficiency, and innovation but also generates pressures for its members to succeed at any cost (Messner and Rosenfeld 2001). The glorification of these traits fosters ambition and mobility, but the means to attain idealized success are not available for everyone—and everyone does not have the capacity.

Although there has been a perceived crisis in American moral values for a number of years (Baker 2005), which could be used to explain increases in crime, empirical evidence does not support this perception. Baker (2005), in a study of American values using World Values Surveys across two decades, concluded that traditional values about religion, morality, and national pride have not changed throughout time, that Americans still subscribe to the same values they did decades ago.

Masculinities and Privilege

Men are generally held more accountable than women for achieving culturally defined success through values emphasized in American culture. Traditional gender role expectations hold men and women accountable for behaving in ways that are deemed socially acceptable for each sex and that perpetuate socially defined masculine and feminine ideals (West and Zimmerman 1987). Men are expected to be unemotional and exhibit aggression, confidence, leadership, intelligence, and dominance, and women are expected to exhibit emotion, passivity, submissiveness, compassion, and nurturance (Connell 1987, 2002, 2005; Henson and Rogers 2001; Jourard 1971; Reisman 1967; Zuo and Tang 2000). Reisman (1967, 41) argues as follows: "Sex in the United States, like other statuses, often seems as much achieved as ascribed," in that men and women cannot assume that masculinity or femininity is biologically given, but must be "proved." Because of these gendered expectations, men may experience enhanced pressure to "win" at all cost—to be smarter, faster, and better than others. Men are rewarded for individualistic and competitive behaviors, while women, who are expected to be more relationship oriented, are discouraged from such behavior. Gilligan (1996, 267) argues that, for men, the "patriarchal code of honor and shame generates and obligates male violence."

Messages about gender in American culture are pervasive and constantly reinforced such that we begin to think of differences between men and women as natural, rather than social, constructions. Therefore, we generally think of being an American as something one must work at, but being men and women as innate. Few men can achieve the idealized version of masculinity in American culture, yet men are expected to strive toward the ideals to be considered masculine. With the patriarchal structure of American society, male dominance is a value in itself, broadcast with others that are compatible, such as individualism, competition, privilege, recognition, wealth, and success.

Although much social research examines gender differences with regard to social development and behavior, these studies infrequently examine *masculinities*. The masculinities perspective is grounded in the feminist notion of power, specifically that the essential nature of the relationship between men and women is one involving domination and oppression (Carrigan, Connell, and Lee 1985, 552). This relationship is embedded in the structures of society, as well as its institutions: the family, schools, the political system, the economic system, mass media, and religion. Masculinities and femininities are constructed through gendered power relations that have a historical dynamic in society as a whole (Carrigan et al. 1985). This conception of gender dimorphism posits that masculinity can only exist in contrast with femininity (Connell 2005), and this relationship is continually reconstituted within the historic system in which dominance is generated (Carrigan et al. 1985; Savran 1998). One of the fundamental "facts" about masculinity is that "men in general are advantaged through the subordination of women" (Carrigan et al. 1985, 590).

As members of privileged groups in society, white men may have acquired a sense of entitlement to the rewards of privilege and become frustrated and angry when they do not reap the benefits (Irvine and Klocke 2001). Johnson (2006, 91) argues that "just because a system is male-dominated doesn't mean all men are powerful" but that "every man can *identify* with power as a value that his culture associates with manhood, and this identification makes it easier for any man to assume and use power in relation to others" (italics in original). Men, especially *white* men, may feel more entitled to subordinate others to feel power—to which they are culturally entitled—when they otherwise would feel powerless because of their position in the social structure.

Masculinities are constructed not only through gendered power relations but also by their integral involvement with the division of labor and with patterns of emotional attachment (Carrigan et al. 1985). It is important to differentiate between hegemonic masculinity and other forms of masculinity. Hegemony is historically mobile—not fixed—with some association between cultural ideals and institutional power. Hegemonic masculinity, then, is a cultural ideal of what it means to be male, but it is a model that changes through time and is not achievable for most men.

Messerschmidt (1993) argues that gender intersects with race and class to create different notions of what it means to be male, thus creating different masculinities or ways for a boy or man to "do gender." In this way, not only does *masculine* mean "nonfeminine," but also, by characterizing the ideal way to do gender, hegemonic masculinity anchors one end of a continuum of masculinities that more or less fit that ideal.

In modern industrialized societies, hegemonic masculinity is realized through participation in the paid-labor market, the subordination of women, heterosexuality, heightened sexuality, and behavior that displays authority, control, competition, individualism, independence, aggressiveness, and the capacity for violence (Messerschmidt 1993, 82). Carrigan et al. (1985, 594) argue that "hegemony means persuasion," and they point to the mass media as influences on conceptions of masculinity and femininity. Advertising promotes ideals of masculinity via the amplification of traditional male gender role expectations (Carrigan et al. 1985, 594). Advertising is, of course, only one example; the mass media are continually reinforcing notions of masculinity and femininity through products and the messages attached to them, characterizing what is appropriate for "doing" maleness and femaleness. Of particular relevance to this study, Eschholz and Bufkin (2001, 655) argue that media may be "influential in establishing values that accept violence as one means to accomplish masculinity."

Hegemonic masculinity is closely aligned with the division of labor, the way of defining what is considered "men's work" and "women's work," and the way of defining what work is more or less masculine than other types. The gendered division of labor not only constructs this notion of men's work and women's work, but also leads to the view that each type of work is not just what men and women do but actually part of *what they are* (West and Zimmerman 1987).

Hegemonic masculinity also is closely involved in and enforced by the state. The political system reinforces and encourages conformity to the hegemonic pattern through economic incentives (e.g., tax incentives and welfare rules) (Carrigan et al. 1985). The media and the state are not the only societal institutions reinforcing hegemonic masculinity. The family also teaches and reinforces ideals of masculinity and femininity. Children learn what it means to be male or female from an early age in the home by the clothes they are given to wear, the toys they play with, the chores they are required to perform, and so on. But, although "people growing up in a gendered society unavoidably encounter gender relations, and actively participate in them" (Connell 2002, 79), participation varies, as does the extent to which messages about gender are consistent. Children encounter mixed messages about gender through parents, grandparents, teachers, classmates, and other peers and adults (Connell 2002). Therefore, in every period there is a hegemonic masculine ideal, but that ideal does not provide a clear-cut definition of what it means to be male for every boy or man, and boys and men for various reasons sometimes do not accept the hegemonic ideal.

Regardless of whether the hegemonic ideal is pursued, male dominance may be pursued. Men's domination over women and the domination of particular men over other men are "sought by constantly re-constituting gender relations as a system within which that dominance is generated" (Carrigan et al. 1985, 598). This reconstitution process is never a smooth one, however; the conditions for its development are ever changing and foment a continuing struggle among subordinated groups. Gendered violence is one outcome of the power struggle among those seeking to achieve the dominance associated with the ideal of hegemonic masculinity (Anderson and Umberson 2001; Atkinson, Greenstein, and Lang 2005; Carrigan et al. 1985).

Men are encouraged to view their masculinity in relation to their position in the social structure and, therefore, their access to power and other resources (Messerschmidt 1993). For many men, their position in the paid-labor market is what they believe defines their masculinity in relation to women and other men. Because women have traditionally been segregated within or excluded from the workplace, paid labor has historically been a means for men to exert their dominance over women for they hold the economic power, and women must then rely on men financially. In the paid-labor market, hegemonic masculinity can be seen in how much power a man holds, which means men in managerial and executive-level positions may be able to achieve masculinity in the workplace more easily than men in other white-collar positions and many in blue-collar positions.

Men do not need to attain high-status positions (e.g., executives) in the workplace to demonstrate masculinity. Particular types of employment—like firefighting, police work, military work, coal mining, factory work, and construction work—that presumably demonstrate endurance, strength, toughness, and bravery are considered "manly" and provide an alternative means for men to demonstrate masculinity (Connell 2005). Some men employ other methods of doing masculinity (Connell 2005; Messner 1992). A sense of being manly may be reached through participation in activities that require skill and emphasize competition or aggression, including sports, video games, gambling, and some community organizations.

Many men are forced to construct alternative masculinities, which generally are considered subordinated to the hegemonic model. Researchers have examined how men form alternative masculinities in various social settings, the consequences of and the relationship between different forms of masculinities, and the relationship between masculinities and femininity. Beal (1996) examined alternative masculinities constructed by skateboarders in Colorado; Irvine and Klocke (2001) examined the construction of alternative masculinities in 12-step programs in New York; Sathiparsad (2008) examined the construction of alternative masculinities by men in South Africa as a strategy to address gendered violence; and Smith and Winchester (1998) examined how Australian men negotiate masculinities at work and home. Although these studies and others find that men in a variety of ways reconstruct and redefine masculinities in their daily lives, their attitudes and behaviors still tended to be based on the hegemonic model and to reproduce patriarchal relations. Therefore, alternative masculinities do not represent a rejection of hegemonic masculine ideals.

Race and class play a role in constructing alternative masculinities (Connell 2005). Although no "black masculinity" or "working-class masculinity" exists, masculinities constructed by marginal groups are related to their position in the social structure and the means available to them. While media may associate black masculinity with violence, irresponsibility, unintelligence, and laziness (Hatty 2000), many black men construct masculinities in opposition to this imagery and focus, at least in part, on attempting to achieve aspects of hegemonic white masculinity within available means. Working-class masculinities may focus on self-respect (making an honest living) and being a family provider (Connell 2005). Although men construct and demonstrate masculinities in a variety of ways, they are produced in the same patriarchal cultural and institutional settings (Connell 2005) and are more or less valued according to how well they fit the ideals of hegemonic masculinity (Connell 1987).

These masculine ideals mesh with American cultural values like individualism, competition, skill, and control. Positive portrayals of frontiersmen and self-made men indicate that men throughout their lives are tested on their individual abilities to prove their manliness. They must prove (mostly to other men) that they are contenders in achieving hegemonic masculinity, or a version close to it, and have the required self-discipline and control (Irvine and Klocke 2001).

Messerschmidt (1993) argues that when legitimate means for achieving culturally defined forms of masculinity are absent, illegitimate means, including criminal offending, may seem a suitable alternative for some men. For these men, deviant means for asserting manliness may include subordinating women (through sexual harassment, domestic abuse, rape, or murder); demonstrating heterosexuality (through harassment, physical abuse, or murder of homosexuals); demonstrating uncontrollable sexuality (through rape, promiscuity, or adultery); or being aggressive and presenting a capacity for violence (through fighting, assault, burglary, rape, or murder). Others argue that aggression and violence are themselves part of hegemonic masculinity (Hatty 2000; Kaufman 1997;

Umberson et al. 2003), which means that men do not necessarily need any reason for aggression and violence other than it being a means in itself to achieve masculinity. Thus, whether aggression is associated with alternative masculinity or hegemonic masculinity, it is tied to masculinity.

Biological arguments frequently portray men as having an aggressive nature and stronger sexual drive than women and that such "naturally" stronger sexual drives require a "release" (Henderson 1992, 136). Variations of this argument often appear in the rape literature. But, biological arguments do not recognize the cultural ideals that promote aggression.

Traditional gender roles, hegemonic masculinity, and dominant-group privilege not only encourage particular behaviors and patterns of thinking for some American men but also may *obligate* white, male violence. For a limited number of men, serial murder may be one channel for constructing and expressing masculinity when other channels have been blocked or found to be unsuccessful through repeated failure.

The Criminal Experience

The experience of crime commission is distinct yet also consonant with both American cultural values and masculine ideals. Components of the criminal experience—including risk taking, thrill seeking, and a desire for power and control—are compatible with American values and masculine ideals. In the United States, thrill seeking is associated with freedom and self-actualization, and those who take big risks that pay off are handsomely rewarded. Because these values mesh well with masculine ideals, men, who are encouraged to be aggressive, competitive, and willing to take risks to gain success, are particularly susceptible to messages about these values.

Although Lyng (1990, 2005) and Katz (1988) do not address serial murder in their theoretical models, Lyng's (2005) concept of "edgework" and Katz's (1988) concept of the "seductions of crime" provide useful ways for conceptualizing the appealing and often-thrilling nature of offending. Both attempt to "link an experiential understanding of crime with the structural conditions of modern social life" (Miller 2005, 157).

Risk Taking and Thrill Seeking

Katz (1988) urges the examination of crime by attempting to understand the *criminal experience*. He focuses on the "seductive," or attractive, components of crime, which can be "moving" and "thrilling" for some. He urges an examination of criminal activity as an emotional process that offers its perpetrators distinctive rewards and sensations. Miller (2005, 155–156) agrees: "From this perspective, crime is seen as a powerful, seductive, emotional experience that allows social actors to transcend their otherwise routine, mundane lives." The recognition of the criminal experience as an emotional, thrilling practice provides another perspective for understanding serial murderers.

Lyng (1990) explores the appeal of risk taking and thrill seeking, whether partaking in adventures like rock climbing, skiing, or skydiving; financial risks like stock trading; or psychological risks like unprotected sex and sadomasochism, and attempts to explain such high-risk behaviors "in terms of a socially constituted self in a historically specific social environment" (Lyng 1990, 852–853). He argues that other models of risk-taking behaviors fail to explain why some people appear to "place a higher value on the *experience* of risk-taking than they do on achieving the final ends of the risky undertaking" (Lyng 1990, 852; emphasis in original).

A common characteristic of edgework activities is that they all include a clear, serious threat to the participant's physical or mental well-being; if he or she fails to meet the challenge, the consequences may include death or debilitating injury. But, edgeworkers frequently claim a high level of expertise or a heightened ability to maintain control in situations most people would classify as uncontrollable (Lyng 1990). To be successful in an edgework activity, participants must maintain constant control, even when faced with the unexpected.

Edgeworkers often describe their activities as constituting a "hyperreality," creating a sense of "self-realization," "self-actualization," or "self-determination" and contend that no words can truly explain the experience; thus, many will not discuss their activities in detail (Lyng 1990, 860–861). Yet, they often feel a special bond with other edgeworkers based on the belief that their activities require an extraordinary skill not possessed—or understood—by most people.

Edgeworkers do not participate in risky ventures to obtain some ultimate benefit; instead, the benefit is found in the experience itself. In edgework, "the seductive quality is in the extreme rush experienced during the event and, subsequent to it, in the reflections on the accomplishments that have taken place under extreme conditions" (Milovanovic 2005, 53). Participation in risky ventures induces an altered state for the production of an adrenaline rush and is a means for proving skill and control. Edgework activities require planning, concentration, and flexibility, and edgeworkers view success as a mark of significant survival skills. As with most thrilling ventures, the excitement eventually lessens with repetition, and edgeworkers need to intensify the risk level periodically to achieve the desired feeling.

Lyng (1990) argues that the alienating nature of modern, industrialized society leads some people to participate in edgework because it offers them the opportunity to feel that they have greater control of their lives or a means to express their "real selves." Some people may only recognize their real selves in "moments of uninhibited behavior, emotional outbursts, or spontaneous expression" (Lyng 1990, 864). Those bound by social constraints may seek spontaneous and emotional activities to "feel like themselves." Lyng (1990, 871) argues that the constraining nature of contemporary work "offers none of the phenomenological experiences that define spontaneous, free activity," so "workers look to leisure time for experience that is self-determining and self-actualizing" and particularly activities that involve both risk and skill.

Lyng further argues that the modern world is full of uncertainty and dangers that generally are beyond people's control, but that participating in edgework activities creates a sense of greater control in such a threatening environment. In addressing the apparent paradox of people participating in dangerous activities "as a response to the threats they confront in an already dangerous world," Lyng (1990, 874) argues that "the absence of control experiences in institutional routines is the direct counterpart of the heightened sense of control experienced in edgework, even if the latter sensation is largely illusory." The sensation is termed *illusory* because many circumstances in edgework activities cannot be anticipated and therefore cannot be controlled, but the edgeworker defines his or her skill in terms of the ability to plan for potential hazards, quickly compensate for unexpected events, and ultimately survive the experience unscathed.

Lyng briefly explores the particularly male preoccupation with skill and control—and edgework activities—and suggests that gender socialization may be responsible. Most edgeworkers tend to be young men, as "males are more likely than females to have an illusory sense of control over fateful endeavors because of the socialization pressures on males to develop a skill orientation toward their environment" (Lyng 1990, 872–873).

The need to express a real self outside an alienating labor force does not push everyone into edgework, and some lower-income edgeworkers may gravitate to high-risk subcultures (e.g., biker groups) or work in high-risk occupations (e.g., police work, firefighting, and combat soldiering) (Lyng 1990). Other people may experience self-actualization in "their commitment to family, occupation, or an ideology like Christian fundamentalism" (Lyng 1990, 879). However, Lyng (1990, 882) concludes: "The fact that many people find this type of experience alluring and seek to repeat it as often as possible is an important statement on the nature of modern social life."

Power and Control

Many serial murderers have described murder as thrilling and providing a great sense of power and control, whether over their victims, by instilling a sense of fear in the community, or over the police by outsmarting them for a time (Fox et al. 2005; Levin and Fox 2007; Levin 2008; Martingale 1993; Ramsland 2006). Levin (2008) suggests that when serial murderers contact the media and taunt police, it is evidence of a desire to establish an image of power and dominance. Some may consider serial murder a path to fame, giving them a sense of domination and immortality. Confessing to or claiming exaggerated numbers of victims occurs as a form of "one-upmanship and the desire for historical notoriety" (Ramsland 2006, 48).

Another means for acquiring power is by demonstrating control or dominance over others. Capitalist societies are stratified by privilege and power, with a small dominant group holding the most power and the rest of the population more or less marginalized, at least partially based on gender, race or ethnicity, and socioeconomic status.

In the U.S. patriarchal society, nonwhites, those in the working or poor class, homosexuals, women, children, and the elderly hold less power than white, middle-class, heterosexual men. Given their relative powerlessness and in some cases higher accessibility (because of a tendency for some to spend more time on the streets), vulnerable-group members make convenient targets for crime. Serial murderers who target members of vulnerable groups may have more control than if they targeted members with equal or higher social status, who may be more difficult to access.

Broadcasting Cultural Values: The Role of the American Mass Media

Widespread media coverage does not create serial murder, but it does keep serial murder on the cultural surface. Through portrayals as savage, elusive beasts to fear *and* corrupt American heroes, serial murderers become mythic cultural monsters. Stories of serial murder are ubiquitous and perpetuate sensational, often exaggerated, representations of serial murderers to maintain public interest. Media representations that create nameless, faceless victims and afford the killers celebrity status may lessen our fear of victimization. Media also benefit from the representations: In-depth, prominent coverage of serial murder and the perpetuation of its sensational image draw consumers (and their money).

Representations of Crime

Most people do not have direct experience with violent offenders or their victims, but they receive media-mediated images of their social and psychological characteristics and their typical behavior, just as they receive images of monsters through legend and myth. The mass media are influential in our understanding of any phenomenon in which we have little direct involvement, including crime, and in shaping our perceptions of crime, criminals, and victims. Ideologies of crime and criminals permeate our culture and are "shaped by popular images about what is criminal, who is more likely to commit a crime and who is more likely to become a victim, what are the connections between criminals and victims, where and when is a crime more likely to occur, and what are the best ways to control or prevent crime" (Madriz 1997,

342). Media inform us about who and what to fear and how we should handle that fear.

Media construct images of crime and criminals that may be distorted versions of reality. Colomy and Greiner (2008) found that continuous and prominent coverage in the 1990s by the *Denver Post* newspaper of a succession of unusual violent events created a sense in the community that a crime wave was taking hold that required urgent attention, yet no increase in violent crime was recorded during that time. Various reasons may account for why one event or type of event receives more media coverage than another.

Media outlets, as for-profit businesses, are likely to cover events or issues that increase newspaper sales or draw an audience to the evening news, and they are cognizant that crime news is inherently newsworthy. Timing of the event or issue also affects its coverage—an event that occurs at a time in which much coverage is devoted to another event or issue (e.g., a national disaster or election) may be ignored because of constraints on reporters' time, publication space, and other resources (Fine and White 2002). Conversely, if the event occurs during periods of "slow news," it may receive more coverage than it normally would be granted. For crime stories, perceptions of the innocence of victims, the seriousness of the offending, and consumer perceptions of their likely victimization also contribute to the extensiveness of media coverage and public alarm (Colomy and Greiner 2008).

Violent criminals may be described in news reports and popular media as insane or out of control, with descriptors such as "monsters," "crazy," "insane," "mad," "maniac," "nuts," "cracked," "bizarre," and "weird" (Madriz 1997, 346). Or, they may be described as animalistic or savage (e.g., Consalvo 2003). Portraying some people as monsters not only dehumanizes them but also separates them from "the rest of us" and casts them as "other." However, the public prefers that the other fit into a particular image already present in the culture; such classification seems less threatening because members of the public perceive that we know what to expect from them. Individuals who seem to deviate from a known cultural type make us more anxious.

Other cultural images of criminals include their supposed tendency to congregate in groups, that they often are immigrants (especially new immigrants), that they lack compassion or other human sentiments (descriptors like "cruel," "inhuman," "immoral," and "evil" are used), that they are poor or on welfare, and that they most often are strangers (Madriz 1997).

Representations of crime also include images of victims. Women are depicted as more likely than men to be victims of violence, even though the opposite is indicated in official reports (Andersen 2000). Women who more closely fit traditional gender expectations are seen as "ideal victims"—"those who, when affected by crime, are more frequently given the 'legitimate status' of victim" (Madriz 1997, 343). Ideal victims are "symbolic icons of community life" (Colomy and Greiner 2008, 153). They embody positive cultural values and personify innocence and morality (Colomy and Greiner 2008; Madriz 1997). Women who violate traditional gender expectations (e.g., alcohol or drug users, strippers, prostitutes, runaways, single mothers, women who dress or act provocatively, or women who stay out late) do not fit the innocent victim ideal and may be discredited or even blamed for the crimes committed against them. As the traditional image of femininity best applies to white, middle-class women, minority women and women in lower classes often are seen as nonideal victims. Madriz (1997, 350) argues: "To be recognized as victims, black and Latina women have to show that they are better than the rest of their kind: better mothers, students, more religious, more virtuous, and so on." This helps explain the invisibility of or disregard for many victims of serial murderers. The most frequent victims of serial murderers are prostitutes and female runaways—in other words, women who do not fit the image of ideal victim.

Images of offenders also tend to be racialized. The predominant images of criminals in American culture are young, African American or Latino men, followed by "white trash" men (Colomy and Greiner 2008; Henderson 1992; Madriz 1997; Young 1985). Colomy and Greiner (2008, 153) argue that this racialization may create a heightened sense of alarm over violent white offenders and the "construction of a more ominous category" for them—like *serial murderer*.

Model of Media Coverage

As described in more detail in Chapter 5, the American media have become an outlet for fame and recognition for many serial murderers, as particular cases are thoroughly covered and given top billing as lead stories. For many serial murder cases, each detail is reported and analyzed by media outlets for a public eager to devour every word, and the killers become infamous. But, not all cases of serial murder receive this treatment in the media; some receive little attention, with stories appearing briefly somewhere off the front page of the daily newspaper or mentioned somewhere in the middle of a news broadcast. Just about every American can identify Ted Bundy and Jeffrey Dahmer, but many have never heard of Dayton Rogers or Eddie Cole. In my study, I explored this discrepancy in media coverage and public recognition and discovered another area in which American media reinforce dominant cultural values.

In my study, the amounts of media coverage each serial murderer received (see Table 6.1) varied dramatically, and this was related to the eventual notoriety of each killer: The more media coverage there was, the more infamous the killer became. The most news articles were found for Dahmer (12,896 articles), followed by Bundy (10,339), Ramirez (6,598), Gacy (4,905), Ridgway (4,816), Wuornos (4,172), and Rader (2,745). Fewer articles were found for Rifkin (974 articles), Black (806), Jesperson (529), Watts (459), Wallace (453), Rogers (433), Berdella (86), and Cole (41). For all the killers in this study, regardless of notoriety, themes emerged in the presentation of information in news stories.

Killers who were active for a longer period of time received more coverage than those who were active for shorter periods, but this did not appear to be because the total number of articles covered a longer period of time.[1] Instead, the killers who were active for the longest periods of time received more coverage at every comparable timeframe after their apprehension than those who were captured more quickly. Long time spans were related to larger numbers of victims, which adds an element of shock and may explain some of the increased coverage. Finally, those who contact the police or media usually receive large amounts of coverage, but some of the most notorious serial murderers (e.g., Bundy, Dahmer, Gacy, and Ramirez) never attempted any contact.

Three components appear to make a serial murder case more or less newsworthy: (1) the social status of the killer, (2) the social status of the victims, and (3) the shock factor of the murders (for information about how these components were measured, see Tables 6.2 and 6.3). For high amounts of media coverage, generally at least two of these

Table 6.1 Number of Articles Found by Database and Search Term; Number and Percentage Used in Analysis

	NEWSBANK NAME	NEWSBANK NICKNAME	FACTIVA NAME	FACTIVA NICKNAME	PROQUEST NAME	PROQUEST NICKNAME	TOTAL FOUND	TOTAL ANALYZED	PERCENTAGE ANALYZED
Bob Berdella	5	N/A	80	N/A	1	N/A	86	22	25.58
Eddie Cole	0	N/A	41	N/A	0	N/A	41	17	41.46
Jeffrey Dahmer	865	0	11,814	9	208	0	12,896	149	1.16
		(1)[a]		(21/12)[a]					
John Gacy	219	N/A	4,505	N/A	181	N/A	4,905	187	3.81
Keith Jesperson	15	0	166	343	3	2	529	71	13.42
		(9)[a]	(477/311)[a]		(4/1)[a]				
Dennis Rader	0	85	164	2,413	0	83	2,745	67	2.44
	(54)[a]	(1,776/1,612)[a]							
Gary Ridgway	6	71	1,574	3,117	8	40	4,816	64	1.33
	(63/57)[a]		(2,337/763)[a]		(14/6)[a]				
Joel Rifkin	37	N/A	797	N/A	140	N/A	974	103	10.57
Dayton Rogers	0	0	405	0	28	0	433	66	15.24
Robert Black	0	N/A	806	N/A	0	N/A	806	35	4.34
Ted Bundy	527	N/A	9,464	N/A	348	N/A	10,339	117	1.13
Richard Ramirez	111	208	1,185	4,502	18	574	6,598	60	0.91
	(161/50)[a]		(2,522/1337)[a]		(45/27)[a]				
Henry Wallace	16	N/A	430	N/A	7	N/A	453	111	24.50
Coral Watts	20	0	433	0	6	0	459	65	14.16
				(2)[a]					
Aileen Wuornos	158	N/A	3,931	N/A	83	N/A	4,172	58	1.39

[a] For cases in which the serial murderer had a widely used nickname, separate searches using the nickname and the real name frequently produced duplicate articles. In such cases, two numbers are listed in parentheses to indicate the total number of articles produced by the search (to the left of the slash) and the number of duplicate articles (to the right). The number outside the parentheses indicates the number of distinct articles produced by the search. For serial murderers with no widely used nickname, a nickname search was not applicable (N/A).

three components also were high. The cases in which this does not hold true are for Dahmer and Ridgway; in these cases, the shock factor was so extreme that it appeared to be the main factor in the enormous amounts of coverage they received.

This relates to valuations of members of high-status and low-status populations. Except for Dahmer's and Ridgway's cases, high amounts of media coverage were generated when the victims' social status was high, but the killers' social status was of limited consequence. A high-status killer apparently warrants more coverage than others, but it is unclear whether this relates to the killer's status, the apparent tendency of a high-status killer to target higher-status victims, or the shock factor of a high-status person committing such offenses.

Narrative Structure

Many social scientists have theorized about the importance of storytelling as a social and cultural phenomenon.[2] Stories serve as a fundamental means not only for making sense of our lives but also for transmitting meaning to others. Given their key role in transmitting culturally valued messages and their massive audience, media may be the ultimate storytellers.

American culture emphasizes the importance of storytelling and establishes what constitutes a "good" story. Through socialization, we learn not only how to tell a story, but also how to evaluate one. Stories have apparent and persistent features that we anticipate and that provide us the tools for interpreting meaning. A story has a distinct beginning, middle, and end, and within the story, a plot is established, characters are introduced, complications arise and are resolved, and some message is transmitted.

Media use narrative tools to draw the public's attention and aid in their understanding and acceptance of the story (and messages about cultural values). News reports—especially human-interest stories—include elements of any good story: an intriguing setting, a compelling cast of characters, conflict, resolution, and significance. Lule (2001) identifies a particular narrative structure commonly used in news stories about heroes: the humble birth, the early mark of greatness, the quest, the triumph, and the return.

Table 6.2 Determining Social Status of Serial Murderers[a]

	EDUCATION		EMPLOYMENT		TOTAL	
	LEVEL	SCORE	TYPE	SCORE	STATUS SCORE	STATUS LEVEL
Bob Berdella	Some vocational	15	Curio shop owner	30	45	Middle-high
Eddie Cole	High school dropout	9	Warehouse worker	10	19	Low
Jeffrey Dahmer	Some college	15	Factory worker	10	25	Middle-low
John Gacy	Some college	15	Construction business owner	20	35	Middle
Keith Jesperson	High school	12	Long-haul truck driver	15	27	Middle-low
Dennis Rader	College degree	18	Compliance officer	30	48	Middle-high
Gary Ridgway	High school	12	Truck painter	15	27	Middle-low
Joel Rifkin	Some college	15	Frequently unemployed landscaper	10	25	Middle-low
Dayton Rogers	High school dropout	9	Engine repair business owner	20	29	Middle-low
Robert Black	Dropout	6	Delivery truck driver	15	21	Middle-low
Ted Bundy	College degree	18	Sometime law student	35	53	Middle-high
Richard Ramirez	High school dropout	9	No history of employment	0	9	Low
Henry Wallace	Some college	15	Fast-food worker	5	20	Middle-low
Coral Watts	Some college	15	Auto mechanic	20	35	Middle
Aileen Wuornos	High school dropout	9	Prostitute	0	9	Low

[a] Scores determined with scale developed by Hollingshead (1975) and updated by Barratt (2006).

Table 6.3 Predictors of Media Coverage

	SOCIAL STATUS OF KILLER[a]	SOCIAL STATUS OF VICTIM[b]	SHOCK VALUE[c]	AMOUNT OF COVERAGE[d]
Bob Berdella	High	Low	High	Low
Eddie Cole	Low	Low	Low	Low
Jeffrey Dahmer	Low	Low	High	High
John Gacy	Middle	High	High	High
Keith Jesperson	Low	Low	Low	Middle
Dennis Rader	High	High	High	High
Gary Ridgway	Low	Low	High	High
Joel Rifkin	Low	Low	High	Middle
Dayton Rogers	Low	Low	Low	Low
Robert Black	Low	High	Low	Middle
Ted Bundy	High	High	High	High
Richard Ramirez	Low	High	High	High
Henry Wallace	Low	Low	Low	Low
Coral Watts	Middle	High	Low	Low
Aileen Wuornos	Low	High	High	High

[a] For consistency and ease of comparison, only three categories—low, middle, and high—are used here for the social status of the killers. "Middle-low" was changed to "low"; "middle-high" was changed to "high"; and "middle" was left unchanged. See Table 6.2.

[b] Determined based on limited demographic, educational, and occupational information about the victims.

[c] The following elements were considered when determining shock value of the murders: evidence of torture, high numbers of victims, degree of overkill, cannibalism, necrophilia, and bizarre explanations for murders. Community involvement and marital status also were considered, as "family man" and "community leader" types of serial murderers appear to be more shocking to most people.

[d] High coverage was considered more than 1,000 articles produced through database searches; middle coverage was considered between 500 and 999 articles produced; and low coverage was considered fewer than 500 articles produced.

There was an apparent and consistent narrative structure in the biographical narratives and newspaper articles about the serial murderers in my study. There is a distinct beginning, middle, and end; an established plot; a cast of characters; complications and resolutions; and messages produced. This structure is apparent within in-depth articles about the cases and descriptive of the overall coverage.

Initial Reports

The media first reported the murders when it was established that they were part of a series[3] or when a defendant became a suspect, by either confession or accusation. Murder, unfortunately, is prevalent enough in the United States that media attention generally requires an unusual or shocking component, which serial murder fulfills. At this point, the known murders are described, the public cautioned, and a sense of urgency established. The reports typically portray the killer as an unpredictable maniac or wild animal "on the loose" and urge people to take precautions. These accounts focus on information about the attacks and connections among attacks. For cases in which the killer had not yet been captured, fear is stoked and advice offered about suitable actions to take (e.g., tips to avoid victimization frequently are found).

Nicknames appear in early coverage of the serial murderers, primarily for those who received media attention before their apprehension. The creation and use of nicknames prior to apprehension is a practical means for referring to the ongoing investigation of a series of known murders when the killer's identity is unknown. The nicknames typically are coined by detectives or the media and commonly identify the geographic location in which the killers committed the murders or left victims' bodies: the "Green River Killer" (Gary Ridgway) and the "Molalla Forest Killer" (Dayton Rogers). Or, they identify a distinctive killing method: the "Night Stalker" (Richard Ramirez) and the "Sunday Morning Slasher" (Coral Watts).[4] Sometimes, the killers create their own nicknames, like the "BTK Killer" (Dennis Rader) and the "Happy Face Killer" (Keith Jesperson),[5] although disseminating their new moniker generally requires contact with media or police. Less common is the creation of a nickname *after* a serial murderer's apprehension. This type of nickname appears to be used not for ease in referring to the case, but for creating meaning about the killer through culturally familiar imagery. Jeffery Dahmer was the only serial murderer in my study with a postapprehension nickname: the "Milwaukee Monster."

Media reports frequently continue using the nicknames in articles written after the killers are captured, convicted, and sentenced. After capture, the real name *and* nickname are used in media stories, but the nickname frequently appears in the headline or before the real name in the story. Exceptions in this study are news coverage of Rogers and Watts; Rogers's nickname was almost exclusively used *before* his capture, and only 2 articles of the 65 used in the sample include a reference to Watts's nickname, never in a headline or beginning paragraph.

Notoriety and Record Setting

Still in the early stages of coverage but after the initial reporting of the murders, articles begin to focus on the growing notoriety of the killers. Stories describe the long lines of cars driving by the killers' homes and neighbors' and family members' complaints of constant phone calls and reporters' questions.

At this point, reporters find a way to describe the murders as record setting and compare the murders and accused killers to past notorious offenders. Dahmer was described as "the man accused of the worst murder spree in the state's history" (Stingl 1992, B1). Rogers was described as "Oregon's worst serial killer" ("Judge formally sentences serial killer to death," 2006). Ramirez's case was described as "the biggest murder investigation in Los Angeles since the 1977–78 Hillside Stranglers" ("Briefly: The Nation" 1985). Watts was described as "the last major serial killer in Houston" (Makeig 1992, 29) and his murders among "the worst crimes in the past 100 years in Houston" (King 1982, A20). Aileen Wuornos was called "one of the most notorious female killers in recent history" (Nesbitt 2005, A1); "one of the nation's only female serial killers" (Briefs: AP report in *Ventura County Star* 2002, A5); and "one of nation's first known female serial killers" ("Photo: Serial Killer Aileen Wuornos" 2001, D7).

John Gacy was frequently compared to Illinois mass murderer Richard Speck. After Gacy's conviction and sentencing, the Illinois corrections director said, "He's the most notorious criminal in Illinois, no doubt about it. I'm sure [Richard] Speck will be happy to see someone more notorious than he" (Rowley 1980). Around the same timeframe, an article published about Gerald Stano, another multiple murderer, compares the killer to well-known Gacy: "If investigators confirm all his confessions, Stano, 31, may go into the record books as the killer with the greatest number of victims in the nation's history, a title now held by Chicago's John Wayne Gacy" (Kemp 1982). Gacy's name and image eventually became signifiers for multiple murders, as demonstrated by one report that describes another serial murderer as a "Gacy-type killer," even though they killed in different ways (McNeil 1983).

Before Ridgway's capture, his murders were described as the "nation's worst unsolved murder case" (Egan 1989, 6) and after capture as "one of the nation's deadliest serial murder cases" (Kershaw 2003, A10) and "perhaps the longest homicide investigation ever undertaken" (Kershaw 2003, A10). A story compares another alleged serial murderer to Ridgway, treating them as rivals for a record: "If [Robert Charles] Browne's confessions prove true, he will surpass Gary Leon Ridgway, the Green River Killer, as the national's worst serial killer" (Langbein 2006).

Representing the killers as extraordinary evil or the murders as somehow unique likely generates more public interest in the stories, as well as revenue. These representations also encourage the application of the hero type to the killers and contribute to their notoriety.

Need to Know Why

Around the start of legal proceedings, the articles begin to focus on the personal lives of the killers, particularly seeking to determine what made them successful killers and whether there were any missed opportunities to stop them sooner. The reports quote experts and community members speculating about explanations for the murders, the killers' sanity, and who else should share the blame. There also is an element of suspense evident in these stories, with speculation about possible additional victims and frequent revelations of ghoulish details.

The articles include detailed information about the killers' childhood, education, employment history, relationships, and what neighbors and co-workers thought about the killers. Sometimes, the killers at this point are cast as victims. Newspapers published many details about Dahmer's childhood and past problems, almost portraying Dahmer as a victim through descriptions of his lifelong feelings of loneliness and alienation, sense of abandonment after his parents' divorce, and guilt about his homosexuality. Wuornos's rough childhood and prior victimization were frequent foci.

The articles also suggest that other people in the killers' lives may be partially responsible for the murders because of alleged negligence or indifference. Community members and officials are given space to level blame at family members, neighbors, the community, police officers, and the criminal justice system. In stories about Dahmer, nearly everyone in the killer's life was blamed for not taking action. The criminal justice system was blamed for not providing Dahmer with treatment on his release for a molestation conviction. Police officers were blamed for their alleged racism and for unknowingly aiding in the murder of one victim when they returned the escapee to Dahmer's apartment after Dahmer convinced them the boy was his lover. Dahmer's probation officer was assigned blame for not making home visits. Neighbors were blamed for not doing anything when they noticed a putrid smell, loud noises, and screaming coming from Dahmer's apartment. Family members were blamed for not seeing supposed "warning signs" in Dahmer's past. The articles portray the murders as an embarrassment for the city of Milwaukee, implying partial blame. Dahmer is credited in several articles for his truthfulness and for accepting blame for the murders, suggesting that others are not accepting their share of the responsibility. A columnist portrays Dahmer as helpless and others as culpable in the murders:

> So Dahmer actually turns out to be the only character in this whole grisly saga to take responsibility for what he did. It's nice someone does. It's too bad nobody else—parents, stepmother, neighbors, prison officials, judge, parole officer—cared enough to stop this refugee from a 1950s horror film before their stupid indifference let him bring his nightmares to life. (Francis 1991, G1)

Race is a frequent issue in media accounts of Dahmer's murders, with most portraying minorities as victims of police and community racism, not necessarily Dahmer's hatred (his alleged hatred of African Americans was mentioned in several articles and later discounted). The fact that Dahmer was white and his victims were mostly African American is acknowledged in many articles. In addition, the murders are seen as an attack on the gay community, which also was portrayed as victimized due to community prejudice and hatred.

In articles about Gacy, police blunders are blamed for not apprehending him sooner:

> Chicago police arrested killer John Gacy more than a year ago when a 19-year-old youth told them Gacy had kidnapped him at gunpoint

and forced him to engage in sexual acts, but no criminal charges were filed, police records show. "I was shocked," the youth told *The Tribune*. "They [the police] would only say there was insufficient evidence. Both the cops and an assistant state's attorney said that he [Gacy] was a solid citizen. I was practically pleading with them. I even told them that he bragged to me that he had killed people and said he was going to kill me, but my pleas didn't do any good." (Gorman 1979, 22)

An article published after Ridgway was apprehended not only suggests that the police made a mistake in the investigation but also implies a sense of apathy by a detective:

More than 20 years ago, a despairing father led a police detective to the Green River Killer's house. But the efforts of the father, Jose Malvar, to help catch his daughter's killer fell short when Gary Ridgway, who has since confessed to the Green River murders, denied knowing her and the detective walked away. ("Early Tip Fell Short in Green River Killings" 2003, A30)

Articles about Rifkin seem to imply that family members should have suspected the murders:

The sheer array of women's belongings raised questions about how Mr. Rifkin collected such a pile of personal effects—much of it left in plain sight in his cluttered room—without arousing the suspicion of his sister, Jan, 31, or his mother, Jeanne, 71, with whom he lived. (Schemo 1993, B5)

Blaming the police is a strong theme in articles published in British media about Black, who killed in Scotland and England. Following are three examples:

[The police] promised us they would learn from their mistakes. Yet 20 years after the Yorkshire Ripper claimed his first victim, police are examining the possibility that another serial killer may be trawling the nation's highways in search of vulnerable women. (Burrell 1996, 1)

One reason that serial killers often evade detection for many, many years is that our police aren't very good at catching them. (Wilson 2007b, 23)

His arrest had as much to do with luck as anything else. (Wilson 2007b, 23)

In Henry Wallace's case, residents lodged accusations of racism against the police, suggesting that, because the victims were all African American and among the working class, police officers considered them low-priority victims and responded to the case slowly.

Anniversary Stories

Finally, stories appeared years and decades after convictions that marked anniversaries of important dates related to the trials—typically when the killer was convicted or sentenced—and these dates are also included in lists compiled of significant historical events, either for a particular state or for the nation. The killers' notoriety is especially apparent in these stories.

Berdella's sentencing is among four events listed for the year 1988 on the "Century's events timeline" for Missouri according to the Associated Press. Gacy's conviction is included on the "This Week in History" feature in *The Commercial Appeal* newspaper in 2006. Rader's apprehension is included in a list of "Across the Nation and Abroad 2005" in the *Wichita Falls Time Record News*. Wuornos's conviction is included in a "Today in History" feature in 1997 in *The Stuart News*.

Missing Victims

A theme found throughout the news coverage of the serial murderers, especially after initial reports, is the invisibility of victims. Nearly all stories mention the number of victims killed, but inclusion of their names or personal information is rare. In some cases, stories featuring victims or a particular victim's family are found, and these stories most frequently appeared while the trial was ongoing. Victims' names are most commonly found in reports that include the formal charges, courtroom testimony, and information about wrongful death lawsuits.

In articles about Dahmer, victims are most frequently mentioned by number and race but not often by name: "Police have identified all the victims found in Dahmer's apartment. Nine were black, one white, and one the Laotian teenager" ("Dahmer Murdered First Victim While in High School, Police Say" 1991, 3A).

The fact that Ridgway's victims were primarily prostitutes is always included, and usually near the beginning, in each article. Their arrest records and histories of drug abuse are frequently included, but they are rarely mentioned by name. Following are three examples:

> A police task force investigating murders of young women, many of them prostitutes, yesterday ... ("Police Probers add to List of 'Green River' Killings" 1984, A20)
>
> All of the victims were last seen in those areas, and all but one, who was a tavern waitress, were young runaway girls or prostitutes. (Turner 1987, A14)
>
> The victims, all killed between 1982 and 1984, were among society's most unfortunate. They were all relatively young women—the oldest was 33—and rootless. They plied the streets as prostitutes, runaways or beggars. When they disappeared they often weren't missed for days. (Gilliem 2001)

Wallace's victims receive considerably more media attention, with several articles listing all victims' names, ages, how they were killed, when they were killed or found, and how they knew Wallace, and others offering in-depth information about one victim's family at a time.

No victim is mentioned by name in any court case or legal journal article analyzed, despite most of the names being known and part of the official charges. The exception is when they were named as plaintiffs in the case or in wrongful death lawsuits. Instead of names, a total number of the killer's victims usually is stated. In one case, each of Berdella's victims is assigned a letter: victims A, B, C, and D (*Economy Fire and Casualty Company v. Betty Ann Haste, et al.*).[6]

The omission of victims' names and personal information suggests that they are relatively unimportant to the narrative of serial murder. The killers clearly are the stars of these stories. As the victims most often are members of vulnerable groups, their exclusion from these stories reinforces the subordination of these groups and seemingly justifies their victimization. In addition, references to deviant behaviors of victims (e.g., prostitution, drug use, and running away) and the absence of humanizing information (e.g., information about their families, friends, and goals) weakens the audience's ability or willingness to identify with the victims, diminishing a sense of their own victimization and shifting their fear.

Social Typing

The values and ideals of a culture are dramatized through its stories, and media perpetuate culturally familiar stories. Social typing is employed by media to increase the likelihood of message reception. Media reports that draw intensive public attention—human interest stories—usually cast the main characters as "ideal" types who, good or bad, reinforce cultural messages. Fine and White (2002) argue that one of the appeals of human interest stories is their ability to draw members of a public together to become a focused community able to express a unified perspective and shared values. When "everyone" is interested in a story, one who speaks of it participates in the community and expresses its values (Fine and White 2002).

Social typing is ubiquitous in U.S. society and evident in all facets of its culture. Klapp (1972, 2) argues, "In our society we do not have, as one might at first suppose, freedom *from* typing but a *choice* of type" (emphasis in original). We routinely attempt to "fit" people we meet and hear about into types, which are culturally defined and encompass groups of characteristics—desirable or not—that we use to understand others. Social typing also is employed to judge others and ourselves according to cultural ideals: Negative types are those who violate cultural values in some way, and positive types are those who uphold cultural values. Thus, we not only praise or degrade a person through the type applied but also send messages to others about which characteristics and behaviors are approved and which are unacceptable. We also type ourselves: Our *self* is a type. Because we type ourselves and others, and others type us, we often develop at least two selves (Klapp 1972, 5), the self we define and the social self defined by others.

Klapp (1972, 16) identifies three main categories of typing (praise, condemnation, and ridicule) and three corresponding social types (heroes, villains, and fools). Most people want to be recognized as fitting the hero type and hope to avoid displaying characteristics of the villain or fool. Heroes are those who uphold cultural values and thus are held up as good examples of appropriate ways to think and behave. Heroes deserve prestige because they are recognized as performing at the highest levels and have talents and dedication reserved for only a few (Goode 1978). They may be "winners," "splendid performers," "heroes of social acceptability," "independent spirits," or "group servants" (Klapp 1972, 27–28).

Klapp argues that, because of inconsistencies in messages in American culture, there may be uncertainty between classifications of heroes and villains. True villains lack redeeming characteristics, violate cultural values and social norms, and threaten the group the hero serves, yet some also have hero characteristics. Robin Hood, for instance, probably should be typed as a villain, but instead he is portrayed as serving a greater good. Klapp (1972, 51) argues that the villain serves society as a scapegoat for aggression and as a hate symbol that builds support for law enforcement and reinforces dominant cultural messages in the community.

Finally, fools are targets of ridicule; they are portrayed as incompetent, "discounting types" (e.g., those who as a group tend to be discounted because of undervalued occupation, gender, age, ability, or some other characteristic), nonconformers, overconformers, and those used for comedic or tension relief (e.g., the butt of jokes and the "clever fool") (Klapp 1972, 69).

In reconciling the frequent confusion between hero and villain types, Klapp (1972) created what he describes as a contemporary hero type: the "corrupt hero," which includes the "tough guy," the "smart operator," the "wolf," the "bad-good guy," and the "false goodfellow." Lule (2001) identifies a similar type, calling it the "modern hero," and agrees with Klapp that this type is a product of contemporary culture. This contemporary hero type characterizes both hero and villain types in certain ways and is praised and degraded at times. Its pervasiveness in American cultural imagery indicates inconsistency in cultural messages and that deviance consequently may be rewarded in America.

In my study, social typing, drawn from culturally familiar imagery and well-known characters in popular culture, is evident in descriptions of the murders. The killers were thus cast into roles that were easily recognized and for which expectations were understood. Elements of all three of Klapp's (1972) types—the (corrupt) hero, villain, and fool—are evident.

The fool type is least frequently found and mostly evident in newspaper reports published soon after the killers' apprehension, when personal information was first being reported. Most of the serial murderers are typed as loners, nerds, "squares" or losers, characteristic of this type and subject to ridicule (in quoted comments from members of the public, as well as editorial commentary and letters to the editor). Once those types were explicated, frequently no other description was offered, which is evidence of the salience of the fool type: It is unnecessary to state defining characteristics of the fool as most people understand that it includes social awkwardness, unkempt appearance, and friendlessness.

Serial murderers are consistently typed as villains in all data collection sources. Although dehumanizing types (such as monster, animal, and beast) are commonly used to classify the killers as villains, a serial murder type (with negative connotations) is evident. The killers are frequently compared to an apparently widely understood set of criteria, presumably drawn from popular images of serial murderers. A newspaper account of Dennis Rader's trial offers models for what the serial murder type is (disenfranchised loner, secret monster), as well as what it is *not* (a churchgoing, married father):

> The allegations that a churchgoing, married father of two was Kansas' infamous BTK murderer have shaken the Hollywood image of the serial killer as disenfranchised loner, and it has people wondering just how many of their mild-mannered colleagues, spouses and fellow parishioners might secretly be monsters. (Breed 2005, 17)

In many cases, the serial murderer type is evident in descriptions of the killers' seeming divergence from it. A description of Gary Ridgway offers criteria of the serial murderer type and an exemplar of serial murder for comparison:

> Gary was not acting like the unfeeling, conscienceless, degenerate serial killer he was supposed to be, at least if one believed in the popular image of such predators. This was definitely not Hannibal Lecter. (Prothero and Smith 2006, 36)

The contradiction between portrayals of Ted Bundy and of "typical" serial murderers is acknowledged:

> The stereotype of mass killers—with minds bedeviled by tumors or hallucinations—is all too familiar to the American public. They were the drifters, the malcontents, the failures and the resenters. Ted Bundy, for all appearances, no way resembled any of them. He had all the personal resources that are prized in America, that guarantee success and respect.

He loved children, read poetry, showed courage by chasing down and capturing a purse snatcher on the streets of Seattle, rescued a child from drowning, loved the outdoors, respected his parents, was a college honor student, worked with desperate people at a crisis center, and, in the words of one admirer, "Ted could be with any woman he wanted—he was so magnetic!" He wanted to become an attorney or a politician, to do something with his life to help others. (Nordheimer 1978, SM24)

Social typing also is widespread in the courtroom, and the imagery used by the prosecution and defense is nearly identical in each killer's case. The prosecution discounted suggestions of insanity and described the defendants as evil, manipulative, calculating, coldblooded, brutal, and savage, conjuring the image of a monster or beast. The defense frequently claimed insanity or at least mental illness and tried to portray the killers as victims themselves—of their mental illness, prior abuse, the exclusive social structure, the criminal justice system, or a number of other people, including family members, friends, and co-workers. The defense, especially, used culturally familiar imagery to cast their clients in an easily understood role. John Gacy's defense attorney quoted from *Dr. Jekyll and Mr. Hyde*, likened the trial to the atmosphere surrounding the Salem witch trials, and said: "A man does not have to look like a bulging-eyed monster to be insane. ... Mr. Gacy is not an evil man. He has done some evil things" (Fritsch 1980, 1).

As Klapp suggests, portrayals of the killers frequently lack distinction between the villain and hero types. Many of the killers are both praised (characteristic of the hero type) and condemned (characteristic of the villain type). The characterization of serial murderers fitting two supposedly incongruent types simultaneously is compatible with Klapp's (1972) corrupt hero type and Lule's (2001) modern hero type. The complicated reconciliation of these two types occurring simultaneously sometimes is acknowledged. Usually, this results in a "split personalities" characterization; the Dr. Jekyll and Mr. Hyde imagery is most common, as well as imagery of a masked figure.

Tuning In: Accepting the Messages

All of the serial murderers in my study to some extent were active participants in their culture, recognizing cultural values and striving for culturally valued goods, yet many appeared to lack the cultural competencies to achieve their goals. The goals they expressed appear ordinary, as they were pulled from the cultural milieu and are shared by much of the population. Their commitments to these pursuits indicate that they continued to adhere to cultural values and the culturally valued means for achieving goals, yet based on the gap between their cultural competencies and their dreams, they formed an alternative line of action (serial murder).

With the exception of Richard Ramirez (who did not appear to have a desire to "fit in" or achieve culturally valued success), these killers tried and failed repeatedly to achieve culturally valued goals through legitimate means, although some had what could be considered success. All except for Ramirez sought employment as a means for gaining income, respect, and success; Ramirez tried to acquire these through burglary and theft. Yet, most were fired from multiple jobs, and approximately half discussed scholastic failures after high school.[7] With the exceptions of Ramirez and Bob Berdella, all sought romantic relationships at some point, but most had trouble maintaining them and suffered perceived betrayals and embarrassments. Several expressed long-held dreams of success, fame, and fortune. Bundy hoped for success in politics and strove to become a governor one day, and Aileen Wuornos dreamed of becoming a movie star or singer. The following sections provide evidence of serial murderers' acceptance of particular American cultural values described previously.

Regard for Violence

Many serial murderers indicate a high regard for violent acts as a means for gaining money or power, as well as an enjoyment of violence in popular culture. About half of the killers in my study showed violent tendencies before they started killing (e.g., a history of violent criminal convictions, animal abuse, or a violent temper). Others indicated a high regard for violence and the recognition that it can be a means for control, companionship, wealth, and fame. This was evident in their expressed admiration or enjoyment of cultural models of violence: other serial murderers and violent offenders, violent films and literature, and violent fantasies.

Wuornos had a longtime fascination with Bonnie and Clyde-type stories, and Eddie Cole enjoyed "gruesome horror shows" at the movies. Joel Rifkin and Berdella claimed that their murders were in some ways inspired by violent films: For Rifkin, it was the 1972 Alfred Hitchcock film *Frenzy*, in which a serial murderer stalks women in London and kills them through strangulation with a necktie, and for Berdella, it was *The Collector*, in which a man kidnaps a woman to hold her hostage in his house for his own enjoyment, although she eventually dies. Most serial murderers in my study (Wiest 2009) who had criminal histories committed minor property offenses, but several were convicted of violent acts before they started killing, and Gacy and Wuornos were known for having violent tempers. In addition, several serial murderers, including Cole, Jeffrey Dahmer, and Keith Jesperson, abused and killed animals while children. In my study, several of the serial murderers indicated that they targeted particular victims because of their resemblance to someone against whom they sought revenge, yet none had a history of committing domestic abuse. Only Cole targeted the source of his anger when he attempted to kill his first wife by setting her hotel room on fire (she escaped) and successfully killed his second wife by strangulation.

Individual Accomplishment and Competition

Most of the serial murderers in my study saw their killing as requiring an abundance of skill and not something of which anyone was capable. Ridgway saw serial murder as his "career" and the thing he did best. He said during sentencing: "Choking is what I did, and I was pretty good at it" (Johnson 2003, A2). The killers frequently described the knowledge, planning, and effort necessary to successfully kill repeatedly and were proud of their accomplishments. Ridgway, who removed clothing, took jewelry, and clipped the fingernails of victims in an effort to avoid capture, said: "Well I was, in a way, a little bit proud of not being caught doing … like removing the clothes. Not leaving anything … and fingerprints on it, using gloves. … Not bragging about it. Not talking about it" (Smith and Guillen 2004, 520).

Some expressed feelings of invincibility and superiority. Bundy's bragging was particularly extreme:

I think that at last I have perspective. And a sort of self-confidence. It may be borne, in part, out of this immense publicity. I don't know. I'm recognized in a terribly bizarre kind of way. I feel immune. I feel nobody can hurt me. (Michaud and Aynesworth 2000, 32)

[Other prisoners] may talk a lot. But they won't say anything to my face. The reputation stops 'em. They're afraid I'll do something to them. And I probably would, if it came down to it. It may be the way I handle the authorities. The way I fucked with them. The way I made them pay to get me. (Michaud and Aynesworth 2000, 34)

Some killers apparently received a great deal of satisfaction from perceiving that they outsmarted those in law enforcement. Ann Rule (2000), a true crime writer and former friend of Bundy's, described his feelings of superiority:

He had been telling me, and I'm sure a number of other people, how much more he knew about serial murder than anyone else did. (Rule 2000, 512)

The surveillance has become a game to him. He found the men tailing him clumsy and awkward and was taking delight in losing them. (Rule 2000, 191)

He was beginning a pattern that he would repeat again and again, a kind of arrogance toward those designated by the state to defend him; if he could not have what he considered the best, then he would go it alone. (Rule 2000, 246)

Rader's boasting also is well documented. Discussing his second commission of murder, during which one of the two people he attacked survived, he said that "if I had brought my stuff and used my stuff, Kevin would probably be dead today. ... I'm not bragging on that. It's just a matter of fact" (*The State of Kansas v. Dennis L. Rader*, 16–17). Gacy made a game out of the surveillance placed on him just before his arrest, introducing the officers as his "bodyguards," often giving them directions to his next destination, sitting with them at restaurants, and inviting them inside his home.

Several considered themselves experts on serial murder and offered lessons and advice. While giving a statement on his guilty pleas, Rader referred to serial murderers as "my kind of person" and calmly explained to the judge how serial murderers choose victims:

Well, I don't know. If—you know, if you read much about serial killers, they go through what they call the different phases. That's one of the phases they go through is a—as a trolling stage. You're lay—basically you're looking for a victim at that time, and that can either be trolling for months or years. But once you lock in on a certain person then you become stalking, and that might be several of them, but you really home in on that person. They—they basically come the—that's—that's the victim, or at least that's what you want 'em to be. (*The State of Kansas v. Dennis L. Rader*, 30)

While still maintaining his innocence, Bundy sent a letter to the Green River Taskforce offering his expert advice in solving the Green River Killer case. Robert Black offered his assistance in solving the 2007 disappearance of British 3-year-old Madeleine McCann from a resort in Portugal.

As does any rising athlete, actor, singer, or professional in competition with others, most of the serial murderers in my study followed and appeared to admire other serial murderers, while some were striving to beat current "records" (e.g., most victims or greatest amount of publicity). Berdella kept a folder filled with news clippings about other serial criminals, including Elmer Wayne Henley of Texas, Charles "Tex" Watson of California (a member of the infamous Manson Family), and Kansas City's "Westport Rapist" James Maynard. Cole said the "Boston Strangler" case "stimulated me beyond description" (Newton 1994, 119), and he collected news clippings about it. While in prison, Keith Jesperson attempted to become pen pals with other serial murderers, although he received little reception from them. Ramirez recognized one of the detectives he met as instrumental in the capture of two other serial murderers. Rifkin compared himself to Ridgway, although his name was not yet known:

> I think I imitated what I read, because a lot of what I told [the psychiatrists] is almost lifted page by page from the [Green River] book. He buried one, I buried one. He went from water to land, I went from water to land. He placed one by an airport, I place one by an airport. He did things in clusters, I did things in clusters. (Mladinich 2001, 93)

Masculinities and Privilege

Egger (1984) encourages an analysis of "maleness and its socialization" in examining serial murder. Serial murder may be an outlet for proving masculinity for some American men, as it can be seen as fulfilling complementary masculine ideals and cultural values such as individualism, competition, dominance, aggression, violence, recognition or fame, and sense of accomplishment.

All of the male serial murderers in my study displayed masculine characteristics but also saw themselves as failing in masculinity. Black's and Coral Watts's athletic abilities were outlets for displaying their masculinity; Jesperson, at 6 foot 6 inches tall, was big and physically powerful; Berdella, Gacy, and Rogers were business owners; and Bundy frequently was described as physically attractive, strong, charming, and sexually appealing. Several of the killers, including Berdella, Gacy, Jesperson, and Rifkin, expressed a desire for their father's attention and approval, yet frequently did not receive it. As a child, Jesperson dreamed of becoming someone who fits the ultimate ideals of hegemonic masculinity, a dream probably parallel to those of many boys striving to be masculine:

> I'd pretend to be a miner or a heavy-equipment operator. I would take my bow and arrow and be a great white hunter in Africa. I stood along our creek and fired torpedoes at enemy U-boats, created the ocean in my mind and sent destroyers off to war. When I finally got my own BB gun, I became a sniper shooting at the enemy. I saw myself as an enforcer for good, a war hero, *superboy*! Keith would save the world. (Olsen 2002, 46; emphasis in original)

Whether or not they felt they could achieve masculine ideals, they were aware of them and strove toward them. All but Ramirez sought legitimate employment; Berdella, Gacy, Rader, and Bundy held positions of leadership in their communities; several regularly displayed aggression and violence; and most sought relationships with—and control over—women. Cole, whose mother was a frequent adulterer, remembered when he was in high school talking to his father about male domination over women and judged his father a failure in this aspect of masculinity. He said his father told him: "No matter what, don't ever let a woman dominate you," and he replied, "And how can *you* say that, for Christ's sake?" (Newton 1994, 77; emphasis in original). Taken aback, his father punched him in the face. Cole later wrote of that incident: "I feel shame and sorrow now, but at the time I hated him. Not because he hit me, but because he let me down. To this day, I regret that night, because I think he really knew about my mother's infidelity" (Newton 1994, 77).

The masculinity of the male serial murderers in my study was challenged in various ways. Berdella and Black claimed to have been raped or sexually assaulted by men when they were children. Three—Jesperson, Rifkin, and Bundy—said that they were self-conscious about lacking athletic ability. Bundy said:

> I always felt I was too small. This feeling began to emerge in junior high school. That I didn't have the weight or physique for sports. It wasn't true, but I never pushed myself. ... I attempted to get on the school basketball team and a couple of baseball teams, but I failed. It was terribly traumatic for me. (Michaud and Aynesworth 2000, 22)

Rather than his large size being a means to display masculinity, Jesperson was teased by other children and called names such as "sloth," "monster man," "fatty," "hulk," and "tubby." Jesperson and Coral Watts both experienced severe and prolonged illnesses as children that made them feel weak and excluded from others. Rifkin endured nearly constant bullying from other male children, and Cole was involved in numerous fights in school and frequently was teased for his "feminine" first name (Carroll). A 1961 psychiatric report about Cole details his struggle with masculine ideals:

> His neurotic conflicts center about three main areas: (1) conflict with authority figures which appears to be a generalized response learned from his interaction with his father; (2) a masculinity conflict where he feels the need to constantly prove to himself and others that he is a "man." This conflict not only is revealed by the testing results, but is reflected in his need to display tattoos on his arms, and the Don Juan behavior with girls that never results in anything but infantile sexplay and flirting; (3) a dependency conflict where he is attempting to give the impression of being independent but wishing to maintain childlike dependency. (Newton 1994, 101)

Masculinity includes the ability to form and maintain relationships with the opposite sex, but many failed in this regard. In several cases, the killers blamed themselves for their relationship failures. Jesperson and Bundy expressed devastation resulting from breakups as young adults; Rifkin said he was more comfortable with prostitutes because they never rejected him; and Black said that he was unable to form close relationships, although he strived for them. Black and Bundy, respectively, articulated this self-blame:

> I've always felt I wanted to be married, have a family. And I tended to look at every relationship as a potential marriage. Whether I put out those sort of vibes or talked about it ... it put the girls off, you know? (Wyre and Tate 1995, 125)

> Her name is Stephanie, and I haven't seen her for a long time. She's living near San Francisco, and she's completely beautiful. She's tall, almost as tall as I am, and her parents are wealthy. She's never known anything but being rich. I just couldn't fit in with that world. (Rule 2000, 30)

Gender-specific images were evoked by several of the serial murderers in my study. Female killer Wuornos's explanation of self-defense points to a traditional female defense for offending. Explanations by Cole, Jesperson, and Rifkin that they killed to take revenge against domineering women in their lives may be understood as a means for restoring elements of their masculinity, as masculinity in American culture includes domination over women.

The Criminal Experience

All of the serial murderers in my study apparently found killing enjoyable. The cultural values most clearly sought by the killers were power and control, yet several also articulated an enjoyment of the risks involved and thrills experienced by committing multiple murders.

Risk Taking and Thrill Seeking

Two of the killers made comments that showed interest in thrill-seeking activities before they started killing. Keith Jesperson was fascinated with Evel Knieval and was excited to watch him complete a daredevil stunt, while Joel Rifkin expressed interest in learning to skydive. Most evidence of thrill-seeking and risk-taking behaviors, however, was in the killers' descriptions of murdering their victims.

Several of the killers described the murders as highly enjoyable, providing a thrill or rush. Others appeared to find their "secret life" thrilling. Gary Ridgway described feeling excited when his wife wore the jewelry he gave her that he took from his victims. Similar to descriptions of edgeworkers, Rifkin discussed having "heightened senses" while killing: "Yeah, it's heightened sense. It's just not your everyday thing" (Mladinich 2001, 130). Robert Black described killing as a "rush of blood" (Wyre and Tate 1995, 48). Ted Bundy's risk taking was well documented: He tried on at least two occasions to outrun police officers trying to pull him over and escaped from jail twice. Bundy described the incredible rush he felt when he escaped from jail in 1977 in Glenwood Springs, Colorado, while awaiting a murder trial:

> It felt just right—the whole time, just perfect. You see, there was nothing clever about the escape. Nothing clever about the engineering. In fact, it was sloppily done. In Ann Arbor, it was just *boom, boom, boom!* I was just cool. I was talking to people in bars. Oh, I felt good! I felt the drive, the power. I had what it took. (Michaud and Aynesworth 2000, 30; emphasis in original)

Four of the serial murderers included in the study—Bundy, Dennis Rader, Richard Ramirez, and Coral Watts—took increased risks by killing in their victims' homes rather than taking them to a location where they may have had more control.[8] Similarly, Jeffery Dahmer, Rifkin, and Ridgway killed in homes they shared with family members, increasing their risk of being caught. Ridgway and Dayton Rogers took risks by continuing to leave bodies in the same locations after some had been discovered and the locations were under surveillance.

Most participants in thrilling ventures express a desire to repeat the activity, with subsequent episodes usually requiring increased risk. Serial murderers commonly take increased risks as they continue killing. For example, Rogers killed all his victims in secluded wooded areas until the last victim, whom he killed inside his pickup truck parked in an empty parking lot across from an occupied restaurant. And, Jesperson began killing more frequently as time passed. Law enforcement officials frequently discuss an escalation over time in the frequency of killing by serial murderers but perhaps without adequate recognition of the thrill seeking that may prompt it.

Power and Control

In my study, the killers' choices of victims appeared to be related to their position in the social structure and access to power. Most of the killers could be classified as of a somewhat low social status,[9] and in most cases, they targeted victims they knew they could control relatively easily. Typically, victims were of a lower social status than the killer, including prostitutes and drug addicts, or were members of vulnerable populations, including children, the elderly, and ethnic minorities. Killers of a relatively higher social status (i.e., Gacy, Rader, and Bundy) targeted victims of a higher status than the other killers' victims but of a lower status than their own. John Gacy, a white, male businessman well known for his involvement in community groups, targeted young, transient white men. Rader, a white, male college graduate with a respectable job and role as a church leader, targeted white, middle-class women. And Bundy, a white, male law student known for community service and political involvement, targeted white, middle- to upper-class women. Ramirez and Wuornos were the only killers to target members of higher-status groups than their own, but they employed killing methods that afforded larger amounts of control (e.g., they relied on surprising their victims and were the only two killers in my study to use guns in the commission of the murders). As members of subordinated groups, targeting members of high-status groups was a way for them to gain power.

Many of the serial murderers in my study also demonstrated a desire for power, dominance, and control over their communities and people who were significant in their lives. Many described this desire in terms of regaining power after they perceived it was taken away from them. Ridgway complained of being "pushed around" by women and said that "I never stand up for myself" (Prothero and Smith 2006, 196) and that he felt in control when he killed his victims, all of whom were women. Bob Berdella also felt that he regained power and control through killing: "Possibly the way I handled situations prior to this, I saw myself in a weak state. This was a way where I was no longer weak and helpless" (Jackman and Cole 1992, 257).

Ridgway and several other killers referred to victims as "property" or "possessions," and in Ridgway's official confession, he said he "placed most of the bodies in groups which I call 'clusters.' I did this because I wanted to keep track of all the women I killed" (*State of Washington v. Gary Leon Ridgway*). He also expressed a sense of loss when the police found the bodies and removed them. Similarly, Jesperson said he would do something unique to the bodies or leave them in a particular way to prove that "she was my kill and not someone else's" (Olsen 2002, 178). Rader admitted that he started communicating with the media again after a long period of quiet because he heard that someone was writing a book about his murders, and he could not let the author tell "his" story (Smith 2006, 307).

A desire for control can also be seen in the killing methods; six of the serial murderers in my study usually bound their victims before killing them, affording the killers a large amount of control. Berdella and Dahmer separately intended to control their victims indefinitely as captives. Restraining victims and targeting members of vulnerable groups also may reduce the likelihood of failure and boost their confidence. The killers most certainly did not seek an even playing field.

Culturally Familiar Imagery

Culturally familiar imagery appears in the killers' explanations of their murders. The most common explanation (insanity) fits with the predominant image of the serial killing "monster": the evil, crazed beast that stalks his victims and viciously pounces through the cover of darkness. The image may be appealing to the relatively powerless as it suggests they single-handedly can terrorize. It also is entangled in the process of creating a legal defense.

In particular crimes, images of a "deserving victim" are summoned. Although this imagery likely did not influence their choice of victims, it is apparent in their descriptions of victims. Ridgway and Rifkin, who killed prostitutes, relied on perceptions of their victims as worthless, trash, or somehow "deserving" of violence. Rifkin said he did not think of his victims as "real people" with families, and Ridgway explained that he was "cleaning up society" by killing them. (Ridgway's explanation, in which he casts himself as a sort of do-gooder or guardian of morality, also is an apparent attempt to gain a sense of achievement when killing "expendable" people generally would not be perceived as much of an accomplishment.) The failure of the media to make the victims seem real also fits with this typing.

The serial murderers also applied social types to describe themselves and their murders. Agreeing with others' typing of him, Rifkin referred to himself during his sentencing as a sometime monster: "You all must think I am nothing but a monster, and you are right. Part of me must be" (Mladinich 2001, 207). Rader made a similar statement in describing one killing to a detective: "I'm sorry. I know this is a human being, but I'm a monster" ("Focus: BTK Killer a 'Monster' Describes Terror Reign" 2005; Hegeman 2005). Ridgway and Bundy, respectively, acknowledged a serial murderer type in suggesting that their dissimilarity to the type may have helped them avoid capture for a while:

> The women, they underestimate[d] me. I look like an ordinary person. ... I acted in a way with the ... with the prostitutes to make 'em feel more comfortable. And I got in their comfort zone, got into the ... ah, 'Here's a guy, he's not really muscle-bound, he's not, ah, [doesn't] look like a fighter, just an ordinary john,' and that was their downfall ... my appearance was different from what I really was. (Smith and Guillen 2004, 520)
>
> Which one do you pick? Do they pick the law student with no criminal background, who was probably even known by some of the prosecutors working the case? Or are they going to go after the types, you know, the guys in the files ... the real weirdos? (Michaud and Aynesworth 2000, 138)

Building Lines of Action: Using Cultural Values

Although an awareness of and adherence to cultural values were apparent for each serial murderer in my study, his or her capacities to utilize them through culturally legitimate means varied. They constructed lines of action in relation to these capacities and their access to power and other resources. Yet, constructing a culturally illegitimate line of action to reach culturally valued goals should not suggest inventiveness on the part of the actor as there are a number of culturally illegitimate paths to social goods available in the cultural milieu. In other words, serial murderers do not create serial murder as a path to social goods; they *select* it from an array of available paths, both legitimate and illegitimate.

American culture is full of inconsistent messages and values that may be utilized in a number of legitimate and illegitimate ways, and it is evidently more important to strive for culturally approved goals (especially if they are actually achieved) than it is to follow a culturally approved path. There are countless examples in American culture that illustrate the ways in which Americans show appreciation for an adherence to cultural values, even if the chosen path was deviant. We splash photos of a bank robber on the front page of U.S. newspapers and call him "creative" for his unique disguise. We marvel at how a Ponzi schemer "got away with it" for so long and analyze his business and personal life in the news. We recognize each anniversary of the 1969 Tate-LaBianca murders with an update on how Charles Manson and his "family" are doing in prison. And, serial murderers are turned into celebrities through widespread media coverage and an overindulgent public fascination.

There also seems to be less cultural consistency in the United States compared to other industrial nations. For example, generally if a German follows expectations, he or she will experience success to some degree (Lehmann 2005), but there are so many contradictions in cultural messages in the United States that some people can experience success by deliberately violating expectations (e.g., outlaws, mobsters, and other famous criminals).

These inconsistent messages have created a cultural environment in the United States of adjustable boundaries and contradictions in which violence is acceptable at times; extreme offending may be rewarded with fame or wealth; violating the law may be seen as honorable; winning at any cost is worthwhile; being known for anything is better than living in anonymity; white, male privilege is pervasive; risks and thrills are emphasized; power and control are accentuated; and the notion of equality of opportunity places the onus of success and failure solely on the individual. This is an environment in which serial murder and its coverage flourish.

Notes

1. All of the articles found about Rader were published after he resurfaced, and the majority found for Ridgway were published after his apprehension.
2. See the work of Berger and Quinney 2005; Ewick and Silbey 1995; Griffin 1993; Harvey 1996; Hollander and Gordon 2006; Maines 1993, 1999, 2000; Maines and Ulmer 1993; McAdams 2001; Ochs and Capps 1996; and Stanley 1993.
3. Preapprehension reports were only found for Jesperson, Rader, and Ridgway.

4. Ramirez broke into his victims' homes at night, and Watts killed mostly during the early hours on Sundays.
5. Rader's nickname described his method of killing: bind, torture, and kill. Jesperson drew a happy face in all his correspondence with the media and police.
6. Further analysis of legal documents regarding different types of cases would help determine whether exclusion of victims' names is commonplace or characteristic of serial murder cases.
7. Berdella dropped out of art school; Rifkin dropped out of college, where he had been studying to be a photojournalist; and Dahmer dropped out of college after failing his first quarter. Jesperson's father refused to pay for him to attend college, even though he expressed interest and his three siblings all attended higher education. Bundy dropped out of law school; Black lost a welding apprenticeship; Wallace failed out of two colleges; and Watts dropped out of college 3 months into his first semester.
8. Wallace also killed his victims in their homes, but, because he was acquainted with all of his victims, in most cases he had been in the homes before.
9. See Table 6.2 for the measured social status of each serial murderer, determined with the scale developed by Hollingshead (1975) and updated by Barratt (2006).

7
IMPLICATIONS

Introduction

The previous chapters present a critique of modern American society for maintaining a culture that fosters serial murder. Emphases in American culture on individualism, competition, and white, male privilege; a strong cultural push for men to strive toward the ideals of hegemonic masculinity; the potential emotional appeal of crime commission; and inconsistent and contradictory cultural messages contribute to the development of serial murderers by making serial murder a path to desired social goods for some men. In addition, economic and social structures that marginalize particular populations and stereotypical representations of crime, criminals, and victims in American media create an environment in which some offenders (e.g., those who do not fit the "ideal criminal" image) may be overlooked or differently regarded, and some victims (e.g., those who do not fit the "ideal victim" image) may be ignored or blamed for their victimization. The components of American culture explored in this text separately offer a deeper understanding of the cultural messages broadcast in the United States and their particular influence on men, yet they are intrinsically intertwined, and together may be used to explain the development of serial murderers in America. However, they also reveal limitations in the study of serial murder in America and clues about possible solutions.

Toward a Deeper Understanding

There is much serial murder researchers can do now to develop a deeper understanding of the phenomenon and start taking steps toward decreasing its incidence. The first step is to increase communication among researchers in hopes of reaching agreement on more aspects of the phenomenon. While different disciplinary perspectives likely will continue to spur disagreements among researchers about the causes of serial murder, exposure to divergent ideas and theories will build knowledge and stimulate innovative ways of thinking.

A valuable first step would be the development of a single definition of serial murder. Such efforts have already begun. In 2005, the Federal Bureau of Investigation (FBI) hosted a symposium, "Serial Murder: Multi-Disciplinary Perspectives for Investigators" in San Antonio, Texas, with the goal of identifying commonalities of knowledge on an array of topics related to serial murder among recognized experts in multiple fields and specialties (i.e., law enforcement, medical, legal, academic, and media). The definition of serial murder developed during that meeting—"the unlawful killing of two or more victims by the same offender(s) in separate events" (Morton and Hilts 2008, 9)—appears to open the door to a number of different types of multiple murderers than would be included in other definitions of serial murder. That door is quickly closed, however, by the restriction appearing further in the document that specifies no relationship between the offender and victim. But, this new definition (without the stranger qualification) is perhaps the best available. It is sufficiently inclusive to allow for additional models of serial murder besides the white, male model, and it eliminates much of the distinction that is so closely related to the term *serial murder*. That distinction, however, will not be easily abandoned by the media and public.

The development of a working definition of serial murder is more difficult—and important—than it may immediately seem. Considering identified common characteristics of serial murder along with existing definitions of the phenomenon exposes a fundamental problem with serial murder research thus far: The definitions of serial murder previously employed, including my own, appear to describe characteristics most associated with white, male serial murderers in the United States and exclude characteristics that may be associated with other groups and people acting with different motivations. Thus, the supposed overrepresentation of white males in serial murder may be explained by the restrictive definitions of serial murder. Slight reformulations of these narrow definitions would fundamentally change the characterization of the "typical" serial murderer. For example, if these definitions were expanded to allow for victims who are known to the killers, a number of African Americans and women would be included. The elimination of some types of multiple murderers (e.g., those who repeatedly kill spouses or children, or hospital or nursing home employees who repeatedly kill patients) from the definition of serial murder may mean that some offenses are not being recognized, potentially putting people at risk. This blindness is related to the power structure in the United States and is (perhaps inadvertently) supported by the mass media and FBI.

The popular representation of serial murderers as highly intelligent, elusive, white men is consistent with the power structure in the United States and notions of whiteness and masculinity. In my study, the influence of power was evidenced in the ways several of the killers differed from the white, male serial murder model, as well as the ways in which the killers were portrayed in the media.

The female and nonwhite serial murderers included in my study were members of subordinated populations (because of race, ethnicity, or gender) and therefore had fewer means for gaining and using power than many of the white men. The variations represented by these killers appeared to be a result of their positions in the social structure and access to power.

Richard Ramirez, Henry Wallace, and Coral Watts, all considered "atypical" serial murderers because of ethnic or racial difference, were the only killers in the study to vary their killing methods. All of the white, male killers used one method of killing—typically strangulation—for every murder. In addition, Wallace exclusively killed people he knew, which under most definitions would exclude him from the serial murderer category. Wallace maintained the general intraracial pattern of violence by killing only African American women, but Watts differed by killing only white women. Ramirez did not fit the profile of the white, male serial murderer, as he generally withdrew from society: He never held a steady job, never showed an interest in dating, had a long history of minor offending and drug use, and did not show any interest in other serial murderers. He also appeared less organized in his killing, did not have one type of targeted victim, and left several victims alive.

Aileen Wuornos, the only woman included in this study, also did not fit the white, male model of serial murder. Not only did her explanation for the murders (self-defense) fit with a traditional female defense, but she also relied on traditionally feminine imagery to carry out the murders. As a prostitute, she recognized the exploitation of women's bodies as an available means of income. She also recognized the cultural imagery of feminine vulnerability and used it to create the element of surprise: She relied on the men who picked her up to trust her because of her gender, and she caught them off guard when she turned violent. In addition, shooting is one of the most common methods used by women in cases of single murder.

The influence of power was clearly evident in media portrayals of the killers. Ted Bundy was the only one of the studied serial murderers who could be considered upper-middle class, and his elevated social status seemed to alter media portrayals of him. In contrast to the "monster," "outcast," and "loser" portrayals of the other killers, the coverage of Bundy depicted him as an "all-American boy," someone who appeared to epitomize American values. He was frequently described as "good looking," "clean-cut," "cool," "bright," and "confident." His status as a former law student was mentioned in nearly every report, and one referred to him as "Kennedyesque." The portrayals of the other white, male serial murderers were not as glamorous, but they were not particularly degrading either.[1]

Bob Berdella was described as a "neighborhood leader" who was instrumental in revitalizing his community and forming a crime watch group. Although also described as having a "gruff, no-nonsense demeanor" and occasionally being abrupt and critical, he was seen as "real pleasant," funny, considerate, helpful, and generous. Jeffery Dahmer was repeatedly described as "normal" and a loner in published comments by community members. John Gacy was depicted as a friendly, neighborly, hard-working businessman, and his popularity as a children's entertainer was frequently mentioned. Dennis Rader was described by those who knew him as well liked and a community leader who also was a church elder and a Boy Scout leader; only one article suggests that his neighbors did not like him. After his apprehension, however, those who did not know him described Rader as "devoid of soul and human feeling" and a "monster." Gary Ridgway was described as an "ordinary Joe." Descriptions of his physical appearance—thick glasses, thinning hair, and slight build—are unflattering in relation to ideal masculine characteristics but may have contributed to the ordinary Joe characterization. Joel Rifkin was described as quiet, respectful, and pleasant. Although he also was described as a loner and "geek," he was generally seen as on the right track. Dayton Rogers was described as "thoughtful and religious," and his roles as husband and father were frequently mentioned.

The media portrayals of the female and nonwhite killers were quite different, particularly in the overwhelmingly negative depictions throughout the coverage. In contrast to most of the white, male serial murderers in this study, Ramirez (born to Mexican immigrants) was never described as "normal" or as having any valuable qualities, although similarly he was described as a "loner." Both before and after his apprehension, he was described as "evil personified," "brutal," and "cold blooded." In addition, his criminal history and link to devil worship were indicated in most of the media reports. Wallace (African American) was most often described as not only a drifter and crack addict but also a good neighbor, charming, attractive, and popular with women. Sometimes, both portrayals were evident in the same article. Watts (African American) was described as ordinary, "pleasant but standoffish," and a loner, although somewhat popular with women. Interestingly, Watts was the only serial murderer in this study never to be called a monster in any of the analyzed data. Two competing portrayals were offered in news accounts of female killer Wuornos: that of a cold-blooded, greedy, evil woman and that of a desperate woman who had been victimized most of her life. Heavy emphasis was placed on her prostitution and childhood abuse and neglect.

More research is needed that examines potential alternative models of serial murder. There may be fundamental differences among various types of serial murderers (especially by race, ethnic origin, and gender) depending on their access to power and other resources. This could lead to a greater understanding of the population and may aid investigations and the improvement of profiling techniques.

Finally, popular representation of serial murder may serve the interests of the elite. Instances of multiple murders—spree and mass murders; mafia murders; murders for hire; and political mass murders—are framed according to the perpetrators' access to power (often, political mass murder is not considered murder at all). Representations of serial murder reinforce and perpetuate the power structure in American society and related values, which sustains an environment for extreme violence and creates a cultural blindness to some perpetrators.

Investigative Considerations

Law enforcement agencies, particularly the FBI, have much to gain from the incidence of serial murder. Criminal profilers receive a large amount of public support for the presentation of themselves as not only experts on serial murder investigation but *the sole authority*, thus establishing a need for their services. They also benefit from popular profiles of serial murderers, for if serial murderers are portrayed as highly intelligent, cunning, and elusive, then those who purport to understand them or are able to capture them are depicted as even more clever. And, the killers' supposed brilliance makes it understandable when FBI agents or profilers experience difficulties in serial murder investigations (and not attributable to law enforcement failure).

The findings in my study differed in several ways from purported characteristics of "typical" serial murderers reported by serial murder researchers and often included in criminal profiles. The differences indicate that there may be fewer commonalities among serial murderers, even among those considered typical. Using a comparison group composed of killers who differed from the prototypical model in various ways also helped deconstruct the typical serial murderer profile. Characteristics of the members in the two groups were much more similar than different, which raises questions about the typical model. Profiles require identifiable similarities, but in cases of serial murder, selecting particular characteristics of a diverse group to force into neat categories is self-serving for those who create the profiles and possibly counterproductive in solving serial murder cases. More research is needed on criminal profiling techniques and how they can be improved to enhance efficiency, accuracy, and general usefulness in investigations.

Decreasing the Incidence of Serial Murder

Steps to reduce the number of future serial murder cases are possible but difficult. As long as inconsistent messages in American culture allow for deviant paths to achieve cultural values, serial murderers are glorified in omnipresent media representations, and groups such as media and the FBI stand to benefit from such representations, the incidence is unlikely to decrease.

Message Consistency

The availability of serial murder as a path to social goods is largely a result of inconsistencies in cultural messages, which are broadcast by the mass media. We can all recognize that serial murder is a means to achieve power, control, recognition, fame, and other values; the evidence is all around us—in the headlines, in our entertainment, and on novelty merchandise. Media representations of serial murderers, along with popular profiles and exclusive definitions, construct a distinct, elite status for serial murderers to which other repeat offenders are not compared.

We receive inconsistent messages about the appropriateness of violence and consistent messages that individualism, recognition, and winning at any cost are valuable. In this context, offending may become a means for achieving cultural values, but *extreme types of offending* are almost guaranteed. Only the worst of the worst offenders—those with the highest body counts, the most vicious and shocking methods, or the most daring schemes to avoid capture—achieve infamy. In a perverse sense, claiming the highest number of the worst type of violent offender may be a perverse source of cultural pride for the United States, an egocentric nation preoccupied with exceptionalism. We must closely examine our cultural messages to uncover what it is we are really saying and whether we want to be saying it.

Several social scientists have examined the treatment in the media of serial murderers as celebrities and hypothesized possible implications. Fox and Levin (2005, 14), for example, sound the alarm, stating that the consequences of granting fame to the killers "may be inadvertently providing young people with a dangerous model for gaining national prominence." Schmid (2005) argues that serial murderers are increasingly aware of their celebrity status, as well as the potential to capitalize from their fame through the market for murderabilia. Drawing conclusions from his studies of the "copycat effect," Coleman (2004) suggests that the publicizing of serial murder actually produces more serial murders and serial murderers.

Protections for All

It is no coincidence that the most frequent victims of serial murderers are women (especially those who do not fit traditional standards of femininity), homosexuals, children, and the elderly. These are populations with few resources and limited access to power. Largely because of the individualistic nature of American culture, members of these groups also are afforded few protections.

Popular images of vulnerable populations frequently are negative, given the tendency to attribute their status to individual flaws or mistakes and to place less value on their lives (Guillén 2007; Sheffield 2004; Wilson 2007a). Members of vulnerable populations sometimes are dehumanized or objectified in American culture, making their victimization seem less important. Serial murderers commonly describe their victims as less than human (Levin and Fox 2007; Martingale 1993), and law enforcement officials and journalists have long been accused of devoting less time and fewer resources to cases in which the victims are members of a vulnerable group. These cultural messages may increase the likelihood of victimization for particular segments of the population.

The dehumanization process has been used by other groups to commit atrocities: During World War II, the Nazis thought of Jews as animals that should be exterminated for the good of society; in 2004, Iraqi militants dragged the mutilated and burned bodies of four American contractors through the streets and suspended them from a bridge as residents cheered; and reports emerged in 2004 of American guards brutalizing inmates at the Abu Ghraib prison in Iraq. Dehumanization of enemies is common, but the process also is evident in the cultural images of some vulnerable populations (e.g., the poor, homeless, and elderly), sending the message that members of those groups can be seen as "asking for" victimization or undeserving of assistance. Thus, poor people may be chastised for accepting welfare or food stamps; homeless people may be overlooked or abused; and elderly people may be exploited or ignored.

Several differences in the economic and social structures of the United States and other industrial societies have been cited as a reason for a higher incidence of violent crime in the United States. Income disparity has been cited as a cause of crime all over the world (Currie

1985; James 1995; Sieber 2005), and the United States has a visible gap between the rich and the poor that is substantial and growing (U.S. Census Bureau 2008). In addition, the exclusionary nature of American society, according to Young (1999), is more severe than in Europe. Following the argument that equality of opportunity is key to the American dream ideology, when people fail, it is blamed on individual qualities; in Europe, individual failures are seen more as the fault of the system. Many other industrialized nations operate under the ideology of mutual responsibility and social obligation and have well-developed social programs and policies that provide income and employment support (Currie 1985; Hickey 2006; James 1995). They also appear to have a much lower incidence of serial murder. More research on the characteristics of serial murder in other nations is badly needed. Until we recognize that components of our cultural ideology and structure are putting some people at greater risk, we will continue to maintain a population vulnerable to victimization. Protecting members of vulnerable groups is one step we can take toward lowering the incidence of serial murder and perhaps violent offending in general.

Note

1. Coverage of serial murderer Eddie Cole differed; most articles merely provided general information about progress made in the case or trial, with little specific information about him, those who knew him, or his victims. It is possible that personal information was difficult for journalists to find because Cole moved from state to state frequently, had no contact with family members, and had no close friends. It also would be worthwhile to examine what other events were covered by news media at the time, as it is possible that the news focus was elsewhere. Fine and White (2002) emphasize the importance of timing in the amount and type of news coverage an event is likely to receive.

Appendix: Methodology

Introduction

Arguments in this book are supported by findings from my 2009 dissertation, which is referenced throughout. The purpose of the study was to identify the ways in which the American cultural milieu fosters serial murder and the creation of white, male serial murderers. Informed by a framework drawn from cultural sociology and gender studies, the study employed a qualitative content analysis of biographical narratives, newspaper articles, and legal documents regarding 15 serial murderers—9 who appear to characterize the "typical" serial murderer and 6 who each represent a variation of one of the prototypical characteristics. Although the purpose of the study was achieved, data analysis also revealed unexpected findings (especially regarding the definition of serial murder, representations of serial murderers, and the implications of each), which were developed further and introduced in this text. Following is a detailed explanation of the methodology employed in that study.

Rationale

Studies of culture examine the symbolic–expressive dimension of social life and view culture as a distinct aspect of social reality (Wuthnow et al. 1984). Wuthnow et al. (1984, 259) argue that a chief aim of cultural analysis is "to identify empirical regularities or patterns in this dimension of reality" and identify features of those regularities that make them meaningful. This can be accomplished by examining the "recorded culture," which "encompasses all the things that record in some way how people thought and felt" in a particular time and place (Inglis 2005, 17). These cultural records, including newspapers, magazines, advertisements, films, government documents, diaries, and letters, offer extraordinary insight into the lived culture of a particular group (Denzin 1992).

To identify aspects of American culture that foster a milieu suitable for serial murder and that influence the reported overrepresentation of men and whites in serial murder, I employed a qualitative content analysis. A variety of cultural records—including biographical narratives, newspaper articles, court cases, legal journal articles, and official confessions—regarding 15 serial murderers was analyzed. Secondary data were used for this study because the representations of serial murder in American culture were of principal interest. The use of primary data could have aided in identifying characteristics of the killers but was unnecessary given the wealth of secondary data available.[1]

Qualitative Content Analysis

The qualitative content analysis approach is commonly used in the analysis of documents and comprises a search for underlying themes in the materials under study (Bryman 2001, 381). In contrast to quantitative content analysis, the process used in a qualitative approach is to extract from texts themes often left implicit, and the processes of conceptualization, data collection, analysis, and interpretation do not necessarily follow a well-defined structure (Bryman 2001, 381). Coding of themes evolves, with the researcher "discovering" themes through analysis, rather than seeking data to fit into predetermined categories. By reading and rereading documents, the researcher tries "to pin down [the] key themes and, thereby, to draw a picture of the presuppositions and meanings that constitute the cultural world of which the textural material is a specimen" (Denzin and Lincoln 2005, 870). The researcher begins with research questions and loose categories, which may be revised, abandoned, or augmented throughout the research process.

Research Questions

1. In what ways does American culture provide a milieu conducive to the generation of serial murderers?
2. In what ways does American culture contribute to the overrepresentation of men in serial murder?
3. In what ways does American culture contribute to the overrepresentation of whites in serial murder?
4. In what ways do media portrayals of serial murderers shape public perceptions about serial murder and characteristics of serial murderers?

Defining Serial Murder

Because of variation in the definition of serial murder, it is necessary to establish the definition employed here. Based on the Federal Bureau of Investigation (FBI) definition, as well as common characteristics established in the literature, *serial murder* is defined in this study as three or more homicides that were intentionally committed by a single offender acting alone for sexual or other personal gratification over a period of weeks, months, or years. The motivational qualifier I included is commonly found in social scientists' definitions of serial murder and helps distinguish serial murder from homicides motivated by material or financial gain, sympathy, revenge, passion, or temporary rage, which I believe can be demonstrated to be qualitatively different types of homicide. A *serial murderer* is defined as a person who has been convicted of serial murder, as defined here. Among types of killers that may be considered serial murderers elsewhere but are not included in this definition are those who have been suspected but not convicted of at least three murders; those who murdered family members or other intimates; those who killed as part of a partnership; and health care or child care workers who killed in those settings or while on duty. These offenders appear to differ in killing methods, targeted victims, and apparent motivation from the "typical" serial murderer[2] and generally are treated as atypical in popular portrayals.

Sample Selection[3]

The number of serial murderers identified varies widely depending on the chosen definition of serial murder, and a comprehensive list of known serial murderers is difficult to compile. By culling information from various books that purport to be comprehensive information sources of serial murder, like *The A to Z Encyclopedia of Serial Killers* (Schechter and Everitt 1997) and the Crime Library (http://www.trutv.com/library/crime/index.html), which includes information about known serial murderers and breaks down the list into categories, including "Most Notorious," "Sexual Predators," "Truly Weird & Shocking," "Unsolved Cases," "Partners in Crime," and "Killers in History," I developed a list of 141 serial murderers.

This list is not exhaustive, and several reasons can account for the discrepancy between estimates of the number of serial murderers and the number included in popular sources. Serial murder sources that are produced for the public generally include cases that are well known (i.e., received vast amounts of media coverage), exceptional in some way, or about which there exists an abundance of information. In addition, information about cases prior to 1960 (before the so-called surge in serial murder) is difficult to find, and some cases from all time periods likely are never documented. (Convicted murderers who would fit the definition of a serial murderer may not have been identified as such, some serial murderers are never apprehended, and variations of record keeping and quality of records may have kept some veiled from public knowledge.) Finally, most "comprehensive" sources of serial murder are compiled and produced in the United States and include mostly American cases; only the most notorious non-American serial murderers are included.

From the 141 serial murderers identified, I extracted the killers who appeared to characterize the typical serial murderer. Typical serial murderers were identified as those who fit my definition of serial murderer (explicated in the previous section), as well as common characteristics established in the literature. This meant excluding unsolved cases; those who were not convicted of at least three murders on separate occasions; those who killed with a partner; those who killed family members, people in their care, or other people who were previously known to them; those who appeared to kill for burglary, sympathy, revenge, or reasons other than personal gratification; and those who were not white, male, and American.[4] After these exclusions, the new list was composed of 22 serial murderers. I selected my typical group of 9 serial murderers[5] from this list, looking for variety in time frame, geographic location, and type of victim. I also ensured that the final sample included a nearly equal mix of notorious[6] and lesser-known murderers.

Comparison groups are useful for better understanding of a phenomenon of interest (Bryman 2001; Creswell 1998; Denzin and Lincoln 2005) because contrasting similar groups can help reveal characteristics and variations of the phenomenon that may be difficult to distinguish otherwise. Denzin and Lincoln (2005, 451) emphasize the importance of selecting cases that offer an opportunity to learn, arguing that "sometimes it is better to learn a lot from an atypical case than a little from a seemingly typical case." Examining serial murderers who do not fit presumably prototypical characteristics may lead to better understanding of the influence of those characteristics within the American cultural context, as well as a revelation of additional characteristics or variations. The inclusion of a comparison group also aids in a critical analysis of those characteristics and their status as typical. I selected six serial murderers[7] for a comparison group, using Internet resources and books and looking specifically for cases that differ by nationality, race or ethnicity, sex, and social status. Each killer in this "atypical" group represents a variation of one of these characteristics, but I did not seek to include all variations of all characteristics.

The inclusion of divergent serial murderers in this study aids in the understanding of presumably prototypical white, American, male serial murderers. But, as only 15 serial murderers are included in the sample, findings from the proposed study will not be generalizable to the serial murderer population but will contribute to an understanding of this population and how culture influences its development.

Although the sample in this study was not randomly selected, the selection process was similar to the approach of previous studies. No study was found that claimed to employ a random selection process. Divergent definitions of serial murder and the unknown reliability of records would limit any sampling frame. Hickey's (2006) study, employing one of the most inclusive definitions of serial murder, is the only one found that purports to offer a comprehensive study of serial murder in the United States, but employment of a different definition would exclude a number of killers from his study.

Typical Group

- **Robert (Bob) Berdella** murdered six men by torture, suffocation, and drug injections from 1980 to 1984 in Kansas City, Missouri.
- **Carroll Edward (Eddie) Cole** murdered 13 women by strangulation from 1971 to 1980 in Dallas, Texas; San Diego, California; and Las Vegas, Nevada.
- **Jeffrey Lionel Dahmer** murdered 17 men and boys by strangulation from 1978 to 1991 in Milwaukee, Wisconsin.
- **John Wayne Gacy** murdered 33 boys and young men by strangulation from 1972 to 1978 in Chicago, Illinois.
- **Keith Hunter Jesperson** murdered at least 4 women (he confessed to 160) by strangulation from 1990 to 1995 in Oregon, Wyoming, Washington, and possibly Florida and California.
- **Dennis Lynn Rader** murdered 10 men, women, and children by strangulation and stabbing from 1974 to 1986 in Wichita, Kansas.
- **Gary Leon Ridgway** murdered 48 women (usually prostitutes and teenage runaways) by strangulation mostly from 1982 to 1984 and also in 1990 and 1998 in Washington.
- **Joel David Rifkin** murdered nine women (mostly drug addicts and prostitutes) by strangulation from 1989 to 1993 in New York City.
- **Dayton Leroy Rogers** murdered seven (possibly eight) women by stabbing in the 1980s in Oregon.

Atypical Group

- **Robert Black** represents a case that differs by nationality. A white, Scottish man, he murdered at least three girls (and is suspected of more) by strangulation from 1982 to 1990 in Scotland and England.
- **Theodore Robert (Ted) Bundy** represents a case that differs by socioeconomic status. A white, upper-middle-class

man, he murdered at least 3 (the actual number of victims is believed to be closer to 35) women by strangulation and bludgeoning from 1974 to 1978 in Washington, Utah, Colorado, and Florida.
- **Richard Munoz Ramirez** represents a case that differs by ethnicity. Born in El Paso, Texas, to Mexican immigrants, he murdered at least 13 women and men by shooting or stabbing from 1984 to 1985 in southern California.
- **Henry Louis Wallace** represents a case that differs by race. An African American man, he murdered at least 9 (but admitted to 10, including 1 prostitute) young African American women, mostly by strangulation but also stabbing, from 1992 to 1994 in Charlotte, North Carolina.
- **Coral Eugene Watts** represents a case that differs by race. An African American man, he murdered at least 14 (but admitted to more than 80) white women by drowning, stabbing, hanging, or strangulation from 1974 to 1982 in Houston, Texas, and Michigan.
- **Aileen Carol Wuornos** represents a case that differs by sex. A white woman, she murdered at least six men by shooting from 1989 to 1990 in Florida.

Data Collection Sources

Data were obtained from a number of sources:[8] biographical narratives, newspaper articles, court cases and legal journal articles, and official confessions.

Biographical Narratives

Biographical narratives of serial murderers in this study were obtained from the Crime Library Web site, which is run by truTV[9] and has been shown to be a dependable resource for detailed accounts of crimes, offenders, and related analysis (Gniewek and Moore 2006), as well as books written by journalists (usually the reporters assigned to cover the cases), law enforcement officers, and academics based on interviews with law enforcement officials, attorneys, victims' families, surviving victims, the murderer's family, and often the murderer.

These narratives provide information about the serial murderer's personal life; dates and locations of the murders; victim background and cause of death; previous arrests and convictions; and details about trials, their time spent in prison, and executions. They also include direct quotations from the killers, which provide insight into how they thought about cultural values, how they understood their cultural competencies, and how they accordingly constructed lines of action.

One Crime Library article (15 total) and at least 1 book (21 total) were used for each killer in this study, except Black. For the lesser-known serial murderers, few books—in Black's case, none[10]—had been published. For the more notorious, there often were several books available, and two or three were selected for analysis. Selection was based on the perceived credibility of the authors and the integrity of the publishers (e.g., overly sensationalized books or ones written by relatively unknown authors generally were not selected).[11] Although different books about the same killer contain a considerable amount of repetitive information, using more than one book when available was useful as it provided a more complete account of the case.

While analyzing these data, I looked for information about each murderer's upbringing, relationships, goals and outcomes, occupations, and pastimes, as well as information about the social environment during his or her childhood, adolescence, and adulthood. I also looked for evidence of perceived failure (e.g., in school, relationships, or occupations); evidence of a desire for power or domination or for fame or distinction; a tendency for violent behavior, risk-taking behaviors; and interest in military or law enforcement. These were general categories I kept in mind while remaining receptive to emerging patterns and themes.

Newspaper Articles

The mass media are an important transmitter of cultural messages, and my analysis relied heavily on newspaper reports. Newspapers, through a complex process of cultural production and consumption, not only report news but also "make news meaningful" (Hall 1975, 21). Cultural values are evoked and narrative structure employed, along with a variety of verbal, visual, and typographical means, to create "signifying meaning-structures" (Hall 1975, 21) through which people understand their world and construct meanings about it (Lule 2001). It is important to look at not only *what* newspaper stories say but also *how* it is presented, as well as how it shapes and is shaped by culture (Hall 1975). Examining media representations of serial murderers aided in understanding the relationship between dominant cultural values and representations of serial murder, as well as the ways in which cultural values are transmitted via these cases and how they may be interpreted in different ways.

A variety of articles published in newspapers across the nation was used for analysis and gathered through three databases of national and international newspapers available through the University of Tennessee libraries: Dow Jones Factiva, Newsbank Incorporated, and ProQuest Historical Newspapers.[12] A search of each database was conducted for each killer using his or her given name.[13] For the seven killers who had a well-known nickname associated with the murders, a second search was conducted using that nickname;[14] results of both searches were then compared and duplicate articles eliminated. A total of 50,252 articles were found: in the typical group, 86 for Berdella, 41 for Cole, 12,896 for Dahmer, 4,905 for Gacy, 529 for Jesperson, 2,745 for Rader, 4,816 for Ridgway, 974 for Rifkin, and 433 for Rogers; and in the atypical group, 806 for Black, 10,339 for Bundy, 6,598 for Ramirez, 453 for Wallace, 459 for Watts, and 4,172 for Wuornos.

To select a sample of articles from the total number found, I looked for variety in information covered,[15] geographic location of the publications, and newspaper size. The sample covers the entire coverage time period produced through the database searches. My aim was to get a sense of the overall picture that emerged from media coverage of serial murderers in America, so it was important to choose as wide a variety of publications as I could find using the databases to which I had access. A total of 1,192 articles were included in the sample: in the typical group, 22 for Berdella, 17 for Cole, 149 for Dahmer, 187 for Gacy, 71 for Jesperson, 67 for Rader, 64 for Ridgway, 103 for Rifkin, and 66 for Rogers; and in the atypical group, 35 for Black, 117 for Bundy, 60 for Ramirez, 111 for Wallace, 65 for Watts, and 58 for Wuornos.

In my analysis, I examined how much coverage each serial murderer received (as measured by numbers of published articles found),[16] how each was portrayed by the coverage,[17] and patterns in how the information was reported. Also important was considering what appeared to be missing from the reports; omission of information by the media indicates value judgments about what is considered unimportant to narratives of serial murder. I also looked for information about how the killers responded to media coverage, as well as whether they apparently sought the coverage.

Court Cases and Legal Journal Articles

Legal documents, including court cases and legal journal articles, also are rich sources of cultural understandings and transmission. In the courtroom, people may be punished for violating the most strongly held values and norms in society, and examining legal documents points to the strong influence of culture in our ways of thinking about the world and our judgments of others.

Federal and state court cases and legal journal articles were obtained from the LexisNexis Academic database available through the University of Tennessee libraries. Searches were conducted for each killer using his or her given name and nickname, where applicable, with duplicate results eliminated, as described for the newspaper articles. Every unique court case that was produced was included in the analysis, and a selection of legal journal articles was included, based on their usefulness in contributing to a cultural argument.[18] A total of 107 court cases was included: in the typical group, 8 for Berdella, 2 for Cole, 10 for Dahmer, 10 for Gacy, 7 for Rifkin, and 4 for Rogers; and in the atypical group, 22 for Bundy, 18 for Ramirez, 14 for Wallace, 6 for Watts, and 6 for Wuornos. No relevant court cases were found for Jesperson, Rader, Ridgway, or Black. A total of 18 legal journal articles were included: in the typical group, 4 for Berdella, 3 for Jesperson, 3 for Rader, 5 for Ridgway, and 3 for Rogers; no relevant legal journal articles were found for Cole, Dahmer, Gacy, or any of the killers in the atypical group.

Official Confessions

Two official confessions were found,[19] those of Rader and Ridgway. The confessions include not only information about the murders and the killers' attempts to offer explanations and justifications for the killings, but also those explanations and justifications incorporate cultural images and indicate the killers' cultural understandings. This discourse provides insight into how the serial murderers thought about cultural values, how they understood their cultural competencies, and how they accordingly constructed lines of action.

Analytical Procedure

For the initial stages of analysis, I established general areas of inquiry based on the information I sought (explained previously by data collection source) and shaped by the theoretical framework. I intended to pay close attention to their social environment from childhood up to the time before their first murder, any evidence of cultural values or familiar imagery conveyed through the documents, and the killers' own explanations and apparent cultural understandings. I then carefully read the Crime Library narratives and books first, then newspaper articles, then court cases and legal journal articles, and finally confessions, highlighting and making notes about information that appeared significant. Patterns and themes began to emerge throughout this process, and I created the following loose categories:

- Relationships with family members
- Relationships with friends
- Goals and their outcomes
- Perceived failures (e.g., in school, relationships, and occupations)
- Favorite pastimes
- Social environment (during childhood, adolescence, and adulthood)
- Evidence of a desire for power or domination
- Evidence of a desire for fame or distinction
- History of violent behavior
- Evidence of risk-taking behavior
- Interest in military service or law enforcement
- Claims made by prosecution before, during, and after trials
- Claims made by defense before, during, and after trials
- References to killers in unrelated newspaper articles or court cases

- Portrayals in newspaper articles, especially through social typing
- Characteristics of the cases that were considered newsworthy or not
- Use of a nickname in newspaper coverage
- Whether and how killers sought media coverage
- Killers' responses to media coverage
- Killers' attention to other serial murderers
- Evidence of feelings of superiority
- Explanations offered by killers
- In confessions and direct quotations, evidence of killers' cultural understandings (how they understood their cultural competencies and subsequent construction of lines of action)

Next, I reread each document and entered relevant information into computer files separated by the newly formed categories. Further analysis led to the revision, abandonment, and augmentation of the categories. The revised set of coding categories included the following:

- Serial murderer characteristics and comparisons[20]
  - Intelligence and school performance
  - Employment
  - Sexuality
  - Age at first murder
  - Previous abuse
  - Criminal history
  - Military service
  - Interest in law enforcement
  - Peer and romantic relationships
  - Failures
  - Trophies
  - Explanations offered
- Cultural values tuned in and utilized
  - Success and recognition
  - Violence
  - Portrayals
  - Social types
    - Fools

- Villains
        - Corrupt hero
- Masculinities
    - The criminal experience
- Thrill seeking and risk taking
    - Power and control
    - Skill or accomplishment
    - Narrative of serial murder

Table A.1 General Information about Serial Murderers in the Sample

	BIRTH	DEATH	SEX	RACE/ ETHNICITY	NATIONALITY	NICKNAME	TIME FRAME	LOCATION	VICTIM TYPE	NO. OF VICTIMS	KILLING METHOD	SENTENCE
Bob Berdella	1/31/1939	10/8/92	Male	White	American	N/A	1980–1984	Kansas City, MO	Gay men	6	Torture, suffocation, drugs	Life in prison
Eddie Cole	5/9/1938	12/6/85	Male	White	American	N/A	1971–1980	Dallas, TX; San Diego, CA; Las Vegas, NV	Women	16	Strangulation	Death, two life terms
Jeffrey Dahmer	5/21/1960	11/28/94	Male	White	American	Milwaukee Monster	1978–1991	Milwaukee, WI	Boys, young men	17	Strangulation	15 life terms
John Gacy	3/17/1942	5/10/94	Male	White	American	Killer Clown	1972–1978	Chicago	Boys, young men	33	Strangulation	Death
Keith Jesperson	4/6/1955	N/A	Male	White	Canadian/ American	Happy Face Killer	1990–1995	Oregon, Wyoming, Washington	Prostitutes	At least 4	Strangulation	2 life terms
Dennis Rader	3/9/1945	N/A	Male	White	American	BTK	1974–1986	Wichita, KS	Women, men, children	10	Strangulation	10 life terms
Gary Ridgway	2/18/1949	N/A	Male	White	American	Green River Killer	1982–1998	Washington	Prostitutes, runaways	48	Strangulation	48 life terms

APPENDIX: METHODOLOGY

Joel Rifkin	1/20/1959	N/A	Male	White	American	N/A	1989–1993	New York City	Prostitutes, drug addicts	9	Strangulation	Life term
Dayton Rogers	9/30/1953	N/A	Male	White	American	Molalla Forest Killer	1980s	Oregon	Prostitutes	At least 7	Stabbing	Death
Robert Black	4/21/1947	N/A	Male	White	Scottish	N/A	1982–1990	Scotland, England	Female children	At least 3	Strangulation	Life, parole possible
Ted Bundy	11/24/1946	1/24/89	Male	White	American	N/A	1974–1978	Washington, Utah, Colorado, Florida	Young women	At least 3	Strangulation, bludgeoning	Death
Richard Ramirez	2/29/1960	N/A	Male	Mexican	American	Night Stalker	1984–1985	Southern California	Women and men[a]	At least 13	Shooting, stabbing	Death
Henry Wallace	11/4/1965	N/A	Male	African American	American	N/A	1992–1994	Charlotte, NC	Young women	At least 9	Strangulation, stabbing	Death
Coral Watts	11/7/1953	9/21/07	Male	African American	American	Sunday Morning Slasher	1974–1982	Texas, Michigan	Young women	At least 14	Drowning, stabbing, hanging, strangulation	60 years, 2 life terms
Aileen Wuornos	2/29/1956	10/9/02	Female	White	American	N/A	1989–1990	Florida	Men	At least 6	Shooting	Death

Note: N/A, not applicable.

[a] Men were attacked if they were with female targets; in such cases, the men usually were attacked first.

Table A.2 Breakdown of Data Collection Sources

	BOOKS	CRIME LIBRARY BY TRUTV	NEWSPAPER ARTICLES	COURT CASES	LEGAL JOURNAL ARTICLES	OFFICIAL CONFESSIONS	TOTALS
Bob Berdella	1	1	22	8	4	—	36
Eddie Cole	1	1	17	2	—	—	21
Jeffrey Dahmer	2	1	149	10	—	—	162
John Gacy	1	1	187	10	—	—	199
Keith Jesperson	1	1	71	—	3	—	76
Dennis Rader	2	1	67	—	3	1	74
Gary Ridgway	2	1	64	—	5	1	73
Joel Rifkin	1	1	103	7	—	—	112
Dayton Rogers	1	1	66	4	3	—	75
Robert Black	1	1	35	—	—	—	37
Ted Bundy	3	1	117	22	—	—	143
Richard Ramirez	1	1	60	18	—	—	80
Henry Wallace	1	1	111	14	—	—	127
Coral Watts	1	1	65	6	—	—	73
Aileen Wuornos	2	1	58	6	—	—	67
Totals	**21**	**15**	**1,192**	**107**	**18**	**2**	**1,355**

APPENDIX: METHODOLOGY

Table A.3 Characteristics of Serial Murderers in the Sample

	IQ	CHILDHOOD SCHOOL PERFORMANCE	EMPLOYMENT	SEXUAL ORIENTATION	AGE AT FIRST MURDER	PREVIOUS ABUSE	CRIMINAL HISTORY	MILITARY SERVICE	INTEREST IN LAW ENFORCEMENT
Bob Berdella	High	Good	Curio shop owner	Homosexual	41	No	Drug arrests	None	None
Eddie Cole	High	Poor	Warehouse worker	Heterosexual	33	Yes	Various: property and conduct	Navy	None
Jeffrey Dahmer	Average	Poor	Factory worker	Homosexual	18	No	Indecent exposure, sexual assault	Army	None
John Gacy	Average	Poor	Construction business owner	Bisexual	30	No	Various: sexual, violence, property	None	Posed as an officer
Keith Jesperson	Average	Poor	Long-haul truck driver	Heterosexual	35	No	None	None	Interest in Royal Canadian Mounted Police or being a game warden
Dennis Rader	Average	Average	Compliance officer	Heterosexual	29	No	None	Air Force	Compliance officer; degree in criminal justice
Gary Ridgway	Low	Poor	Truck painter	Heterosexual	33	No	Patronizing prostitutes	Navy	None

Continued

APPENDIX: METHODOLOGY

Table A.3 (Continued) Characteristics of Serial Murderers in the Sample

	IQ	CHILDHOOD SCHOOL PERFORMANCE	EMPLOYMENT	SEXUAL ORIENTATION	AGE AT FIRST MURDER	PREVIOUS ABUSE	CRIMINAL HISTORY	MILITARY SERVICE	INTEREST IN LAW ENFORCEMENT
Joel Rifkin	High	Poor	Frequently unemployed landscaper	Heterosexual	40	No	Patronizing a prostitute	None	None
Dayton Rogers	High	Poor	Engine repair business owner	Heterosexual	~27	Yes	Accused of violent assaults	None	None
Robert Black	Average	Average	Delivery truck driver	Heterosexual	35	Yes	Pedophilia, theft, auto theft, assault	None	None
Ted Bundy	High	Good	Sometime student	Heterosexual	28	No	None	None	Posed as an officer; worked in security
Richard Ramirez	Average	Poor	No history of employment	Heterosexual	24	No	Petty theft, auto theft	None	None
Henry Wallace	Average	Poor	Fast-food worker	Heterosexual	27	No	Arrested for rape	Navy	None
Coral Watts	Average	Poor	Auto mechanic	Heterosexual	21	Yes	Harassment, theft, assaults	None	None
Aileen Wuornos	Low	Poor	Prostitute	Homosexual	33	Yes	Disorderly conduct, driving under the influence, weapons	Tried to join	Tried to work in corrections

APPENDIX: METHODOLOGY

PEER AND ROMANTIC RELATIONSHIPS

	CHILDHOOD	ADULTHOOD	TYPE OF FAILURES[a]	TROPHIES	EXPLANATIONS OFFERED[b]
Bob Berdella	Loner/outcast	Seen as community leader; few dates; never married	Scholastic	Photographs, body parts	Movie *The Collector*
Eddie Cole	Loner/outcast	Loner; divorced	Scholastic, relationships	None known	Revenge for domineering mother, prior victimization
Jeffrey Dahmer	Loner/outcast	Loner; poor relationships; never married	Scholastic, relationships	Photographs, body parts	Fear of abandonment, insanity
John Gacy	Seen as well adjusted	Active in community; divorced	Arrest	Small personal items (e.g., wallets and clothing)	Ridding society of its "bad element," mental illness
Keith Jesperson	Loner/outcast	Loner; divorced	Relationships	None known	Revenge for domineering ex-wife
Dennis Rader	Loner/outcast	Active in community; married at time of arrest	None identified	Photographs and small personal items (e.g., driver's licenses)	"Demon" inside him
Gary Ridgway	Loner/outcast	Loner; married at time of arrest	Scholastic	Photographs	Cleaning up society

Continued

Table A.3 (Continued) Characteristics of Serial Murderers in the Sample

	PEER AND ROMANTIC RELATIONSHIPS				
	CHILDHOOD	ADULTHOOD	TYPE OF FAILURES[a]	TROPHIES	EXPLANATIONS OFFERED[b]
Joel Rifkin	Loner/outcast	Loner; never married	Scholastic	Lingerie and small personal items (e.g., driver's licenses, library cards, credit cards)	Revenge against biological mother (whom he never met), movie *Frenzy*, insanity
Dayton Rogers	Loner/outcast	Loner; married at time of arrest	None identified	Clothing, jewelry	Self-defense for one murder, strict religious upbringing
Robert Black	Loner/outcast	Loner; never married	Occupational	None known	Uncontrollable sexual desire
Ted Bundy	Seen as well adjusted although described feeling like an outcast	Active in community; few friends; never married	Scholastic, relationships	None known	None offered; pornography alleged as influence
Richard Ramirez	Loner/outcast	Loner; never married	None identified	Stole items of value	None offered
Henry Wallace	Loner/outcast	Few close friends; never married	None identified	None known	Insanity
Coral Watts	Loner/outcast	Divorced	Scholastic	Small personal items, which he disposed of within days	Said victims had "evil eyes"
Aileen Wuornos	Loner/outcast	Divorced	Occupational, relationships	Stole items of value	Self-defense, prior victimization

[a] Types classified by specific failures described by the killers as most significant to them.
[b] Including explanations offered by the killers or through their legal defense.

Notes

1. Primary-data collection also was not possible or feasible in all cases because several of the killers included in this study are dead, and others are known for their unwillingness to discuss their offending.
2. A "typical" serial murderer, as suggested by previous studies, is considered to be a white, American man of middle-to-low socioeconomic status who killed alone; was convicted of killing at least three people previously unknown to him on separate occasions; and who did not steal items of value from his victims or kill for any apparent reason other than personal gratification.
3. Table A.1 contains a breakdown of general information about the serial murderers in the sample.
4. No sexual orientation was established as typical in the literature, although all serial murderers in the typical group fit identified patterns of sexuality in serial murder.
5. The qualitative researcher often must use personal judgment, based on a set of criteria, to select a sample size that will aid in understanding (Creswell 1998; Denzin and Lincoln 2005). Based on my prior knowledge and research, and given the large volume of data available, I felt that nine serial murderers would compose a small enough group to be manageable yet large enough to get a good sense of the phenomenon, how it is represented in American culture, and possible variation.
6. Notorious serial murderers are those who attained celebrity status through large amounts of media attention and broad public recognition. They continue to be widely recognized long after publicity subsides and often after death. They are referenced in media accounts of current serial murderers and often are used as a measuring stick by which other offenders are judged. They also are included in a number of compilations, such as truTV's Crime Library list of the "Most Notorious" or "Truly Weird & Shocking" crimes.
7. For reasons stated previously, I felt that six serial murderers composed a reasonable group in size and offered enough variation to aid in understanding the phenomenon.
8. Table A.2 contains a breakdown of data collection sources for each serial murderer in this study.
9. At the time of data collection, this channel and corresponding Web site were known as Court TV. The name change occurred January 1, 2008.
10. No book was found that was exclusively about Black, yet one focused on British serial murderers devoted substantial space to his case.
11. Convenience and availability also were considered in the selection process, so books that were not selected for analysis did not necessary fail to meet these criteria.
12. Table 6.1 (Chapter 6) contains a breakdown of the number of articles found and selected for the sample, organized by database and search terms.

13. The first and last names were entered into the search field as a nonphrase, thereby retrieving articles that contained both names but not necessarily appearing consecutively. This search method made it possible to find articles that contained variations of the killers' names (i.e., inclusion of a middle name or nickname that separates the first and last names). However, this search method produced unrelated articles that also included both names anywhere in the text; those articles were excluded from the study and from the article totals reported herein.
14. Using a well-known nickname as a search term made available articles published about the murders before the killers were identified. For those without a well-known nickname, no preapprehension coverage could be found. However, for most of the killers without a nickname, their murders had not been detected until their apprehension, making it unlikely that much or any preapprehension coverage exists. Before being identified as a serial murderer, Bundy was simply called "Ted," the name reported by witnesses and too ordinary to be used as a search term. However, a number of articles were available starting from when he was arrested on an unrelated charge and first became a suspect in the serial murders.
15. Because many newspapers use wire services (e.g., Associated Press or Reuters) as a news source, the same article frequently appeared in multiple publications. Therefore, on significant dates in the cases, a widely distributed article from a wire service was published by multiple newspapers, and it was unnecessary to include all of these versions. Although not every article about every key development in the case was selected, the sample includes at least one article about every key development (as defined by information about plea deals or significant dates in the trial—jury selection, opening arguments, presentations of evidence, key witness testimony, closing arguments, conviction, and sentencing—and other new information that generates large amounts of publicity, like the discovery of additional victims, courtroom outbursts, or new explanations offered). In some cases, multiple versions of a wire service article were included if it was significantly altered by one or more newspapers or if it appeared in vastly different newspapers (in size or geographic location). Altered articles indicate differences in story valuation among newspapers, and examining article publication by geographic location or newspaper size indicates similarities in story valuation despite differing audiences. The cases with the fewest articles in the sample are those with the most articles containing duplicate information.
16. I am interested in determining whether the amount of coverage is related to culturally influenced judgments made in the media about the "newsworthiness" of the murders. The number of published articles found is a crude measure of the amount of coverage received by each killer, primarily because the amount of time that lapses between the awareness of the media that a serial murderer is active and his or her capture likely skews the volume of articles published; a longer time frame likely means more articles and a shorter time frame likely means fewer articles. In addition,

more articles may be published about the killers who sought the coverage by calling or sending letters to the media, and some articles may have been excluded from the databases for various unknown reasons.
17. As newspaper reporters typically are assigned a "beat," or area of specialty, the same reporter often writes many of the stories published about a serial murder case in a particular source. Although enough variety of sources is used to avoid a singular portrayal of each killer, the portrayals may represent fewer perspectives than seems apparent, especially because articles from wire services are included.
18. Creswell (1998) provides a rationale for this selection.
19. Transcripts of court proceedings frequently are available only to those who request them in person from the appropriate courthouse. The documents used in this analysis are scanned copies obtained from The Smoking Gun Web site (http://www.thesmokinggun.com), albeit with permission from the original sources.
20. Tables A.3 and A.4 were created based on data in this category.

References

Across the nation and abroad 2005. 2007. *Wichita Falls Times Record News*, May 14, N7. Accessed January 17, 2008, from Newsbank.

Adler, P. A. and P. Adler. 1989. The glorified self: The aggrandizement and the constriction of self. *Social Psychology Quarterly* 52(4):299–310.

American Psychiatric Association. 2000. *Diagnostic and Statistical Manual of Mental Disorders*, 4th ed. Washington, DC: American Psychiatric.

Andersen, M. L. 2000. *Thinking about Women: Sociological Perspectives on Sex and Gender*, 5th ed. Needham Heights, MA: Allyn & Bacon.

Anderson, K. L. and D. Umberson. 2001. Gendering violence: Masculinity and power in men's accounts of domestic violence. *Gender and Society* 15(3):358–380.

Arrigo, B. A. and A. Griffin. 2004. Serial murder and the case of Aileen Wuornos: Attachment theory, psychopathy, and predatory aggression. *Behavioral Sciences and the Law* 22(3):375–393.

Athens, L. H. 1992. *The Creation of Dangerous Violent Criminals*. Urbana, IL: University of Illinois Press.

Atkinson, M. P., T. N. Greenstein, and M. M. Lang. 2005. For women, breadwinning can be dangerous: Gendered resource theory and wife abuse. *Journal of Marriage and Family* 67:1137–1148.

Baker, W. 2005. *America's Crisis of Values: Reality and Perception*. Princeton, NJ: Princeton University Press.

Barratt, W. 2006. *The Barratt Simplified Measure of Social Status*. Terre Haute, IN: Indiana State University. Accessed February 17, 2009, from http://wbarratt.indstate.edu/socialclass/Barratt_Simplifed_Measure_of_Social_Status.pdf.

Beal, B. 1996. Alternative masculinity and its effects on gender relations in the subculture of skateboarding. *Journal of Sport Behavior* 19(3):204–221.

Beasley, J. O. 2004. Serial murder in America: Case studies of seven offenders. *Behavioral Sciences and the Law* 22:395–414.

Berger, R. J. and R. Quinney. 2005. The narrative turn in social inquiry. In *Storytelling Sociology: Narrative as Social Inquiry*, edited by R. J. Berger and R. Quinney, 1–11. Boulder, CO: Rienner.

Brantley, A. G. and R. H. Kosky, Jr. 2005. Serial murder in the Netherlands: A look at motivation, behavior, and characteristics. In *FBI Law Enforcement Bulletin* 74(1), edited by R. S. Mueller, 26-31. Accessed February 27, 2011, from http://www.fbi.gov/stats-services/publications/law-enforcement-bulletin/2005-pdfs/jan05leb.pdf.

Breed, A. G. 2005. Serial-killer stereotypes not valid. *Ventura County Star*, March 6, 17. Accessed January 17, 2008, from Newsbank.

Briefly: The Nation. 1985. *The Record*, August 14, A7. Accessed January 17, 2008, from Dow Jones Factiva.

Briefs: AP, *Ventura County Star*, October 1, A5. Accessed January 17, 2008, from Newsbank.

Brogan, R. 2006. Serial arson. In *Serial Crime: Theoretical and Practical Issues in Behavioral Profiling*, edited by W. Petherick, 225–245. London: Academic Press.

Bryman, A. 2001. *Social Research Methods*. New York: Oxford University Press.

Burgess, A. W., C. R. Hartman, R. K. Ressler, J. E. Douglas, and A. McCormack. 1986. Sexual homicide: A motivational model. *Journal of Interpersonal Violence* 1(3):251–272.

Burrell, I. 1996. Why can't we catch these serial killers? *The Sunday Times*, January 7. Accessed January 16, 2008, from Dow Jones Factiva, p 1.

Canter, D. 2000. Offender profiling and criminal differentiation. *Legal and Criminal Psychology* 5:23–46.

Canter, D., T. Coffey, M. Huntley, and C. Missen. 2000. Predicting serial killers' home base using a decision support system. *Journal of Quantitative Criminology* 16(4):457–478.

Capp, B. 1996. Serial killers in 17th-century England. *History Today* 46(3):21–26.

Caputi, J. 1989. The sexual politics of murder. *Gender & Society* 3(4):437–456.

———. 1993. American psychos: The serial killer in contemporary fiction. *Journal of American and Comparative Cultures* 16(4):101–112.

Carlo, P. 1996. *Night Stalker: The Life and Crimes of Richard Ramirez*. New York: Pinnacle Books.

Carlo, P. 2006. *Ice Man: Confessions of a Mafia Contract Killer*. New York: St. Martin's Press.

Carrigan, T., B. Connell, and J. Lee. 1985. Toward a new sociology of masculinity. *Theory and Society* 14(5):551–604.

Castle, T. and C. Hensley. 2002. Serial killers with military experience: Applying learning theory to serial murder. *International Journal of Offender Therapy and Comparative Criminology* 46(4):453–465.

Cawelti, J. G. 1984. *The Six-Gun Mystique*. Bowling Green, OH: Bowling Green State University Popular Press.

REFERENCES

Century's Events Timeline. 1999. *Associated Press Newswires*, December 25. Accessed January 17, 2008, from Dow Jones Factiva.

Cerulo, K. A. 1998. *Deciphering Violence: The Cognitive Structure of Right and Wrong*. New York: Routledge.

Claus, C. and L. Lidberg. 1999. Serial murder as a Schahriar syndrome. *The Journal of Forensic Psychiatry* 10(2):427–435.

Coleman, L. 2004. *The Copycat Effect: How the Media and Popular Culture Trigger the Mayhem in Tomorrow's Headlines*. New York: Paraview Pocket Books.

Colomy, P. and L. R. Greiner. 2008. Criminalizing transgressing youth: A neofunctionalist analysis of institution building. In *Illuminating Social Life: Classical and Contemporary Theory Revisited*, 3rd ed., edited by P. Kivisto, 133–167. Thousand Oaks, CA: Pine Forge Press.

Collins, R. 2008. *Violence: A Micro-sociological Theory*. Princeton, NJ: Princeton University Press.

Connell, R. W. 1987. *Gender and Power*. Stanford, CA: Stanford University Press.

———. 2002. *Gender*. Malden, MA: Blackwell Publishing Inc.

———. 2005. *Masculinities*, 2nd ed. Berkeley: University of California Press.

Consalvo, M. 2003. The monsters next door: Media constructions of boys and masculinity. *Feminist Media Studies* 3(1):27–45.

Creswell, J. W. 1998. *Qualitative Inquiry and Research Design: Choosing among Five Traditions*. Thousand Oaks, CA: Sage.

Cullen, D. 2009. *Columbine*. New York: Twelve.

Currie, E. 1985. *Confronting Crime: An American Challenge*. New York: Pantheon Books.

Dahmer murdered first victim while in high school, police say. 1991. *The Baltimore Sun*, July 28, 3A. Accessed January 17, 2008, from Dow Jones Factiva.

Daniels, J. 1997. *White Lies: Race, Class, Gender and Sexuality in White Supremacist Discourse*. New York: Routledge.

Davis, C. A. 2001. *Women Who Kill: Profiles of Female Serial Killers*. Brixton, UK: Allison & Busby.

Denzin, N. K. 1992. The many faces of emotionality: Reading persona. In *Investigating Subjectivity: Research on Lived Experience*, edited by C. Ellis and M. G. Flaherty, 17–30. Thousand Oaks, CA: Sage.

Denzin, N. K. and Y. S. Lincoln. 2005. *The Sage Handbook of Qualitative Research*. Thousand Oaks, CA: Sage.

Douglas, J. and M. Olshaker. 1995. *Mindhunter*. New York: Pocket Books.

Douglas, J. and M. Olshaker. 1997. *Journey into Darkness: The FBI's Premier Investigator Penetrates the Minds and Motives of the Most Terrifying Serial Killers*. New York: Mindhunters.

Douglas, J. and M. Olshaker. 1998. *Obsession*. New York: Pocket Books.

Douglas, J. E., A. W. Burgess, A. G. Burgess, and R. Ressler. 1997. *Crime Classification Manual: A Standard System for Investigating and Classifying Violent Crimes*. San Francisco: Jossey-Bass.

Egan, T. 1989. After 7 years, a 'viable suspect' in murders of 48. *New York Times*, July 15, 6. Accessed July 17, 2008, from ProQuest Historical Newspapers, *The New York Times*.

Early tip fell short in Green River killings. 2003. *New York Times*, December 26, A30. Accessed July 17, 2008, from ProQuest Historical Newspapers, *The New York Times*.

Economy Fire and Casualty Company v. Betty Ann Haste, et. al., 824 S.W.2d41 (Mo. 1991).

Edward D. Cowart, 62, judge in Florida trial of Ted Bundy. 1987. *New York Times*, August 4, B9. Accessed July 17, 2008, from ProQuest Historical Newspapers, *The New York Times*.

Egger, S. A. 1984. A working definition of serial murder and the reduction of linkage blindness. *Journal of Police Science and Administration* 12:348–357.

———. 1998. *The Killers among Us: An Examination of Serial Murder and Its Investigation*. Upper Saddle River, NJ: Prentice-Hall.

Eschholz, S. and J. Bufkin. 2001. Crime in the movies: Investigating the efficacy of measures of both sex and gender for predicting victimization and offending in film. *Sociological Forum* 16(4):655–676.

Ewick, P. and S. S. Silbey. 1995. Subversive stories and hegemonic tales: Toward a sociology of narrative. *Law & Society Review* 29(2):197–226.

Ezekiel, R. S. 1995. *The Racist Mind: Portraits of American Neo-Nazis and Klansmen*. New York: Viking.

Ferber, A. L. 2004. Introduction. In *Home-Grown Hate: Gender and Organized Racism*, edited by A. L. Ferber, 1–18. New York: Routledge.

Ferber, A. L. and M. S. Kimmel. 2004. "White men are this nation": Right-wing militias and the restoration of rural American masculinity. In *Home-Grown Hate: Gender and Organized Racism*, edited by A. L. Ferber, 143–160. New York: Routledge.

Ferguson, C. J., D. E. White, S. Cherry, M. Lorenz, and Z. Bhimani. 2003. Defining and classifying serial murder in the context of perpetrator motivation. *Journal of Criminal Justice* 31:287–292.

Fine, G. A. and R. D. White. 2002. Cresting collective action in the public domain: Human interest narratives and the rescue of Floyd Collins. *Social Forces* 81(1):57–85.

Finkelhor, D. and S. Araji. 1986. Explanations of pedophilia: A four factor model. *The Journal of Sex Research* 22(2):145–161.

Focus: BTK killer a "monster" describes terror reign. 2005. *The Commercial Appeal*, August 18, A8. Accessed January 17, 2008, from Newsbank.

Former Los Angeles prosecutor Phil Halpin dies at 65. 2003. *Associated Press*, July 26. Accessed January 17, 2008, from Dow Jones Factiva.

Fox, J. A. and J. Levin. 1998. Multiple homicide: Patterns of serial and mass murder. *Crime and Justice* 23:407–455.

———. 2005. *Extreme Killing: Understanding Serial and Mass Murder*. Thousand Oaks, CA: Sage.

Fox, J. Alan, J. Levin, and K. Quinet. 2005. *The Will to Kill: Making Sense of Senseless Murder*. Boston: Pearson Education Group.

Francis, S. 1991. Brutal signs long ignored. *The Washington Times*, July 30, G1. Accessed January 17, 2008, from Dow Jones Factiva.

REFERENCES

Freund, K. and R. Watson. 1990. Mapping the boundaries of courtship disorder. *The Journal of Sex Research* 27(4):589–606.

Freund, K., R. Watson, R. Dickey, and D. Rienzo. 1991. Erotic gender differentiation in pedophilia. *Archives of Sexual Behavior* 20(6):555–566.

Fritsch, J. 1980. Gacy called "worst of all murderers." *Chicago Tribune*, March 12, 1. Accessed July 17, 2008, from ProQuest Historical Newspapers, *Chicago Tribune*.

Fryer, A. and C. M. Ostrom. 2001. Cost of trying Ridgway likely in the millions. *The Seattle Times*, December 8. Accessed October 30, 2010. http://community.seattletimes.nwsource.com/archive/?date=20011208&slug=cost08m0.

Garfinkel, H. 1949. Research notes on inter- and intra-racial homicides. *Social Forces* 27(4):369–381.

Gilliem, J. 2001. Murders have dogged Seattle police for decades. *Scripps Howard News Service*, November 30. Accessed January 17, 2008, from Newsbank.

Gilligan, J. 1996. *Violence: Our Deadly Epidemic and Its Causes*. New York: Putnam.

Gniewek, D. and N. Moore. 2006. *True Crime Resources*. American Library Association. http://www.ala.org/ala/aasl/aaslpubsandjournals/kqweb/kqarchives/volume35/351gniewekmoore.htm.

Godwin, M. 1998. Victim target networks as solvability factors in serial murder. *Social Behavior and Personality* 26(1):75–84.

Goldsworthy, T. 2006. Serial rape: An investigative approach. In *Serial Crime: Theoretical and Practical Issues in Behavioral Profiling*, edited by W. Petherick, 161–188. London: Academic Press.

Goode, W. J. 1978. *The Celebration of Heroes: Prestige as a Control System*. Los Angeles: University of California Press.

Gorman, J. 1979. Gacy seized year ago but freed, record show. *Chicago Tribune*, January 7, 22. Accessed July 17, 2008, from ProQuest Historical Newspapers, *Chicago Tribune*.

Graham, H. D. 1970. The paradox of American violence: A historical appraisal. *Annals of the American Academy of Political and Social Science* 391:74–82.

Griffin, L. J. 1993. Narrative, event-structure analysis, and causal interpretation in historical sociology. *The American Journal of Sociology* 98(5):1094–1133.

Grover, C. and K. Soothill. 1999. British serial killing: Towards a structural explanation. *The British Criminology Conferences: Selected Proceedings Volume 2*. Belfast, Ireland: British Society of Criminology.

Guillén, T. 2007. *Serial Killers: Issues Explored through the Green River Murders*. Upper Saddle River, NJ: Pearson Prentice Hall.

Hall, S. 1975. Introduction. In *Paper Voices: The Popular Press and Social Change, 1935–1965*, edited by A. C. H. Smith, 11–24. Totowa, NJ: Rowman and Littlefield.

———. 1997. Introduction. In *Representation: Cultural Representations and Signifying Practices*, edited by S. Hall, 1–11. Thousand Oaks, CA: Sage.

Harbort, S. and A. Mokros. 2001. Serial murderers in Germany from 1945 to 1995. *Homicide Studies* 5(4):311–334.

Harvey, J. H. 1996. *Embracing Their Memory: Loss and the Social Psychology of Storytelling*. Needham Heights, MA: Allyn & Bacon.

Hatty, S. E. 2000. *Masculinities, Violence, and Culture*. Thousand Oaks, CA: Sage.

Hegeman, R. 2005. Details of killer's brutality emerge. *Ventura County Star*, August 18, 10. Accessed January 17, 2008, from Newsbank.

Heide, K. M. and B. T. Keeney. 1994. Gender differences in serial murderers: A preliminary analysis. *The Journal of Interpersonal Violence* 9:383–398.

Henderson, L. 1992. Rape and responsibility. *Law and Philosophy* 11(1/2):127–178.

Henson, K. D. and J. K. Rogers. 2001. "Why Marcia you've changed!" Male clerical temporary workers doing masculinity in a feminized occupation. *Gender and Society* 15(2):218–238.

Hickey, E. W. 2006. *Serial Murderers and Their Victims*. Belmont, CA: Thomson Wadsworth.

Hodgskiss, B. 2004. Lessons from serial murder in South Africa. *Journal of Investigative Psychology and Offender Profiling* 1(1):67–94.

Hollander, J. A. and H. R. Gordon. 2006. The processes of social construction in talk. *Symbolic Interaction* 29(2):183–212.

Hollingshead, A. B. 1975. Four factor index of social status. New Haven, CT. Unpublished manuscript. Accessed February 17, 2009, from http://www.yale.edu/sociology/faculty/docs/hollingshead_socStat4factor.pdf.

Holmes, R. M. 1985. Profiles in terror: The serial murderer. *Federal Probation* 44(3):29–34.

Holmes, R. M. and J. De Burger. 1988. *Serial Murder*. Newbury Park, CA: Sage.

Holmes, R. M. and S. T. Holmes. 2002. *Profiling Violent Crimes: An Investigative Tool*. Thousand Oaks, CA: Sage.

Holmes, S. T., R. Tewksbury, and R. M. Holmes. 1999. Fractured identity syndrome: A new theory of serial murder. *Journal of Contemporary Criminal Justice* 15(3):262–272.

Inglis, D. 2005. *Culture and Everyday Life*. New York: Routledge.

Irvine, L. and B. Klocke. 2001. Redefining men: Alternative masculinities in a twelve-step program. *Men and Masculinities* 4(1):27–48.

Jackman, T. and T. Cole. 1992. *Rites of Burial*. New York: Pinnacle Books.

James, O. 1995. *Juvenile Violence in a Winner-Loser Culture: Socio-Economic and Familial Origins of the Rise in Violence Against the Person*. New York: Free Association Books.

Jenkins, P. 1994. *Using Murder: The Social Construction of Serial Homicide*. New York: de Gruyter.

Johnson, A. G. 2006. *Privilege, Power, and Difference*. New York: McGraw-Hill.

Johnson, G. 2003. Man confesses to 48 killings. *The Cincinnati Post*, November 6, A2. Accessed January 17, 2008, from Newsbank.

Jourard, S. M. 1971. *The Transparent Self*. New York: Litton Educational.

Judge formally sentences serial killer to death. 2006. *Associated Press*, March 7. Accessed January 15, 2008, from Dow Jones Factiva.

Katz, J. 1988. *Seductions of Crime: Moral and Sensual Attractions in Doing Evil*. New York: Basic Books.

Kaufman, M. 1997. The construction of masculinity and the triad of men's violence. In *Gender Violence: Interdisciplinary Perspectives*, edited by L. O'Toole and J. R. Schiffman, 30–51. New York: New York University Press.

Kemp, L. 1982. Florida killer's toll may be a record 39. *Chicago Tribune*, October 13, A5. Accessed July 17, 2008, from ProQuest Historical Newspapers, *Chicago Tribune*.

Kershaw, S. 2003. New discoveries move Green River case to fore again. *New York Times*, September 22, A10. Accessed July 17, 2008, from ProQuest Historical Newspapers, *The New York Times*.

King, W. 1982. Suspect in Texas slaying was under police surveillance in 2 states. *New York Times*, August 12, A20. Accessed July 17, 2008, from ProQuest Historical Newspapers, *The New York Times*.

Klapp, O. E. 1972. *Heroes, Villains and Fools: Reflections of the American Character*. San Diego, CA: Aegis.

Kocsis, R. N., A. F. Hayes, and H. J. Irwin. 2002. Investigative experience and accuracy in psychological profiling of a violent crime. *Journal of Interpersonal Violence* 17(8):811–823.

Kraemer, J. D., W. D. Lord, and K. Heilbrun. 2004. Comparing single and serial homicide offenses. *Behavioral Sciences and the Law* 22:325–343.

Lane, R. 1997. *Murder in America: A History*. Columbus, OH: Ohio State University Press.

Langbein, S. 2006. Profilers wary of murder claims; Experts: Professed serial killers often exaggerate claims. *Rocky Mountain News*, August 1, 19A. Accessed January 17, 2008, from Newsbank.

Lee, R. A. 1988. A motive for murder. *Police Times* July/August:6.

Lehmann, W. 2005. Choosing to labour: Structure and agency in school-work transitions. *Canadian Journal of Sociology* 30(3):325–350.

Levi-Minzi, M. and M. Shields. 2007. Serial sexual murderers and prostitutes as their victims: Difficulty profiling perpetrators and victim vulnerability as illustrated by the Green River case. *Brief Treatment and Crisis Intervention* 7(1):77–89.

Levin, J. 2008. *Serial Killers and Sadistic Murderers: Up Close and Personal*. Amherst, NY: Prometheus Books.

Levin, J. and J. Fox. 2007. Normalcy in behavioral characteristics of the sadistic serial killer. In *Serial Murder and the Psychology of Violent Crimes*, edited by R. N. Kocsis, 3–14. Totowa, NJ: Humana Press.

Lewis, N. D. C. and Yarnell, H. 1951. Pathological firesetting (pyromania). In *Nervous and Mental Disease Monographs*, Monograph No. 82. New York: Coolidge Foundation.

Leyton, E. 1986. *Hunting Humans: The Rise of the Modern Multiple Murderer*. Toronto, Ontario, Canada: McClelland and Stewart.

Lieberson, S. 2000. *A Matter of Taste: How Names, Fashions, and Culture Change*. New Haven, CT: Yale University Press.

Lloyd-Goldstein, R. 2000. Serial stalkers: Recent clinical findings. In *Serial Offenders: Current Thought, Recent Findings*, edited by L. B. Schlesinger, 167–185. Boca Raton, FL: CRC Press.

Long, W. R. 2002. A time to kill? Reflections on the Oregon death penalty. *The Oregon State Bar Bulletin* 62:9.

Lule, J. 2001. *Daily News, Eternal Stories: The Mythological Role of Journalism*. New York: Guilford Press.

Lundrigan, S. and D. Canter. 2001. Spatial patterns of serial murder: An analysis of disposal site location choice. *Behavioral Sciences and the Law* 19(4):595–610.

Lyng, S. 1990. Edgework: A social psychological analysis of voluntary risk taking. *The American Journal of Sociology* 95(4):851–886.

———, ed. 2005. *Edgework: The Sociology of Risk-taking*. New York: Routledge.

Madriz, E. I. 1997. Images of criminals and victims: A study on women's fear and social control. *Gender and Society* 11(3):342–356.

Madsen, D. L. 1998. *American Exceptionalism*. Jackson, MS: University Press of Mississippi.

Maines, D. R. 1993. Narrative's moment and sociology's phenomena: Toward a narrative sociology. *The Sociological Quarterly* 34(1):17–38.

———. 1999. Information pools and racialized narrative structures. *The Sociological Quarterly* 40(2):317–326.

———. 2000. The social construction of meaning. *Contemporary Sociology* 29(4):577–584.

Maines, D. R. and J. T. Ulmer. 1993. The relevance of narrative for interactionist thought. *Studies in Symbolic Interaction* 14:109–124.

Makeig, J. 1992. Serial killer is sentenced to die by injection; Louisiana man has now been formally charged with five murders. *Houston Chronicle*, May 7, 29. Accessed January 17, 2008, from Dow Jones Factiva.

Martingale, M. 1993. *Cannibal Killers*. New York: Carroll & Graf.

Mavromatis, M. 2000. Serial arson: Repetitive firesetting and pyromania. In *Serial Offenders: Current Thought, Recent Findings*, edited by L. B. Schlesinger, 67–101. Boca Raton, FL: CRC Press.

McAdams, D. P. 2001. The psychology of life stories. *Review of General Psychology* 5(2):100–122.

McNeil, E. 1983. Body identified as uptown boy. *Chicago Tribune*, November 15, N1. Accessed July 17, 2008, from ProQuest Historical Newspapers, *Chicago Tribune*.

Messerschmidt, J. W. 1993. *Masculinities and Crime: Critique and Reconceptualization of Theory*. Lanham, MD: Rowman & Littlefield.

Messner, M. A. 1992. *Power at Play: Sports and the Problem of Masculinity*. Boston: Beacon Press.

Messner, S. F. and R. Rosenfeld. 2001. *Crime and the American Dream*, 3rd ed. Toronto, Ontario, Canada: Wadsworth Group.

Michaud, S. G. and H. Aynesworth. 2000. *The Only Living Witness: The True Story of Serial Sex Killer Ted Bundy*. Irving, TX: Authorlink Press.

Miller, W. J. 2005. Adolescents on the edge: The sensual side of delinquency. In *Edgework: The Sociology of Risk-Taking*, edited by S. Lyng, 153–171. New York: Routledge.

Milovanovic, D. 2005. Edgework: A subjective and structural model of negotiating boundaries. In *Edgework: The Sociology of Risk-Taking*, edited by S. Lyng, 51–72. New York: Routledge.

REFERENCES

Mladinich, R. 2001. *From the Mouth of the Monster: The Joel Rifkin Story*. New York: Pocket Books.

Morton, R. J. and M. A. Hilts, ed. 2008. Serial murder: Multi-disciplinary perspectives for investigators. Behavioral Analysis Unit, National Center for the Analysis of Violent Crime. Accessed September 17, 2010, from http://www.fbi.gov/publications/serial_murder.htm.

Mott, N. L. 1999. Serial murder: Patterns in unsolved cases. *Homicide Studies* 3(3):241–255.

Mount, C. E., Jr. 1981. American individualism reconsidered. *Review of Religious Research* 22(4):362–376.

Myers, W. C. 2004. Serial murder by children and adolescents. *Behavioral Sciences and the Law* 22:357–374.

Myers, W. C., E. Gooch, and J. R. Meloy. 2005. The role of psychopathy and sexuality in a female serial killer. *Journal of Forensic Sciences* 50(3):652–657.

Myers, W. C., D. S. Husted, M. E. Safarik, and M. E. O'Toole. 2006. The motivation behind serial sexual homicide: Is it sex, power, and control, or anger? *Journal of Forensic Science* 51(4):900–907.

National Institute of Justice. 2002. Preventing school shootings: A summary of a U.S. Secret Service Safe School Initiative report. *NIJ Journal* 248:11–15. Accessed February 27, 2011 from http://www.ncjrs.gov/pdffiles1/jr000248c.pdf.

Nesbitt, J. 2005. Women who kill are rare group. *Evansville Courier & Press*, October 19, A1. Accessed January 17, 2008, from Newsbank.

Newton, M. 1991. *Hunting Humans: An Encyclopedia of Modern Serial Killers*. Port Washington, WA: Loompanics Unlimited.

———. 1994. *Silent Rage: The 30-Year Odyssey of a Serial Killer*. New York: Dell.

Nordheimer, J. 1978. All-American boy on trial. *New York Times*, December 10, SM24. Accessed July 17, 2008, from ProQuest Historical Newspapers, *The New York Times*.

Ochs, E. and L. Capps. 1996. Narrating the self. *Annual Review of Anthropology* 25:19–43.

Olsen, J. 2002. *"I" The Creation of a Serial Killer*. New York: St. Martin's Press.

Palmer, C. T. and R. Thornhill. 2000. Serial rape: An evolutionary perspective. In *Serial Offenders: Current Thought, Recent Findings*, edited by L. B. Schlesinger, 51–65. Boca Raton, FL: CRC Press.

The People v. Richard Ramirez, LEXIS 8638 (Cal. 2006).

Photo: Serial killer Aileen Wuornos. 2001. *Naples Daily News*, July 21, D7. Accessed January 17, 2008, from Newsbank.

Police probers add to list of "Green River" killings. 1984. *Washington Post*, November 18, A20. Accessed July 17, 2008, from ProQuest Historical Newspapers, *The Washington Post*.

Powell, D. 2000. Can't get away from Ted Bundy; long-dead serial killer still plays a part in true-crime writer's life. *The Commercial Appeal*, November 9, F1. Accessed January 17, 2008, from Newsbank.

Protection of Children from Sexual Predators Act of 1998, Pub. L. no. 105-314, H. R. 3494 (1998). Accessed February 27, 2011 from http://www.gpo.gov/fdsys/pkg/BILLS-105hr3494enr/pdf/BILLS-105hr3494enr.pdf.

Prothero, M. and C. Smith. 2006. *Defending Gary: Unraveling the Mind of the Green River Killer*. San Francisco, CA: Jossey-Bass.

Ramsland, K. 2006. *Inside the Minds of Serial Killers: Why They Kill*. Westport, CT: Praeger.

———. n.d. Criminal profiling: Part 1, history and method. truTV Crime Library. Accessed October 29, 2010, from http://www.trutv.com/library/crime/serial_killers/predators/baton_rouge/6.html.

———. n.d. The profile evaluated. truTV Crime Library. Accessed October 29, 2010, from http://www.trutv.com/library/crime/criminal_mind/profiling/history_method/index.html.

———. n.d. Serial killer art. truTV Crime Library. Accessed October 29, 2010, from http://www.trutv.com/library/crime/criminal_mind/psychology/serial_killer_art/index.html.

Ramsland, K. and K. Pepper. N.d. Serial killer culture. truTV Crime Library. Accessed October 29, 2010, from http://www.trutv.com/library/crime/criminal_mind/psychology/s_k_culture/3.html.

Reisman, D. 1967. Some questions about the study of American character in the twentieth century. *Annals of the American Academy of Political and Social Science* 370:36–47.

Ressler, R. K., A. W. Burgess, and J. E. Douglas. 1992. *Sexual Homicide: Patterns and Motives*. New York: Free Press.

Ressler, R. K. and T. Schachtman. 1992. *Whoever Fights Monsters*. New York: St. Martin's Press.

Ressler, R. K. and T. Schachtman. 1997. *I Have Lived in the Monster*. New York: St. Martin's Press.

Rhodes, R. 1999. *Why They Kill: The Discoveries of a Maverick Criminologist*. New York: Vintage Books.

Rossides, D. W. 2003. *Communication, Media, and American Society: A Critical Introduction*. Lanham, MD: Rowman & Littlefield.

Rowley, S. 1980. Gacy horror grips two more families. *Chicago Tribune*, March 11, 3. Accessed July 17, 2008, from ProQuest Historical Newspapers, *Chicago Tribune*.

Rule, A. 2000. *The Stranger Beside Me*. New York: W.W. Norton & Company. First published 1980 by W.W. Norton & Company.

Rule, A. 2004. *Green River Running Red*. New York: Free Press.

Samenow, S. E. 2004. *Inside the Criminal Mind*. New York: Crown.

Sathiparsad, R. 2008. Developing alternative masculinities as a strategy to address gender-based violence. *International Social Work* 51(3):348–359.

Savran, D. 1998. *Taking It Like a Man*. Princeton, NJ: Princeton University Press.

Schechter, H. and D. Everitt. 1997. *The A to Z Encyclopedia of Serial Killers*. New York: Pocket Books.

Schemo, D. J. 1993. Police list items from search of home of suspect in killings. *New York Times*, July 13, B5. Accessed July 15, 2008, from ProQuest Historical Newspapers, *The New York Times*.

Schlesinger, L. B. 2000. Serial burglary: Spectrum of behaviors, motives, and dynamics. In *Serial Offenders: Current Thought, Recent Findings*, edited by L. B. Schlesinger, 187–206. Boca Raton, FL: CRC Press.

Schlesinger, L. B. and E. Revitch. 1999. Sexual burglaries and sexual homicide. *Journal of the American Academy of Psychiatry and Law* 27:227–238.

Schmid, D. 2005. *Natural Born Celebrities: Serial Killers in American Culture*. Chicago: University of Chicago Press.

Schudson, M. 1989. How culture works: Perspectives from media studies on the efficacy of symbols. *Theory and Society* 18(2):153–180.

Seltzer, M. 1995. Serial killers (II): The pathological public sphere. *Critical Inquiry* 22:122–149.

Sheffield, C. J. 2004. Sexual terrorism: The social control of women. In *Oppression, Privilege, and Resistance: Theoretical Perspectives on Racism, Sexism, and Heterosexism*, edited by L. Heldke and P. O'Connor, 164–182. New York: McGraw-Hill.

Shipley, S. L. and B. A. Arrigo. 2004. *The Female Homicide Offender: Serial Murder and the Case of Aileen Wuornos*. Upper Saddle River, NJ: Pearson Prentice Hall.

Sieber, S. D. 2005. *Second-Rate Nation: From the American Dream to the American Myth*. Boulder, CO: Paradigm.

Silvio, H., K. McCloskey, and J. Ramos-Grenier. 2006. Theoretical consideration of female sexual predator serial killers in the United States. *Journal of Criminal Justice* 34:251–259.

Singer, S. D. and C. Hensley. 2004. Applying social learning theory to childhood and adolescent firesetting: Can it lead to serial murder? *International Journal of Offender Therapy and Comparative Criminology* 48(4):461–476.

Skilling, T. A., G. T. Harris, M. E. Rice, and V. L. Quinsey. 2002. Identifying persistently antisocial offenders using the Hare Psychopathy Checklist and *DSM* antisocial personality disorder criteria. *Psychological Assessment* 14(1):27–38.

Skrapec, C. A. 2001. Phenomenology and serial murder. *Homicide Studies* 5(1):46–63.

Slotkin, R. 1992. *Gunfighter Nation: The Myth of the Frontier in Twentieth-Century America*. New York: Harper Perennial.

Smith, C. 2006. *The BTK Murders: Inside the "Bind, Torture, Kill" Case that Terrified American's Heartland*. New York: St. Martin's Press.

Smith, C. and T. Guillen. 2004. *The Search for the Green River Killer: The True Story of America's Most Wanted Serial Killer*. New York: New American Library. First published 1991 by Onyx.

Smith, G. D. and H. P. M. Winchester. 1998. Negotiating space: Alternative masculinities at the work/home boundary. *Australian Geographer* 29(3):327–339.

Snook, B., D. Canter, and C. Bennell. 2002. Predicting the home location of serial offenders: A preliminary comparison of the accuracy of human judges with a geographic profiling system. *Behavioral Sciences and the Law* 20:109–118.

Stanley, L. 1993. The knowing because experiencing subject: Narratives, lives, and autobiography. *Women's Studies International Forum* 16(3):205–215.
The State of Kansas v. Dennis L. Rader. Transcript of pleas of guilty. District Court, Sedgwick County, Kansas Criminal Department, Case No. 05 CR 498.
State of Washington v. Gary Leon Ridgway. Statement of defendant on plea of guilty. Superior Court of Washington for King County, Cause No. 01-1-10270-9 SEA.
Stingl, J. 1992. Unusual security for unusual trial. *The Milwaukee Journal Sentinel*, January 12, B1. Accessed January 17, 2008, from Dow Jones Factiva.
Swidler, A. 1998. Culture and social action. In *The New American Cultural Sociology*, edited by P. Smith, 171–187. Cambridge, UK: Cambridge University Press.
Today in history. 1997. *The Stuart News*, January 27, A2. Accessed January 17, 2008, from Newsbank.
Torres, A. N., M. T. Boccaccini, and H. A. Miller. 2006. Perceptions of the validity and utility of criminal profiling among forensic psychologists and psychiatrists. *Professional Psychology: Research and Practice* 37(1):51–58.
Turner, W. 1987. Search for killer of 37 in Seattle area cut back. *New York Times*, July 7, A14. Accessed July 17, 2008, from ProQuest Historical Newspapers, *The New York Times*.
Turvey, B. 1999. *Criminal Profiling: An Introduction to Behavioral Evidence Analysis.* San Diego, CA: Academic Press.
Umberson, D., K. L. Anderson, K. Williams, and M. D. Chen. 2003. Relationship dynamics, emotional state, and domestic violence: A stress and masculinities perspective. *Journal of Marriage and Family* 65:233–247.
United States of America, ex rel. John Gacy N-00921 v. George Welborn, Warden, Menard Correctional Center, and Roland W. Burris, Attorney General of the State of Illinois, LEXIS 12498 (U.S. Dist. 1992).
U.S. Census Bureau. 2000. Census 2000. Accessed February 17, 2009 from http://www.census.gov/main/www/cen2000.html.
U.S. Census Bureau, *Housing and Household Economic Statistics Division*. 2008. Income inequality (middle class)—narrative. Accessed February 17, 2009 from http://www.census.gov/hhes/www/income/midclass/midclsan.html.
U.S. Department of Justice. 2006. Homicide trends in the U.S. Accessed February 17, 2009 from http://www.ojp.usdoj.gov/bjs/homicide/gender.htm.
U.S. Department of Justice. 2006. Homicide trends in the U.S. Accessed February 17, 2009 from http://www.ojp.usdoj.gov/bjs/homicide/race.htm.
Vecchi, G. M. 2009. The FBI Behavioral Science Unit's Evil Minds Research Museum. *Annals of the American Psychotherapy Association* 12(4):14–15.
Vronsky, P. 2004. *Serial Killers: The Method and Madness of Monsters.* New York: Berkley.
———. 2007. *Female Serial Killers: How and Why Women Become Monsters.* New York: Penguin Group.

Walsh, A. 2005. African Americans and serial killing in the media: The myth and the reality. *Homicide Studies* 9(4):271–291.
Warren, J., R. Hazelwood, and P. E. Dietz. 1996. The sexually sadistic serial killer. *Journal of Forensic Science* 41:970–974.
West, C. and D. H. Zimmerman. 1987. Doing gender. *Gender and Society* 1(2):125–151.
Wiest, J. B. 2009. Creating cultural monsters: A critical analysis of the representation of serial murderers in America. PhD diss., University of Tennessee.
Wille, W. S. 1975. *Citizens Who Commit Murder: A Psychiatric Study*. St. Louis, MO: Green.
Williams, R. M., Jr. 1962. Are Americans and their cultural values adaptable to the concept and techniques of unconventional warfare? *Annals of the American Academy of Political and Social Science* 341:82–92.
Wilson, D. 2007a. *Serial Killers: Hunting Britons and Their Victims 1960–2006*. Hampshire, UK: Waterside Press.
Wilson, D. 2007b. Why serial killers find it so easy to evade blinkered police forces; trail of a killer. *The Times*, November 20, 23. Accessed January 16, 2008, from Dow Jones Factiva.
Woman described as killer like Bundy. 1998. *The Stuart News*, August 7, A5. Accessed January 17, 2008, from Newsbank.
Woodworth, M. and S. Porter. 1999. Historical foundations and current applications of criminal profiling in violent crime investigations. *Expert Evidence* 7:241–264.
Wuthnow, R., J. D. Hunter, A. Bergesen, and E. Kurzweil. 1984. *Cultural Analysis: The Work of Peter L. Berger, Mary Douglas, Michel Foucault and Jurgen Habermas*. Boston: Routledge & Kegan Paul.
Wyre, R. and T. Tate. 1995. *The Murder of Childhood: Inside the Mind of One of Britain's Most Notorious Child Murderers*. London: Penguin Books.
Young, J. 1999. *The Exclusive Society: Social Exclusion, Crime and Difference in Late Modernity*. London: Sage.
Young, R. L. 1985. Perceptions of crime, racial attitudes, and firearms ownership. *Social Forces* 64(2):473–486.
Zimbardo, P. 2007. *The Lucifer Effect: Understanding How Good People Turn Evil*. New York: Random House.
Zuo, J. and S. Tang. 2000. Breadwinner status and gender ideologies of men and women regarding family roles. *Sociological Perspectives* 43(1):29–43.

Index

A

A to Z Encyclopedia of Serial Killers, 166
Abu Ghraib prisoner abuses, 84
Abusive parents, 14, 44, 60, 61, 82, 174, 179–180
Academic research, 25
   differences from mass media portrayals, 37, 44
   disagreements with FBI techniques, 24
   individual focus, 25
   need for cooperation with FBI profilers, 17
   prominent researchers, 26
   psychology focus, 25
Adolescent serial murderers, 48
Adoption, 61, 75
African American serial murderers, 64, 132, 155
   increases in, 64
   reasons for underrepresentation, 66–67

Age
   at first killing, 46, 48, 50, 52, 60, 62, 67, 68, 174, 179–180
   of serial murderers, 45
Aggression, 117
   demonstrating masculinity through, 116
Alcohol, as facilitator, 81
Algorithms, criminal profiling via, 35
Alternative masculinities, 115, 116
American culture
   applying model of, 107
   contextual cultural values, 107–121
   and creation of serial murderers, 108
   critique, 153
   dominant values, 104
   emphasis on white, male serial murderers, 4
   exceptionalism and violence, 159
   exclusionary nature of, 161

fostering of serial murder by, 87, 153, 163, 165
and incidence of serial murder, 1
income disparity and crime, 160–161
model, 102, 103, 105
and overrepresentation of men in serial murder, 165
responsibility for serial murder, xi
white male serial murderers and, 163
Anniversary stories, 134
Anonymity, in urban life, 108
Artifacts, 96. *See also* Murderabilia
Atlanta Child Killer, 14, 64
Attachment theory, 82
Authority
American aversion to, 111
and hegemonic masculinity, 113

B

Bates, Norman, true-life sources, 46
Baton Rouge Serial Killer, 16
Behavioral analysis, academic researcher expertise in, 17
Behavioral Analysis Unit--East/West Regions, 11
Behavioral perspective, 13
Behavioral Science Instruction, 11
Behavioral Science Research, 11
Behavioral Science Unit, 11
Evil Minds Research Museum, 97
Beheading, 69
Berdella, Robert, 144, 168
anniversary stories, 134
challenges to masculinity, 145
data sources, 178
media portrayals, 156
number of media articles, 125
power through killing, 148
predictors of media coverage, 128
profile, 46–47
social status, 127
Berkowitz, David, 106
Biographical narratives, 164, 169–170
Biological explanations, 3, 81, 86
Bisexuality, 50
Black, Robert, 144, 147, 168
boasting behavior, 143
challenges to masculinity, 145
data sources, 178
number of media articles, 125
predictors of media coverage, 128
profile, 75–76
social status, 127
Black-on-black crime, 66
Boasting behaviors, 141–142
Body disposal sites, identifying motives through, 83
Bonnie and Clyde, 110, 141
Broadcasting
anniversary stories, 134
crime representations, 121–123
of cultural values, 107, 121–139
initial reports, 128–130
media coverage model, 123–126
missing victims, 134–135
narrative structure, 126, 128
need to know why, 131–134
notoriety, 130–131
record setting, 130–131
social typing in, 136–139
Brussel, James A., 11
BTK Killer, xi, 1, 52, 53, 129
Buffalo Bill character, 46
Bundy, Carol M., profile, 69–70
Bundy, Ted, xi, 1, 27, 39, 44, 77, 138, 150, 168–169
boasting behavior, 141–142, 143
challenges to masculinity, 145
data sources, 178
escape from Pitkin County Courthouse, 41

FBI photo, Most Wanted
   Fugitives list, 40
Florida mug shot, 41
media attention quest, 93
media coverage, 124
murderabilia, 96
number of media articles, 125
postmortem celebrity, 94
predictors of media coverage, 128
profile, 40, 42
risk taking, 147
social status, 127, 156
socially valued goals, 140
Burgess, Ann, 11

C

Cannibalism, 45, 46, 74
Carlo, Philip, 27
Carpenter, David, 14
Cassidy, Butch, 110
Cat-and-mouse games, with law
   enforcement, 44
Celebrity status, 3, 183
   acknowledgment by courts, 94
   of serial murderers, 92–95
   serial murderers' search for,
      93–94, 159
   social need for, 92
   valuation in American culture,
      109
Chikatilo, Andrei, profile, 74–75
Child Abduction Serial Murder
   Investigative Resources
   Center, 11
Child care workers, as serial
   murderers, 165
Child molestation, 45
Childhood symptoms, 61
Childhood trauma, 37
Children
   as sexual objects, 73
   as victims, 30, 40, 73, 74, 76

Cho, Seung-Hui, 31
Clark, David, 69, 70
Classification systems, 15
   for sexual homicide, 16
Close relationships, 67, 170, 173,
   174, 181–182
   difficulties in, 44, 49, 50, 61, 62,
      66, 68, 76, 145–146
Coding
   categories, 174–175
   of themes, 164
Coed Killer, 48
Cole, Carroll Edward, 124, 168
   data sources, 178
   enjoyment of horror shows, 141
   media attention quest, 93
   media coverage, 161
   motives, 146
   number of media articles, 125
   predictors of media coverage,
      128
   profile, 59–60
   social status, 127
Collector, The, 141
Communication
   increasing among researchers,
      153
   lack of, between law enforcement
      agencies, 10
Community leadership, 144
Compartmentalization, 83
Competition, 108, 153
   as cultural value, 109–111
   male rewards for, 112
   serial murderers' valuation of,
      141–143
Computer modeling, 11
Conde, Rory, 68
Confessions, 164, 174, 178
   official, 172–173
Confluence-of-components theory,
   86
Conscience, in serial murderers, 82

Control, 3, 151, 175
    achieving through serial murder, 159
    as cultural value, 120–121
    and edgework, 118
    male preoccupation with, 120
    need for, 79
    through edgework, 119
    valuation by serial murderers, 147–149
    in white supremacy movement, 79
Cooling-off period, 32
Copycat, 37
Copycat effect, 159
Corona, Juan, 68
Corrupt heroes, 175
Corruption, by social system, 85
Court cases, 164, 172, 178
    transcripts, 185
Court TV, 183
Crawford, Jack, 12
Crime
    and income disparity, 160–161
    media construction of, 122
    newsworthiness, 122
    seduction of, 117, 118
Crime characteristics, identifying, 13–14
Crime Library by TruTV, 169, 170, 173, 178
Crime representations, by mass media, 121–123
Crime scene evidence, 13
    photographic, 13
Criminal experience, 175
    as cultural value, 117
    understanding, 118
    valuation by serial murderers, 146
Criminal profiling, xi, 10. *See also* Profiling
    1980s successes, 16
    creators of, 13
    and development of typologies, 15
    disputes over utility, 24
    failures, 16
    future considerations, 158
    glamour accorded to, 158
    identifying motive via, 83
Criminals, mass media portrayals, 122–123
Critical Incident Report Group (CIRG), 25
CSI: Crime Scene Investigation, 39
Cultural analysis, aims, 164
Cultural blindness, 5
Cultural competencies, 101–104
    killers' understanding of, 173
    and selection of cultural values, 103
    variations in, 105, 107
Cultural competency filter, 102, 103
Cultural context, 91, 100–106, 105. *See also* Sociocultural context
    broadcasting culture, 101
    cultural competencies, 101–104
    and cultural values, 103
    and lines of action, 104–106
Cultural expectations, violation of, 151
Cultural messages
    broadcasting by mass media, 101
    enhancing reception, 136
    inconsistencies, 105
    tuning in to, 139–150
Cultural monsters, 92. *See also* Monsters
Cultural objects
    five dimensions, 102
    shared meanings about, 100
Cultural records, 164
Cultural values, 150
    American, 104

building lines of action with, 150–151
competition, 109–111
contextual features for serial murder, 107–108
criminal experience, 117
dependence on cultural competencies, 103
dominant, 104
individual accomplishment, 109–111
killers' acceptance of, 139–150, 174
killers' use of nondivergent, 107
lines of action for realizing, 104
masculinities, 111–117
media broadcasting, 121–139
murderers' thoughts on, 173
power and control, 120–121
privilege, 111–117
regard for violence, 108–109
risk taking, 118–120
selective attention to, 102
thrill seeking, 118–120
tuned in and utilized, 174–175
violation of, 136
Culturally familiar imagery, killers' use of, 149–150
Culture. *See also* American culture
broadcasting, 101, 102
discounting in research, 83
influence on serial murder, 3, 100
operational model, 4
patriarchal, 86
serial murder and, 3

D

Dahmer, Jeffrey Lionel, xi, 1, 48, 73, 168
characterization of victims, 134
court-acknowledged celebrity, 94–95

data sources, 178
media blame, 132
media coverage, 124
media descriptions, 130
media portrayals, 156
number of media articles, 125
postapprehension nickname, 129
predictors of media coverage, 128
profile, 48–49
risk taking, 147
shock factor, 126
social status, 127
Data collection, 13
Data sources, 169, 178
biographical narratives, 169–170
court cases, 172
legal journal articles, 172
newspaper articles, 170–172
official confessions, 172–173
De Burger, James, 26
Death, social need for representations of, 92
Defense claims, 173
Dehumanization, 108
of enemies, 160
historical examples, 160
of victims, 63, 82, 135, 160
Depp, Johnny, 96
Detection
ability to avoid, 61
avoiding via impression management, 84
Deviant behavior
circumstances legitimizing, 108
as path to achieve social goods, 158
Dexter Morgan character, 40
Dominance, 3
Doss, Nannie, 70
Douglas, John, 11, 12
Dragnet, 25, 84
Drifters, serial murderers as, 37
Dropout status, 47–48, 59, 61, 67, 68

Drowning, 67
Drug addicts, as victims, 47
Drug injections, 46
    by female serial murderers, 71, 72
Drugs, as facilitators, 81
Durousseau, Paul, 64–65
    mug shot, 65
Dysfunctional childhood, 82

E

Earl Brooks character, 40
Edgework, 117–118, 119, 147
    male preoccupation with, 120
Egger, Steven A., 26
Elderly, as victims, 30, 33
Emotional cooling-off period, 32
Employment history, 16, 17, 42, 49, 52, 59, 66, 67, 68, 69, 74, 76, 144, 170, 174, 179–180
    of identified serial murderers, 49
    in serial stalkers, 78
England, 75
    cultural differences from U.S., 76
    serial murders in, 73
Entitlement, in white males, 112
Enuresis, in history of serial killers, 61
Environmental factors, 81, 85
Equal opportunity, 161
Ethnicity
    response to cultural messages, 105
    of serial killers, 176–177
Europe, serial murders in, 73
Evil Minds Research Museum, 97
Exceptionalism, in American culture, 159
Explanations
    biological, 81
    psychological, 82–84
    for serial murder, 81
    social psychological, 84–85
    sociocultural context, 86–87
    sociological, 85–86

F

Facilitators, 81
Failures, 174
    perceived, 170, 173
    types of, 181–182
Fair fights, *vs.* unfair fights, 108–109
Fame, 3
    15 minutes of, 109–110
    achieving through serial murder, 159
    American striving for, 104
    as cultural value, 151
    desire for, 79, 170, 173
    serial murder as path to, 120
Family history, 60
Family members, as victims, 70, 72, 166
Fan clubs, of serial murder topics, 91
Farley, Richard, 30
FBI agents, as all-American heroes, 12
FBI headquarters, 10
FBI representations, 44
    differences from popular representations, 37
Federal Bureau of Investigation (FBI), 5, 9
    claims to authority, 10
    development of serial murder definitions, 154, 165
Fetishism, 60
Fiction
    cat-and-mouse games in, 44
    celebration of serial murder in, 91
    roots of profiling in, 11
    serial murder representations in, 39
Financial gain, as motive, 71, 72

Fire-starting, 61
Fish, Albert, profile, 45–46
Fish, Hamilton Howard. *See* Fish, Albert
Fools, 174
  social typing, 136, 137–138
  as targets of ridicule, 137
Fox, James Alan, 26
France, serial murders in, 73
Frenzy, 141
Frontier ethic, 109, 111

G

Gacy, John Wayne, xi, 1, 73, 144, 148, 168
  anniversary stories, 134
  comparisons to Richard Speck, 130
  data sources, 178
  media portrayals, 156
  notoriety, 130, 131
  number of media articles, 125
  political activities, 51
  predictors of media coverage, 128
  profile, 50–51
  profits from murderabilia sales, 96
  sale of clown suit, 96
  social status, 127
  socially valued activities, 50
Gains, psychological, 83
Gang fights, 109
Gein, Ed, 46
Gender
  intersection with race and class expectations, 113
  and portrayal or serial murderers, 43
  and response to cultural messages, 105
  of serial murders, 69–72
Gender role expectations, 111–112
  violations by victims, 123
Genetic predisposition, 81
Genocide, and mass murder, 31
Geographic profiling systems, 25, 84
Geographical locations, in serial killings, 33
Germany
  comparison with U.S., 76
  serial murders in, 73
Gilbert, Kristen, 71
Green River Killer, xi, 1, 95, 129
  atypical profile, 16–17
  failures of criminal profiling in, 16
  true crime writings about, 27
Guilt, reducing by dehumanization, 83
Guy-next-door image
  increased representation, 39
  in mass media, 37

H

Hannibal Lecter character, 40, 138
Hannibal Rising, 40
Hansen, Robert Christian, 14, 15
Happy Face Killer, 62, 129
Harris, Eric, 30
Hazelwood, Roy, 11
Health care workers, 165
  as serial murderers, 69, 72
Hedonistic typology, 16
Hegemonic masculinity. *See* Masculinity
Heroes, 136
  conflation with villains, 137, 139
  mass media stories about, 126
Heroism, inducement by social system, 85
Heterosexual tendencies, 48, 52, 61, 62, 67, 68, 73, 76
  and hegemonic masculinity, 113

Hickey, Eric W., 26
High culture, celebration of serial murder in, 91–92
Holmes, Ronald M., 26
Holmes, Stephen T., 26
Homeless persons, as victims, 33
Homicide, overrepresentation of men, 64
Homophobia, in Britain, 76
Homosexuals, 30
  as serial killers, 47, 49, 50, 73
  as stalker victims, 78
  as victims, 28, 76, 132, 160
Hoover, J. Edgar, 12
Hospital settings, 155
  serial murders in, 70, 71
Huberty, James, 30

I

Iconic status, xi, 91
Implications, 153–161
Impression management, serial murderers' skill in, 84
Income disparity, and crime, 160–161
Inconsistent messages, 4, 150, 153, 158, 159
Indecent exposure, 49
Individual accomplishment, 108, 153
  as cultural value, 109–111
  male reward for, 112
  serial murderers' acceptance of, 141–143
Infernal Comedy, 91–92
Informers
  distrust of police, 29
  fear for safety, 29
Innocent victim ideal, 123
Insanity, 37, 66
  pleas of, 139

Intelligence characteristics, 42, 43, 46, 47, 49, 50, 52, 59, 61, 62, 66, 67, 68, 75, 174
  of identified serial murderers, 49
Internet. *See also* Web sites
  murderabilia sales, 96
Intraracial homicide, 63, 155
Investigative perspective, 13
  future considerations, 158
Investigative Support Unit, 11, 12
Isolation, 82
Italy, Serial Killer Museum, 98, 99

J

Jack the Ripper
  1888 letter, 38
  "from hell" letter, 39
  role in mass media image, 37
Jekyll and Hyde imagery, 139
Jenkins, Philip, 26
Jesperson, Keith Hunter, 129, 144, 168
  challenges to masculinity, 145
  data sources, 178
  fascination with Evel Knieval, 146
  media attention quest, 93
  motives, 146
  number of media articles, 125
  predictors of media coverage, 128
  profile, 62–63
  risk taking, 147
  social status, 127
Journalists, research on serial murderers, 27

K

Kaczynski, Ted, 110
Kemper, Edmund, 48
Killer Clown, 50

Killing method, 176–177. *See also* Modus operandii
Klebold, Dylan, 30

L

Law & Order: Special Victims Unit, 39
Law enforcement
 blame leveled at, 132, 133
 future considerations, 158
 interest in, 174, 179–180
 research implications for, 2
 serial murderer interest in, 51, 52, 170, 173
Leatherface character, 46
Lee, Derrick Todd, 16
Legal journal articles, 164, 172, 178
Legal system, informers' distrust of, 29
Lesbian lifestyle, of serial murderers, 44
Levin, Jack, 26
Lewisburg Federal Penitentiary, 15
LexisNexis Academic database, 172
Leyton, Elliott, 26
Lines of action
 alternative, 140
 building, 104–106
 constructing according to cultural competencies, 107
 deviant, 107
 and differential cultural competencies, 105
 killers' construction of, 173
 using cultural values to build, 150–151
Local officials, 9
Loner status, 24, 42, 44, 49, 50, 52, 60, 61, 62, 66, 67, 69, 76
 in mass media portrayals, 37
 rebellious, 109

M

Mad Bomber case, 11
Madoff, Bernard, 110
Mafia fights, 109
Malkovich, John, 92
Malvo, Lee Boyd, 31
Manson, Charles, 151
Marginalization, 153. *See also* Vulnerable populations
Marital status, 16, 17, 24, 59, 61, 62, 66, 67, 68, 69, 74, 76
Masculinity, 108, 175
 alternative, 115
 construction through gendered power relations, 112
 as cultural value, 111–117
 hegemonic, 4, 109, 113, 114, 153
 illegitimate means for achieving, 116
 in marginal groups, 116
 need to prove, 111–112
 proving through serial murder, 3
 serial murderers' valuation of, 143–146
 state enforcement of hegemonic, 114
 violence and hegemonic, 116
 in white supremacy movement, 79
 working-class, 116
Mass media
 and aggression/violence, 81
 anniversary stories, 134
 attractive portrayals of serial murderers, 93
 broadcasting of cultural messages, 100
 broadcasting of cultural values by, 121–139
 coverage of high-status killers, 126
 crime newsworthiness and, 122

differences from FBI/academic representations, 37
discrepancy in coverage of criminals, 124
failure to humanize victims, 149
fostering of serial murder by, 159
images of serial murder, 1
increased attention to serial murders, 28
initial reports, 128–130
missing victims stories, 134–135
model of coverage, 123–126
narrative structure, 126, 128
need to command attention from, 79
need to know why, 131–134
notoriety and, 130–131
number of articles, 125
portrayals of typical serial murderers, 37–45, 172
power and portrayals of white male killers, 156
predictors of coverage, 128
record setting, 130–131
research implications for, 2
shaping of public perceptions by, 165
social typing in, 136–139
Mass murder, defined, 30–31
Mass murderers, 30
differentiation from serial murderers, 30
Maternal relationships, 37
abusive, 60
as causes of violence, 82
revenge against, 63
McVeigh, Timothy, 30
Media coverage model, 123–126
Medical examiner reports, 13
Memorabilia. *See also* Murderabilia
sales of, 91

Men
overrepresentation as serial murderers, 165
as victims, 49, 50, 68, 73
Mercy homicide, 71
Methodology, 163
analytical procedure, 173–175
data collection sources, 169–173
defining serial murder, 165
qualitative content analysis, 164–165
research questions, 165
sample selection, 166–169
study rationale, 163–164
Migrant workers, as victims, 33
Military service, 59, 66, 174, 179–180
interest in, 170, 173
Military service killings, exclusion from serial murder, 34
Milwaukee Monster, 48, 129
Missing victims, 134–135
Mission oriented typology, 16
Mobility
role of spatial, 108
of serial killers, 62
Modus operandii, 14
beheading, 69
and desire for control, 149
drowning, 67
drug injections, 46
exceptions among nonwhite killers, 155
in female killers, 71
nicknames and, 129
poison, 71
shooting, 68
smothering, 71
stabbing, 52, 60, 66, 67, 68
strangulation, 17, 40, 50, 52, 59, 66, 67, 74, 75
suffocation, 46
torture, 46, 74

Molalla Forest Killer, 60, 95, 129
Monsters, xi
   mass media portrayals, 122, 157
   serial murderer image as, 92–95
   use of term, 92
Monstropedia Web site, 92
Most Wanted Fugitives list, 40
Motivational model, 83
Motive, 47, 48, 49, 51, 52, 60, 61, 66, 68, 76, 174
   difficulty in finding, 28
   discrepancies in definitions, 29
   excluding killers based on, 167
   financial gain, 71, 72
   identifying via criminal profiling, 83
   irrelevance to new FBI definition, 32–33
   killers' explanation, 174, 181–182
   lack of traditional, 63
   mass media fascination with, 131–134
   personal gratification, 34
   religious upbringing, 60, 61
   revenge, 63
   sexual, 72
   in single *vs.* serial murder, 30
Muhammad, John Allen, 31
Mullaney, Patrick, 11, 13
Multiple murders, 154
Murder
   contributions to understanding, 2
   distinguishing serial from other types, 30–32
Murderabilia
   collectors, 96
   marketing, 95–100
Museums
   Evil Minds Research Museum, 97
   Museum of Death, 97
   Serial Killer Museum of Florence, 97, 98, 99
Mutilation, 74

Mutual responsibility, 161
Mythic creatures, 92

N

Narrative structure, 126, 128
National Center for the Analysis of Violent Crime (NCAVC), 11, 25
National resources, 10
Nationality, 176–177
   of serial murderers, 73–77
Nazism, dehumanization process, 160
Neglect, 82, 131
   by parents, 14
Newspaper articles, 164, 170–172, 171, 178
   killer portrayals in, 174
Newsworthiness, 124, 184
   timing and, 161
Ng, Charles, 68
Nicknames, 129, 174, 184
   court use of, 95
   for serial murders, 93
Night Stalker, xi, 1, 95, 129
Noe, Marie, 70, 71
Nonwhite killers, 16, 155
   media portrayals, 157
Normalcy, in killer portrayals, 156
Norman Bates character, 46
Notoriety, 130–131
   predicting for serial murderers, 4
Novels. *See also* Fiction
   serial murderer representations in, 39

O

Obscene letters, 45
Offenders
   background, 14
   physical characteristics, 14

On-the-job killers, 69
Opera, serial murder themes in, 91–92
Organized crime, exclusion from serial murder, 34
Organized/disorganized typology, 15–16
Ostracism, 50
Outcasts, 44, 49, 50, 60, 61, 62, 66, 69
    serial murderers as, 37
Outlaw myth, 109

P

Paid labor, 115
    exertion of dominance via, 115
    hegemonic masculinity and, 113
Parental absence, 82
Parental effects, 81
Partner serial killings, 69, 165, 166
Pasttimes, 170, 173
Patriarchal culture, 86
Pedophiles, 73
Personal gratification
    killing for reasons other than, 167
    as motive, 34
Pioneer myth, 109
Pitkin County Courthouse, 41
Plainfield Ghoul, 46
Poison
    as choice of female killers, 71
    women's preference for, 72
Police, informer distrust of, 29
Police reports, 13
Political activities, Bundy, Ted, 42
Ponzi, Charles, 110
Popular culture
    redundant violence and dehumanization in, 107–108
    serial murder in, 5, 91–92
    serial murderers as monsters and celebrities in, 92–95
Pornography, as facilitator, 81
Power, 3, 151, 175
    access to, 115
    achieving through serial murder, 159
    American striving for, 104
    as cultural value, 120–121
    culture and forms of social, 100
    desire for, 63, 170, 173
    male identification with, 113
    and media portrayals of killers, 156
    as motive, 63
    need for, 79
    race and class associations, 121
    in serial arsonists, 78
    valuation by serial murderers, 147–149
    via paid labor, 115
    in white supremacy movement, 79
Power/control oriented typology, 16
Power structure, media representations and perpetuation of, 157–158
Primary data, 164, 183
Prior arrests/convictions, 48, 49, 50, 51, 60, 66, 67, 76, 179–180
Privilege, 108
    as cultural value, 111–117
    serial murderers' valuation of, 143–146
Profiles, 3
    discrepancies between popular and scientific, 5
    limitations in case-solving, 13
Profilers
    chemistry students experiment, 24
    glorified media image, 16
    investigative process, 13–14

need for cooperation with
  academic researchers, 17
 specialized training, 13
 as superagents, 16
Profiling. *See also* Criminal
  profiling
 criminal, 5
 race, 63–68
 roots in 19th-century fiction, 11
 typical serial murderers, 37
Prostitutes, 30, 123, 149
 patronization of, 48
 as serial murderers, 42, 43, 156
 as victims, 28, 33, 47, 70, 135
Protection, for vulnerable
  populations, 160–161
Protection of Children from Sexual
  Predator Act of 1998, 32
Psychiatric disorders, 60
 as cause of violence, 82
 in serial arsonists, 78
Psychological explanations, 82–84,
  86
 dominance of, 81
Psychology
 academic researcher expertise in,
  17
 as dominant research perspective,
  25
 and serial murder analysis, 2, 3

Q

Qualitative content analysis,
  164–165

R

Race
 and construction of alternative
  masculinities, 116
 in Dahmer's murders, 132
 and killing methods, 155

 and response to cultural
  messages, 105
 of serial killers, 176–177
Racial characteristics
 of serial murderers, 63–68
 of victims, 63
Rader, Dennis Lynn, 51, 129, 138,
  149, 168
 boasting behavior, 142
 confession, 172
 data sources, 178
 guilty plea transcript excerpts,
  53–58
 media portrayals, 156
 number of media articles, 125
 predictors of media coverage, 128
 profile, 52
 risk taking, 147
 social status, 127
Rage, in serial rapists, 78
Rambo, 110
Ramirez, Richard Munoz, 77, 129,
  130, 155, 169
 court use of nickname, 95
 data sources, 178
 differences from white male
  profile, 155
 media portrayals, 157
 number of media articles, 125
 predictors of media coverage, 128
 profile, 68–69
 risk taking, 147
 social status, 127
Rape, serial, 78
Rate of killing, 83–84
Reality television, 109–110
Rebellious loner type, 109
Recognition, 174
 achieving through serial murder,
  159
 American striving for, 104
 desire for, 79
 valuation in U.S. culture, 109

Record setting, 130–131
Red Dragon, 37
Redundant violence, 107–108
Regard for violence, 108–109
  by serial murderers, 140–141
Rehabilitation efforts, 85
Rejection, as precipitator, 82
Remorse, capacity for, 82
Research. *See* Serial murder research
Research questions, 164, 165
Ressler, Robert K., 10, 11, 12
Revenge, against powerful females, 63
Ridgway, Gary Leon, 17, 24, 44, 129, 138, 143, 146, 150, 168
  atypical profile, 16–17, 24
  confession, 172
  data sources, 178
  as do-gooder, 149
  guilty plea statement, 18–23
  media comparison with Rogers, 95
  media portrayals, 156
  number of media articles, 125
  predictors of media coverage, 128
  prostitute victims, 135
  risk taking, 147
  shock factor, 126
  social status, 127
Rifkin, Joel David, 46, 61, 143, 144, 168
  challenges to masculinity, 145
  data sources, 178
  media attention, 94
  media blame, 133
  media portrayals, 157
  as monster, 149
  motives, 146
  number of media articles, 125
  predictors of media coverage, 128
  profile, 47–48
  social status, 127

Risk taking, 170, 173, 175
  as cultural value, 118–120
  need to intensify, 119
  by serial murderers, 146–147
Ritualized performance, 63
Robin Hood, 110
Rogers, Dayton Leroy, 124, 129, 144, 168
  data sources, 178
  media comparison with Ridgway, 95
  media coverage, 130
  media portrayals, 157
  number of media articles, 125
  predictors of media coverage, 128
  profile, 60–61
  risk taking, 147
  social status, 127
Rule, Ann, 27, 142
Runaways, 30, 123
  as victims, 28, 70, 135
Russia, serial murders in, 73

S

Sadism
  in childhood history of serial killers, 61
  in fantasy of killers, 63
  in serial murder, 32
Sadomasochistic pornography, 60
Sample selection, 166–168
  atypical group, 168–169
  general information, 176–177
  typical group, 168
Sample size, 183
Satisfaction, 3
  American striving for, 104
Schechter, Harold, 26
School performance, 42, 43, 46, 47, 49, 50, 52, 59, 61, 62, 66, 67, 68, 69, 75, 174, 179–180

of identified serial murderers, 49
  in serial stalkers, 78
School shootings, 78–79
Scientific procedures, profiling via, 25
Secondary data, 164
Self-actualization, 118
  through thrill seeking, 117
Self-defense, 156
Self-injury, 46
Seltzer, Mark, 26
Serial arsonists, 78
Serial crimes, 77–78
Serial killer groupies, 93
Serial Killer Museum, 98
Serial murder
  alternative models, 157
  American fascination with, 86
  analysis of definitions, 4–5
  analytical procedure, 173–175
  contextual cultural values facilitating, 107–108
  coverage and interests of elites, 157
  cultural context, 91
  as cultural phenomenon, 3–4
  decreasing incidence, 158–161
  deepening understanding of, 153–158
  defined, 32–34, 165
  definitions, 29–34
  definitions associated with white males, 154
  differentiation from single murder, 30
  difficulty of solving, 28
  distinguishing from other types, 30–32
  enhanced record keeping, 28
  existing explanations, 81
  FBI claims to authority on, 10
  FBI definition, 32
  financial resources expended on, 2
  fostering by American culture, 153
  fostering through publicity, 159
  fundamentals, 9
  higher U.S. incidence, 3
  implications for law enforcement and media, 2
  inaccurate representations, 5
  increased awareness, 28
  increased media attention, 28
  law enforcement personnel and, 9–17, 24–25
  mass media images, 1
  media representations, 171
  multiple killers in, 33
  and murderabilia marketing, 95–100
  narrative, 175
  noninclusion in official crime statistics, 28
  nonwhite, 5
  and other serial crimes, 77–78
  as path to social goods, 107, 153, 159
  perception as American phenomenon, 97
  in popular culture, 5, 91–100
  popular definitions, 4–5
  prevalence, 28–29
  psychological explanations, 82–84
  representations perpetuating power structure, 157
  research contributions, 2–5
  restrictive definitions, 154
  and school shootings, 80–81
  similarities with other types of offenses, 77–79
  single definition, 154
  as skill, 142, 143
  social psychological explanations, 84–85
  sociocultural approach, 89

sociocultural context, 5, 86–87
sociological explanations, 85–86
students of, 9
unique investigative challenges, 10
updates to FBI definition, 32
working definition, 34
Serial murder research
academic researchers, 25
journalists and true crime writers, 27
prominent FBI contributors, 12–13
Serial murderers, 1
absence of relationship with victims, 154
academic researcher-identified characteristics, 45–63
adolescent, 48
American culture and creation of, 106
attention to other, 174
atypical, 163, 167, 168–169
awareness of celebrity status, 159
background and physical characteristics, 14
Berdella, Robert, 46–47
Black, Robert, 75–76
building lines of action, 150–151
Bundy, Carol M., 69–70
Bundy, Ted, 40, 42
Carpenter, David, 14
categories, 166
characteristics in sample set, 179–182
Chikatilo, Andrei, 74–75
childhood symptoms, 61
Cole, Carroll Edward, 59–60
common characteristics, 5
comparison group, 167
competition values, 141–143
criminal experience, 146
Dahmer, Jeffrey Lionel, 48–49
defined, 165
Durousseau, Paul, 65
emphasis on white, male, 4
FBI-identified characteristics, 45–63
Fish, Albert, 45–46
Gacy, John Wayne, 50–51
Gein, Ed, 46
gender characteristics, 69–72
general information about, 176–177
goals and outcomes, 173
Hansen, Robert Christian, 15
homosexual tendencies, 47
impediments to identifying, 63
impression management by, 84
individual accomplishment values, 141–143
Jesperson, Keith Hunter, 62–63
lack of criteria for classifying, 29
mass media portrayals, 37–45, 172
media coverage, 171–172
mobility, 62
nationality characteristics, 73–77
Noe, Marie, 71
numeric estimates, 29
as perverse icons, xi, 91
popular nicknames, 93
popular representations, 155
popularity in prison, 93
portraying as victims, 139
postmortem celebrity, 94
power and control valuation, 147–149
predicting home location, 84
predicting home locations of, 25
predicting potential notoriety, 4
prerequisites for decreasing incidence of, 5

profit from notoriety, 97
racial characteristics, 63–68
racialized images of, 123
Rader, Dennis Lynn, 52
Ramirez, Richard Munoz, 68–69
regard for violence, 140–141
relative ages, 45
Ridgway, Gary Leon, 17, 24
Rifkin, Joel David, 47–48
risk taking by, 146–147
Rogers, Dayton Leroy, 60–61
search for celebrity status, 93–94, 174
sexual characteristics, 72–73
similarities to edgeworkers, 147
social status, 127, 148
split personalities characterization, 139
stuttering in, 14, 15
supposed brilliance, 158
thrill seeking by, 146–147
tuning in to cultural messages, 107, 139–150
typical, 37, 163, 166, 167, 168, 183
typing as villains, 138
typologies, 15–16
use of culturally familiar imagery, 149–150
valuation of masculinities and privilege, 143–146
Wallace, Henry Louis, 66
Watts, Coral Eugene, 67–68
Williams, Wayne, 65
Wuornos, Aileen Carol, 43–44
Serial rape, 78
Serial stalkers, 77–78
Sexual abuse, 82
history of, 44, 76
Sexual assault, 49
Sexual homicide, 16
serial murder classification as, 32

Sexual orientation, 174, 179–180, 183
of serial murderers, 72–73
Sexuality, demonstrating masculinity through, 116
Shared meanings, via culture, 100
Sherlock Holmes stories, 11
Shock factor, 4, 124, 126, 129
Shooting, 68
Silence of the Lambs, 12, 16, 40
true-life sources, 46
Single murder, differentiation from serial murder, 30
Situational justification, 108
Skill, 175
killing as, 141
Smith, Carlton, 27
Smoking Gun Web site, 185
Smothering, 71
Social awkwardness, 42, 48, 52, 62, 67, 76
Social class, 59
of identified serial murderers, 49
internationally, 75, 77
and media portrayals of killers, 156
and response to cultural messages, 105
role in constructing alternative masculinities, 116
Social environment, 173
Social goods, 105
achieving through serial murder, 3
deviant paths to achieving, 158
serial murder as path to, 107, 153, 159
Social obligation, in Europe *vs.* U.S., 161
Social status
of killer and victims, 4, 124
of serial murderers, 127, 148
Social typing, 136–139, 174–175
courtroom, 139

Socialization, downplaying effects of, 85
Socially valued activities, participation in, 50, 51
Sociocultural approach, xi, 89
Sociocultural context, 3, 86–87. *See also* Cultural context
Sociological explanations, 3, 85–86
Sociopathy, in serial murderers, 82
Sodomy, 50
Son of Sam laws, 97, 106
South Africa, serial murders in, 76
Speck, Richard, 30, 130
Split personalities, 139
Spree murder, defined, 31–32
Spree murderers, 31
    differentiation from serial murderers, 30
Stabbing, 52, 60, 66, 67, 68
Stano, Gerald, 130
State resources, 10
Storytelling, 126. *See also* Narrative structure
Strangers, as victims, 33
Strangulation, 17, 40, 50, 51, 52, 59, 62, 66, 67, 74, 75, 141
    by white male killers, 155
Stress, 82
Study rationale, 163–164
Stutter
    David Carpenter case, 14
    Robert Hansen case, 15
Success, 3, 174
    American striving for, 104
    at any cost, 111
    male accountability for, 111
Sudden infant death syndrome (SIDS), 71
Suffocation, 46
Sunday Morning Slasher, 67, 129
Sunset Strip Killers, 69
Superagent mystique, 16
Sweeney Todd, 91

T

Tate-LaBianca murders, 151
Teasing, in murderers' history, 15
Television shows, 39
    celebration of serial murder in, 91
Terrorist acts, 31
    exclusion from serial murder, 34
Teton, Howard, 11, 13
Thrill seeking, 108, 117, 151, 175
    as cultural value, 118–120
    by serial murderers, 146–147
    through murder, 120
Torture, 46, 74
Trailside Killer of San Francisco, 14
Trophies, 42, 44, 47, 48, 49, 51, 52, 61, 68, 174, 181–182
True crime genre, popularity, 91
True crime writers
    Carlo, Philip, 27
    research on serial murderers, 27
    Rule, Ann, 27
    Smith, Carlton, 27
    well-known, 27
Typologies, 15
    general murders, 16
    serial murders, 15–16

U

Unabomber, 110
Unfair fights, 108–109
United States
    comparison of murderer characteristics, 75
    cultural differences from Britain, 76
    prevalence internationally, 73
    surge in serial murders, 28
Unsolved cases, 166
Unterweger, Jack, 92
Untraceable, 37, 39

U.S. Secret Service Safe School Initiative Report, 80

V

Values, tuning in to cultural, 100
Vendetta fights, 109
Victim behaviors, 14
Victim identification, difficulties surrounding, 28
Victim statements, 13
Victims
  absence of killer relationship with, 154
  African American, 66
  audience lack of identification with, 135
  blaming, 153
  choice of, 143
  dehumanization of, 63
  deserving, 149
  difficulty in identifying, 28
  elderly, 33
  failure to find, 28
  family members as, 70
  identifying motive through, 83
  international comparisons, 75
  interracial, 67
  invisibility of, 123, 134, 135
  known to killers, 154–155
  lack of prior relationship to killer, 33
  low-priority, 134
  migrant workers, 33
  number of, and media coverage, 124, 176–177
  number required for serial murder, 32
  numeric estimates, 29
  overrepresentation by gender, 64
  perception as powerless, 33
  prestigeless, 33
  as property, 148
  restraint of, 149
  secretive lives, 28
  social status, 4, 26, 124, 148
  strangers as, 33
  symbolic value, 33
  targeting of higher-status, 148
  transient lifestyles, 29
  types, 176–177
  violation of gender expectations, 123
  vulnerable, 37
  from vulnerable populations, 30
  white race, 63
Villains, 136, 175
  conflation with heroes, 137, 139
Violence, 117, 174
  capacity for, 113
  circumstances legitimizing, 108
  as cultural value, 108–109
  due to patriarchal code, 112
  gendered, 114
  and hegemonic masculinity, 116, 117
  history of, 173
  inconsistent messages, 159
  mass media descriptions, 122
  as means to accomplish masculinity, 113
  as means to control, wealth, fame, 140
  normalization of, 108
  obligation to, 117
  redundant, 107–108
  rewards for extreme types, 159
  serial murderers' regard for, 140–141
  in sports, 108
  tendency to, 170
Violent behavior
  contributions to understanding, 2
  and media consumption, 81
  as outcome of social experiences, 86

Violent Criminal Apprehension
    Program, 11, 12
Visionary typology, 16
Voyeurism, 60
Vulnerable populations, 84, 160
    crime targets, 121, 135
    cultural protections, 160–161
    exploiting images of, 156

W

Wallace, Henry Louis, 155, 169
    data sources, 178
    law enforcement blame, 134
    media portrayals, 157
    number of media articles, 125
    predictors of media coverage, 128
    profile, 66
    social status, 127
Watts, Coral Eugene, 129, 144, 155, 169
    data sources, 178
    media descriptors, 130
    media portrayals, 157
    number of media articles, 125
    predictors of media coverage, 128
    profile, 67–68
    risk taking, 147
    social status, 127
Wealth, American striving for, 104
Web sites
    Monstropedia, 92
    sale of murderabilia, 96
    serial murder-based, 91
Western genre, 109
White male privilege, 4, 108, 153
    defining serial murder by, 154
    and fostering of serial murderers, 163
    sense of entitlement, 112
White males
    creation of predator image, 87
    failure of psychological
        explanations to account for, 82
    international prevalence of, 75, 77
    overrepresentation in serial
        murder, xi, 165
    as serial arsonists, 78
    serial murderers as, 44, 45, 63
White supremacy, 79
Whitman, Charles, 31
Wiest, Julie B., 203
Williams, Wayne, 14, 64
    mug shot, 65
Winning, at any cost, 112
Wire service articles, 184
Witness statements, 2
Women
    African American, 65, 66
    interracial victims, 67
    media portrayals of killers, 157
    as rape victims, 78
    as serial murderers, 69, 155
    subordination of, 113, 116
    terrorizing through fascination
        with serial murder, 86
    underrepresentation in homicide, 64
    as victims, 15, 17, 47, 48, 52, 59,
        60, 62, 65, 67, 68, 69, 73,
        74, 78, 160
Women serial murderers, shift in
    portrayal, 42
Wuornos, Aileen Carol, 72, 131, 146, 169
    competing media portrayals, 157
    data sources, 178
    differences from typical profile, 155–156
    fascination with Bonnie and
        Clyde, 141
    mass media portrayal, 42
    media descriptors, 130

mug shot, 43
number of media articles, 125
predictors of media coverage, 128
profile, 43–44
social status, 127
socially valued goals, 140
targeting of higher-status victims, 148

Y

Yorkshire Ripper, 133

Author

Dr. Julie B. Wiest is an assistant professor of strategic communication at High Point University in High Point, North Carolina, with a part-time appointment in the Department of Human Relations, Sociology, and Nonprofit Studies. She earned a doctorate in sociology from the University of Tennessee and a master's degree in journalism and mass communication from the University of Georgia. Wiest also has nearly a decade of experience in print and electronic journalism and published a book in 2006 titled *We Were There*, a compilation of the World War II narratives of 30 veterans. She is originally from Vail, Colorado, but calls Knoxville, Tennessee, home.